THE STILL SINGLE PAPERS

For my folks, for everything. As I've been saying in your birthday cards since I first learned to write, you are officially 'the Best Mum and Dad in the World'.

Now, don't read this . . .

THE
STILL SINGLE
PAPERS

The Fearless Musings of a Romantic
Adventurer Aged 32½

ALISON TAYLOR

MAINSTREAM
PUBLISHING

EDINBURGH AND LONDON

First published in Great Britain in 2012 by
MAINSTREAM PUBLISHING COMPANY
(EDINBURGH) LTD
7 Albany Street
Edinburgh EH1 3UG

ISBN 9781780575582

This book is a work of non-fiction based on the life, experiences and recollections
of the author. In some cases, names of people, profile names, places, dates or details
of events have been changed to protect the privacy of others. The author has stated
to the publishers that, except in such respects, the contents of this book are true.

A catalogue record for this book is available
from the British Library

Printed in Great Britain by
CPI Group (UK) Ltd, Croydon, CR0 4YY

1 3 5 7 9 10 8 6 4 2

Acknowledgements

First up, I must thank the blokes who've given me so many text messages, bizarre behaviours and misdemeanours to analyse over the years. I couldn't have written this book without their mind-fucking input.

Thanks to Jane Graham Maw, my brilliant agent, who first took on the idea that my ridiculous stories might be worth committing to a manuscript. And my publisher, Mainstream, particularly Bill – for drunken Groucho dinners and hung-over Wolseley breakfasts – and Debs, my editor, for keeping me straight, narrower and ever so slightly paranoid.

My biggest debt is to those amazing friends of mine who've signed disclaimers and let me plunder their lives, jokes and debauched behaviours for the sake of good yarn. Bottom of my heart thanks to:

Mrs Patz – for holding my head up when I needed it, for being my smoking pal in the office and for her marvellous mind of filmic references.

Rubles – for loving *Diagnosis Murder* and expensive deli foods as much as I do.

Pfeiffer – for being single at the same time and sharing in email/ text post-mortems at ridiculous hours.

Rockstar – for coaxing me back to life on more than one occasion, soothing words and sofa time. And for keeping telling me I'm 'fit'.

Angel – for the good times, the 'don't tell anyone else' times and the living-next-door times. For being my true love.

Lady Jane – for encouraging me, and encouraging me, and

encouraging me. If anyone should get famous off the back of this book, it's you, because you're a fucking genius. Am always and constantly in awe. Respec'.

Contents

SUMMER, 2009

summer *(n)* the warmest season of the year, between spring and autumn; astronomically from the June solstice to the September equinox; a time of youth, blossoming, greatest happiness

summer *(n)* the most hedonistic season of the year between Glastonbury and Bestival; a time of boozing and sunbathing in beer gardens and parks; impromptu parties, barbecues, lido swimming and misguided adventures with boys . . .

Guest list:
1. Gay Dad
2. Power Boy
3. Mr Scissors
4. Smiler
5. Cartoon Boy
6. American Boy
7. Music Man
8. Fantasy Boy

JUNE
Getting Rid

Tuesday, 23 June

Today I was asked if I was happy being single. I said I'm not *unhappy* being single but that I would like to meet someone.

'Why?'

'Because I want to love someone and I want them to love me.'

Simple.

Or not.

Wednesday, 24 June

The last guy I 'dated', let's call him 'Gay Dad', called me neurotic. I was naked at the time. We were unsuccessfully post-coital, which is what made it so galling. I pride myself on my quick-wittedness and batted back, 'What? Like Woody Allen?'

Now, I don't want to give him too much credit, but he inspired me to start keeping a diary of what happens in my love life. Mainly because in the three-plus years that I've been single, I find myself thinking WTF? *a lot*. It helps to write it all down to try to make sense of it. Is there a pattern? Is it me? Is it them? There's definitely a pattern in terms of the number of duds and disappointments. There are the flakes, the weirdos, the hot-then-colds, the full-of-shits, the insecures, the ex-obsessed. Then there's the minefield that is texting, the horrors of internet dating, intimacy issues, grooming etiquette . . . I could go on, and I will.

I should say, underpinning all of this 'research' (read moaning) is the fact that I am a manic romantic, a self-confessed love fool. I *do* want to find love. I crave intimacy and I miss kissing so much; I love that first flash of romance when you truly find a connection with somebody, when you really let go, when you go giddy over a text, when your skin prickles and your insides shudder. I want all of this. I do. I'm chasing it. It's addictive – when you don't have it, you crave it and do daft things to try and get it. I'm like Patrick Swayze in *Point Break*, but where he's tripping for the ultimate wave, I'm tripping for the ultimate love.

The problem is, being this switched on gets me in trouble sometimes. It fogs my perception and expectations, for a start – how could it not? Half the time I'm playing out wild relationships in my head. It's like I've got a head start on the blokes. How can they possibly live up to the dream? Was Gay Dad right? Am I neurotic? Maybe I am, but in the best possible way: the angst-y, antsy (and hopefully funny) Woody Allen way. So, in the spirit of the King of Neurotica, imagine, if you will, a voiceover. Welcome to My Particular Love Story . . .

Thursday, 25 June

It's a warm evening and, as is often the way, I'm sitting on the garden steps with my best mate 'Angel', sipping from bottles of Peroni and smoking roll-ups. She's unusually quiet, pensive almost. Then it comes. She exhales and reveals:

'You know what was wrong with Gay Dad?'

'What?'

'He wasn't fit enough.'

Pause.

We crack up, knowing how bad it sounds. The *not fit enough* comment is something of a running joke between Angel and me. It's not wholly serious, but useful shorthand for someone who hasn't quite made the grade. Every time she says it, it makes me laugh, which, of course, is the point. If I had been brooding, I wasn't any more.

I've known Angel for twelve years, lived in London with her for eight and right next door for five. She is not a part of my life; she is a part of me. She rents one flat on the ground floor of an elegant white Victorian house on top of a green hill in South London and I rent the other. We have identical French doors, which lead, via three stone steps, into – and I am not exaggerating here – the most beautiful, three-tiered archetypal English garden. The fact that we live literally side by side, mirrored, in a leafy idyll, could not be a more appropriate metaphor. We've been through a lot together over the years, from Liverpool, where I met her when I was at uni, to now, as best-friend-neighbours who see each other every day. She's my rock. My soulmate.

We meet up most nights for a pint and counsel in our ramshackle local pub, the Cave, she on her way back from the primary school she slaves in as a bloody brilliant teacher, me having spent the day at home, in the flat I procrastinate in as a freelance journalist. We fondly call the pub the Cave because it's the sort of place you go for a pint at teatime and emerge 12 hours later. Our friend 'Elvis' is behind the bar and tends to be involved when anything good goes down.

That's where I met Gay Dad a few months back. He was playing pool with his bumbling but likeable friend who was a spit for the Christian triple-jumper Jonathan Edwards. I was with Angel, my cousin 'Rubles' and our make-up artist friend 'Brigitte'. I noticed him for a number of reasons. I'd never seen him in the pub before, he had an interesting look (or so I thought . . .) and I was in that sort of mood: flirty. I was propping up the bar, wearing a rather fetching pink vintage dress, and it was a bordering-on-raucous gathering. Brigitte is always good value – she's also a singer, so not averse to prancing about for no good reason. I like that in a drinking pal.

With the benefit of hindsight (the most precious commodity for those of us in the dating world?), Gay Dad was one of the classic mistakes: giving someone far more credit than he deserves. I imagined him to be better than he was, practically willing it to be so. Emotional beer goggles.

'Go and talk to him, go and talk to him!'

Brigitte is practically throwing me at him, between songs.

The truth is, I wasn't even sure if I fancied him. I don't know if it was the drink, the constant friend pestering or the marching powder that ultimately made me eye him up across the bar like some kind of demon, but it worked, which must be a relief for all those 'flirt coaches' out there because I'm pretty sure that's very high on the 'how to ensnare a man' manifesto, along with sucking seductively on your finger (or something).

We got chatting. He had a slightly whiney Estuary accent, but I overlooked that, along with the fact that his retro '90s skater look – blond quiff, backpack, baggy pants – perhaps wasn't as cool as I'd previously thought. The girls were hustling me on, though. This is what happens when you're single; your mates get wind of the fact you might fancy someone even a tiny bit and they set to work like Cilla's elves to encourage you (*Yes, he's definitely got an interesting look . . . he definitely likes you . . .*) and, eventually, plot to get you alone with him, which is exactly what happened.

We all ended up going back to mine to continue drinking and in no time at all Brigitte has shepherded his hapless mate off with the promise of some weed, leaving us all alone. Me, Gay Dad and his silly backpack. He went straight in for the kiss, which is fair enough, but, geez, it's not good. *Really* not good. He penetrated my mouth with his tongue like some kind of demented animal, leaving me with a crick in my neck. And suddenly I'm thinking, oh God, this isn't good. Maybe he's not the cool, retro stranger I thought he was. Illusion shattered.

It gets worse. We're sitting on the sofa and because it's all been so blatantly orchestrated I think I feel some obligation to go a bit further with him. There's a sick part of me, as well, that's curious. Well, it can't be any worse than the kiss, can it? None of these, I realise, are solid reasons to sleep with someone, but hey, it's the noughties.

Anyway, it's a disaster. For him. He can't get it up. Probably because he's been sniffing crap coke that doesn't particularly get you high but has a disabling effect on your dick. He's mortified and, weirdly, I actually like him more in flaccid failure mode. His full-on guttedness makes me respect him for being so open. Always seeing the best in people – it's a curse. He says sweet things like, 'I can't believe this – I'm here with a hot girl and this happens.' Whatcha gonna do? He also asks to see me again. This is when I merrily jot down my number on a Post-it, naked, and he responds, laughing, with: 'You're a bit neurotic, aren't you?' Eh? You're the one disintegrating before me, all floppy and useless, and you're calling *me* neurotic!

Didn't stop me texting him, though, did it? That was my second mistake.

*

I opted to text Gay Dad on the Sunday afternoon after our Thursday night fail. Before I press send, I tend to enlist the help of my great and formidable friend Lady Jane of Manchester. It's fun, after all, to discuss in ridiculous levels of detail what to put in a text message to a supremely average guy, isn't it? Lady Jane is brilliant for this because she respects the art of text as I do, but also acts as my filter, which I need when I'm hovering over the send button about to release an SMS bomb. 'Weapons of mass destruction in your send box,' she mock scolds.

Lady Jane wasn't keen on me contacting him rather than the other way around but agreed that a jaunty 'Fancy an afternoon pint?' text was acceptable and possibly even cool. So that's what I sent. Since losing his job at a magazine, he'd been working behind the bar in a local restaurant and it turned out he was working. He sent me a nice text back, saying he'd love to but couldn't. How about in the week?

I want to reply, 'Fuck you, then!' as a joke, but, as usual, I get three strikes. One from Angel, when we discuss it over cups of tea and rollies on her step; one from cousin Rubles, who's also sitting with us, by way of a bemused shake of the head; and a final big, fat nooooooo from Lady Jane, the most vocal objector of all, and she's not even in the same freakin' city. I opt for a boring 'Yes, a night in the week would be good. I can do Wednesday.' You see, bor-ing.

Texting. Part 1.

Where to start? You know those surveys that come out every now and then about how much time, over a lifetime, we cumulatively spend/waste on getting ready (two years), cooking (three years), watching TV (thirteen years! I reckon I could top that), scratching our bums . . . ?

Well, Ms Survey Woman, I would like someone to investigate how much time we spend texting, thinking about texting, analysing texts, composing texts, texting friends about why someone hasn't yet texted . . . I could go on, but you see what I'm getting at? A LOL situation this is not.

Friday, 26 June
Planning the first date

Of course, the fantasy is that a guy will come up with a great suggestion of something to do and be reasonably assertive about it, but, as we know, that rarely happens. I'm not talking *Darling, I'm taking you to Claridge's* levels of chivalry – though that wouldn't go amiss . . . I never go out with *that* guy – just some thought and a bit of interest, rather than a half-arsed text sent about two hours before you're due to go out. Then you end up meeting at a tube station and wandering aimlessly to find somewhere you can sit down or actually hear each other. Is it too much to ask?

Gay Dad suggested 'an old-fashioned movie', by which I think he meant movie-watching is old school rather than we go see *Casablanca*. This worked for me. I like the way he editorialised his choice with a nod to dating etiquette. Plus, cinema – why not? I love the pictures and it seems to have gone out of fashion a bit of late. Let's bring it back! Me and him dating renegades! OK, that's an exaggeration, but there's a lot to be gleaned from what to the naked eye might seem like an off-the-cuff suggestion. I took that as my cue to decide on the movie and had a squiz to see what was showing at the Curzon, the arty cinema on Shaftesbury Avenue (cool films, good downstairs bar and, in my experience, no ASBO kids lobbing food at you). That docu-film *Anvil! The Story of Anvil* was on – about a Canadian metal band – and I really wanted to see it. I'd read about it and thought it looked funny-as. Like *This Is Spinal Tap*, but true.

Now, this was a risk because it was a wee bit obscure and I didn't want to have to go into why I wanted to see it. You'd either get it or you wouldn't. I mean, what if he thought I was a card-carrying metaller? That wouldn't be very representative, would it? There wasn't much else I fancied seeing, though, so I thought, what the hell, and suggested it. His response? 'Nice one! I've been wanting to see that!' Result. A common love of films with a cultural bent . . . (*strokes chin pensively*).

Films with a Romantic Angle. Part 1.

There was a news story recently stating that the genre known as romantic comedy is giving women unrealistic expectations when it comes to love. In case you were wondering, this does not affect men; they have different celluloid-inspired afflictions pertaining mainly to violence and the objectification of women.

I must say, I prefer my rom-coms with a cold hard slab of reality, which is to say the films I enjoy are usually themed around romantic disappointment and Allen-inspired anxiety rather than some kind of Aaron Eckhart wank-off. In some cases, like *The Way We Were*, watched for the severalth time recently, I adopt them like therapy. I have these eureka moments, shrieking 'Yes' to myself – cause I'm a saddo who watches movies alone – 'That's me! That's him! That's why that happened!'

So, not unrealistic expectations, rather food for thought. Let's ponder issues of fate via *Sliding Doors* and that other piece of cinematic genius *Serendipity* (why did you do it, Mr Cusack? You were so cool in *High Fidelity*!). Or unrequited longing – see *Vanilla Sky* and *Elegy*, that dark-and-brooding film where Penelope Cruz is shagging her paranoid college tutor Ben Kingsley and all hell breaks loose.

Sometimes, though – gasp! – I'll just watch films for fun. On a recent duvet day shared with Rubles, my number one loafing pal, we revisited *Cry Baby*, or 'early Johnny Depp', as we like to call it. So exciting were the scenes where he's showing his 'stiff' girlfriend how to French kiss, I took pictures on my phone and sent them to friends I knew would appreciate it.

Saturday, 27 June
The Big Date

When date night with Gay Dad came around, the Wednesday after our initial fumble (if that's not putting too fine a point on it), I was feeling pretty nervous. During the day I was working in the fashion office where I sometimes get called in to cover for gallivanting editors.

As offices go, it's A-OK. I've met some really lovely people, number one of whom we'll call 'Mrs Patz' (in her other life, she's married to a certain R-Patz). She's my new friend and we're still in the honeymoon stage. We exchange witty emails back and forth, smoke together, lunch together; it's the perfect office affair. On date day, it seems perfectly reasonable to me to suggest that she come along. Not for the date, of course, but for a drink before he arrives because I've got some time to kill. Blatantly, she wants to check him out, too. I've since found out that this is a bad move from the guy's point of view because, well, it's scary enough meeting someone for a first date without having their mate there too, grinning inanely. I was the inane grinning friend when Angel met her boyfriend 'G' for their first official date. Some time afterwards he told her that me being there was really off-putting. Oops.

Funnily enough, it was even the same place, a little Spanish bar just off Oxford Street, with cute snogging booths and a great jukebox. It's a good date pub. Mrs Patz and I are enjoying a pint in one of the booths and I'm watching the clock nervously. He'll be here any minute. What did he look like again? I've described him to her as I (vaguely) remember him – you know, working that sort of hip '90s American look – blond quiff à la Vanilla Ice, but not as ridiculous. Cool sneakers. Etc. I nip off to the loo and when I get back Mrs Patz tells me she thinks she's seen him. 'Is he short?' she asks, her Glaswegian accent making it sound even funnier. Not the most promising start and if I'm totally honest I can't actually remember. I don't think he was freakishly short. Oh God, was he freakishly short? 'And he's wearing a backpack?' she continues. Now I really am nervous. The perils of pulling while far from sober: you can't remember shit. I can tell Mrs Patz doesn't think he's all that. She's almost surprised that I would've gone for him, though she's too gracious to say. He reappears at the stairs and I wave hello. Gulp . . .

Monday, 29 June
The Big Let-Down

It was on the journey back from our cinema date that the alarm bells started to ring. The cinema part of the date was fine; the film was brilliant, we held hands in the dark, had a bit of a snog. Fine. Then, heading south on the bus across Southwark Bridge, the London Eye all lit up to my left, I give Gay Dad an excitable squeeze around his shoulders. I'm quite touchy-feely, I guess, and crossing the river always sends a shiver through my bones. What I couldn't have guessed was that Gay Dad would be visibly, physically, freaked out by it. Me putting *my* arms around *him* was, quote, 'too masculine'. WTF? Strike 1.

Four or so dates in, Strike 2. Also related to his insecurity. Despite the fact that I encouraged his magazine design aspirations by urging him to get back in touch with his old contacts, you know, rather than continue to fester in the bar where he was working, he couldn't return the supportive favour. A common theme in modern relationships, I think, is the guy who can't handle a successful woman (or, perhaps more accurately, a woman with balls). Case in point: when I was chatting to him about my upcoming trip to the desert in Egypt, a story earned all by myself for *Elle* magazine and to be taken with Lady Jane, he replied, 'Ooh, get you!' in that camp-and-whiney voice I'd become accustomed to. I let that one slide, but I knew something was very wrong (with him) when he practically had a nervous breakdown because I'd got us into a Pete Doherty gig on the guest list. I smelled a rat: an insecure, jealous, petty rat. He spent the entire gig sulking. I didn't get it. What's not to love about a free gig? Strike 3.

Add to this the fact that he was actually a bit boring, wore terrible underwear (tight Lycra boxers with hideously faded '70s-style swirly patterns), had no spontaneity and carried that bloody backpack around with him everywhere. It was time to part company. I saw him about a week later when he dared to show his face in the Cave. I was with Angel, as usual. She turned her back on him at the bar and mouthed to me, 'Not fit enough.'

Tuesday, 30 June

I realised over the weekend – Glastonbury weekend – that my attitude towards men has much in common with my attitude towards music festivals. It's all about unfulfilled longing. You look forward to them for ages, build them up in your stupid over-active mind to be this fantastical, life-changing wonder-thing, only to find they're actually a bit of a let-down. All these hopes, just waiting to be rained on.

So that's Gay Dad – a big, fat let-down. But I woke up today with a sense of newness hanging in the air. Glastonbury is officially over, the rubbish is being cleared from Worthy Farm as we speak and I no longer have to sulk because I'm not there.

Instead of Glastonbury (where I wanted to be) I ended up at a different festival, in Hyde Park, for one night. It was fun enough because I was with Angel, Rubles and an old London College of Fashion mate, 'Pfeiffer'. We had a laugh, saw a couple of good bands, spotted – wait for it – Ben Fogle in the 'guest/press'/poncy food area (woo hoo!), but I couldn't help muttering to myself, *you wouldn't get that at Glastonbury*. I kid you not; there was a woman watching Echo and the Bunnymen on a footstool. It's no wonder Ian McCulloch was in a rock-star bad mood. It's like the crowd had kitted themselves out with accessories from the Betterware catalogue.

So you see, I might be with X, but I secretly, heck, brazenly, want to be with the cooler, more rock 'n' roll Y. It's the 'grass is always greener' quandary. Since you ask, there were no fit men at the festival. None at all. Just groovy dads and a lot of short people. To be precise, short men on the shoulders of their larger friends. I felt sorry for that guy, actually. Not because of his height but because he was twatted in the back of his head by a flying beer bottle. He got down after that.

JULY
Picking Up

Thursday, 2 July

'Still single' should be a marital status all of its own. When people declare, 'You're *still* single!' or 'I can't believe you're still single', as they tend to when you've been perishing in the wilderness for as long as I have, it's difficult to know what to say back, especially if they're not a really good mate.

I guess it's sort of a compliment (*you're so gorgeous, there's no way you should be single!*), or at least a declaration of pity, but, for me, its emphatic tone always leaves a freakish residue in the air. You know, where I'm the freak.

In the case of 'Yorkshire', my bearded and bolshie ex four times removed, his angle was genuinely puzzled. When we went out for a curry last night (he lives in New York now but comes back to Blighty from time to time), he was reeling off my positive attributes to make his case:

1. Good-looking (can't remember his exact words because I think he felt awkward saying it)
2. Funny (I know!)
3. Intelligent (to be sure!)

Then he paused for a sec before flourishing, '*And you can cook!*' Ha. Well, quite. I felt like adding 'solid hindquarters' into the mix but decided against it.

Joking aside, because Yorkshire and I are such compatible sparring partners and I know he accepts me wholly for who I am, I was able to spit out my naan bread in mock disgust and gesticulate wildly along the lines of: '*I know! What's wrong with them! They don't know what they're missing*,' etc., etc. With Yorkshire, my First Proper Boyfriend and *one and only* successful boyfriend-to-friend, he kind of does know what he's missing and still thinks I'm a good bet, so that makes it kind of nice. He'd make a good pimp.

But with somebody who doesn't know you quite so well, like an old journo friend who emailed me today, the implications are slightly different. When she declared, 'You're still single!' (yep, she did use an exclamation mark), I was tempted to go back with something ridiculous like, 'It's difficult to find men who are adequately endowed' or 'After my court case, it's been so much more difficult to make them stick, you know?', just 'cause it's so damned patronising!

So how do you turn this around, reclaim it and make it positive? I'm thinking a 'Still Single' T-shirt line, or setting up in the burgeoning logo jewellery business so we can hang our status around our necks. You know, just to be clear.

Do guys ever get asked if they are still single?

Friday, 3 July

Dull? Limp? Lifeless? Yes, yes and yes! It's on days like today that I'm so glad to be freelance. Working in an office does not sit well with midweek hedonism. Nor do the Metropolitan Police, for that matter, which is exactly what crossed my mind while I was standing in Brixton, shifty as hell, waiting for the night bus. But still, beyond working for myself for reasons related to variety of work and an enhanced sense of creativity (ahem), blatantly it's pretty sweet being able to get trolleyed on a Thursday night and not get sacked the next day. You just have to not do it all the time. Repeat after me: *You just have to not do it all the time!*

So, last night at a grimy music venue in Camden I re-met a guy with the best name in the world. I can't share it here, so we'll call him 'Power Boy'. He was playing a gig with his Scottish punk-rock band.

Before you ask, no, they're not famous. They're at the stage where they're playing little gigs to a few people in beer-soaked indie haunts and spend a lot of time arguing with each other in a shitty people carrier. They're also mental because they're Glaswegians.

I first met Power Boy over the May bank holiday weekend. Angel and I took a road trip together for some valuable bonding time. The first leg was to her parents' place in the Northumberland hills to generally loll in the garden; the second, to Glasgow, to stay with her trippy-hippy mate 'Starlight' for a spot of fun. Scotland's best city is perfect for such adventures of abandonment, which is exactly how I came to meet Power Boy.

We were in a bar that turned into a rave that turned into a party back at Starlight's place. Fuelled by some gorgeous little blue pills and the goadings of the boys we invited back to Starlight's, I donned my bikini for some dancing. Ridiculous. By noon the next day, Power Boy, who had delighted us with tales of his misadventures around Glasgow and amazing repertoire of funny faces, was the lone boy left with four girls. We moved the party on to what Starlight calls 'the meadow' just down from her tenement. It's actually a field with a few allotments, but the perfect spot for post-party lazing in rare Glasgow sunshine.

It was while lying in the meadow that I developed my affection for Power Boy. We didn't even kiss, but he did show me his and I showed him mine. And we held hands and stared at the blue sky together on our backs. When he finally staggered on his way late into the Saturday night, we vowed to meet up in London at his next gig. Which was last night.

Angel and I watch him gurn out his set before adjourning to the taproom for beers. It was funny seeing him in lead singer mode, all commanding and staccato, when last month he could barely take two steps without assistance. It's clear we're going to get on as we head to the roped pen outside to smoke, but then we suddenly become weirdo magnets. My favourite: a speed-ravaged crusty from Bournemouth who's keen to tell us all about a rave she *nearly* attended back in '93 . . . it was massive!

Anyway, he could see the funny side, which is encouraging. This boy has everything – cute indie boy good looks (skinny jeans, plaid shirt and floppy fringe), a gift for the absurd and a naughty side. He's also completely unsuitable boyfriend material because he spends half his time crammed in a van traipsing up and down the country and he doesn't have a mobile phone. It was run over by a drunk driver, he reckons. I even like this guy's bullshit! Last night, because he had to sleep in said van all the way back to Glasgow, I wasn't able to tempt him to my love nest, though we did try and persuade his manager. We settled for sharing a pill, kisses and sweet nothings instead. Next time, Power Boy, next time.

And now I need to get my shit together for Manchester – a weekend with Lady Jane.

Saturday, 4 July

Saturday morning and Lady Jane wakens me in the living room by rustling a Sainsbury's bag in my face. 'Pork products!' she says in her shrillest Julie Andrews voice. A surefire way to get me up, especially in this flat, where one half, her other half, is vegetarian. Having me and my meat-loving ways in residence is the perfect excuse for her to indulge. When she comes to mine, she calls herself a meat tourist. You just have to follow the crumbs to find her chowing down on a hunk of bread caked in chorizo.

While she's cooking the juicy meat sausages and putting the sorry-looking frozen Linda Ms under the grill, I tell her the Power Boy story and sense her stifling a groan: *not another silly band boy who lives at the other end of the country*. Now, Lady Jane has her own silly band boy, as it happens, but he's outgrown the silly phase to become a fully fledged, money-earning, of-sensible-age 'Rockstar', who's actually a total gem, and they're completely in love and settled. They even have pet names for each other, which could make you gag but strangely it doesn't with them because they're so damn cool.

This difference in our relationship status – her moving towards settling down in a big house and having a baby with the man of her dreams, me copping off in fields with young wannabes for the hell of it – has various implications:

1. She loves the vicarious pleasure of my sometimes ridiculous adventures. Whenever I've been on a date, she'll be the first to text '???' in the morning if she hasn't heard from me.
2. Whenever she comes to see me in London, she goes wild. Wild with meat and recreational activities, *not* other men.
3. She worries about me, and so does Rockstar. From their ivory penthouse in central Manchester, I think they consider me to be reckless, with my fast living and fast loving.

Ultimately, along with Angel, she knows and loves me better than anyone and is, I'd say, desperate for me to meet somebody who 'deserves me' (her words).

I met Lady Jane at university. She was immaculate, like properly 'done', to the point of wearing lip liner every day and crayoning on her eyebrows. She's still the same except she's done away with the blonde highlights, embraced her gingerness and her dress sense is more boho blue-stocking than Manchester shop girl (she used to work in the hell hole that was Morgan).

We were on the same course – English and communication studies. When we first met, I was intimidated by her knowledge of literature. I still am, actually. She's a super-brain. And a brilliant cook. She's not that posh, really, but showed a touch of class from an early age, with pesto and pimento olives crowding our shared student fridge. How do you repay the woman who introduced you to pesto?

She's also the funniest person I know. A total potty mouth. And creative. And passionate. She's mad about outer space, a fierce protector of birds and a brilliant friend. If I'm feeling down or ill or a bit mental, as well as her wonderful words she'll always offer something practical too, like 'Get comfy, eat some nice food and watch a great film.' She's soothing. She's also a demon when she's had a drink.

Sunday, 5 July

Ugh. That thing about Lady Jane being a demon on the booze? She was dancing with a mop at 4 o'clock this morning. To 'Blueberry Hill'. Though if anyone could feasibly look good dancing with a Vileda, it's her. Sexy almost. Rockstar certainly seemed to think so. He just kept slurring 'fit' in his soft Manc accent over and over again as she writhed against the pole. We drank *shitloads*. Drinking is not my best sport, in that after a certain point I will puke. I managed to hold it together, just, but felt decidedly queasy come the small hours. There's a former public convenience that's been turned into a bar near their place and we always end up bunkered in, downing vodka after vodka, or in Rockstar's case Guinness with a whisky chaser. Then, because it's so damned convenient, the bar comes back to theirs. That's how we came to be dancing to 'Blueberry Hill'. Now? I think I might puke.

Monday, 6 July

Back in London. I always feel a bit sad making the journey south. I love London and I've been here close to ten years, but my heart's in the north. I wish Lady Jane and I were in the same city. We often say that to each other over the phone, or ask, wishfully, 'Do you want to come over for a cup of tea?' What larks!

Tuesday, 7 July

I've been seeing a guy every few months for the last six or so years. He's attentive, funny, smart, good with his hands. He's my hairdresser. I've got a crush. A big one. And no, he's not gay. I went into the Bond Street salon recently and, with his guidance, went for shorter underneath with a kind of trendy bird's nest on top. This involved a lot of scrunching on his part, which was most enjoyable for me. OK, this is starting to sound a bit pervy. *If only*. It is a bit confusing, though. He kisses me on my lips when I arrive and leave. Is that just a hairdresser thing? We laugh all the time. Oh, how we laugh! We have loads in common – you know, films, music, preferred holiday destinations (he recommended a hotel in Barcelona). He looks a bit like Mike Skinner from The Streets, wears cool Young Casual clothes, is a part-time DJ and a mountain-bike enthusiast. He's also single at the moment, so I've been wondering, how do I take the relationship from the chair to the bedroom? Ha.

It's this kind of forward thinking that finds me bereft on my sofa at three o'clock Waiting For A Text when I should be typing up an interview that's due in the next day. There have been developments. Last time I was in the salon, let's call him 'Mr Scissors' was scolding me for my lack of interest in Wimbledon. For me, once Nadal's injury was announced I tuned out. I know I should've been rooting for grumpy Murray, but I just couldn't. Nadal, on the other hand – he's fit! I love his petulant, muscly ways. As for patriotism – I'm a citizen of the world, baby. Plus, I am rather a fan of Nadal's homeland, Majorca, as a holiday destination. Anyway, Mr Scissors seemed to think I should've been gripped to the late-night floodlit match that got Murray's Mound all excited the other night (I ask you, Murray's Mound?), so he instructed me to watch the semi-final. Whatever you say, sir.

The next day, I watch it and see it as the perfect opportunity to text him. I got his number at some point in our history, but we never usually communicate between cuts.

Me: 'Guess what I'm watching? x.'

Wait. Wait. He's probably in the middle of a cut. He can't text back straight away . . . Wait. Bleep.

Mr Scissors: 'Well done x.'

Hooray! A response. A bit brief . . . It does have a kiss, though. Then, an hour or so later: bleep.

Mr Scissors: 'Fucking hell . . . hope you haven't got a heart condition x.'

Witty response, witty response???

Me: 'My heart has served me well thus far. I am suffering from an unsteady drinking hand, though x.'

Ooh, that was good, even if I do say so myself. Bleep!

Mr Scissors: 'I knew you had a drinking problem x.'

Me: 'I've got a problem keeping my drinks chilled x.'

Mr Scissors: 'Drink faster x.'

You can imagine, this was all very exhilarating. Flirty? I think so, but I can't be sure. It's text tennis! But what's the next move? Well, quite: the tricky second move. Like with the difficult second album, your innocence is gone. What if the first one was just a fluke? Only one way to find out! So, yes, in a crazy fit of spontaneity I opted to text him on my way back from Manc yesterday. Now, I love a bit of spontaneity but find that a lot of my spur-of-the-moment thoughts and actions don't turn out so well. Such is the life of a romantic.

It was innocent enough: 'How was the seaside?' was my brief and breezy offering. He was at some dance festival on the Essex coast, I'd learned when he was scrunching me. And nothing. No response. The cruellest blow! What does it mean? It's almost 24 hours since I sent it. He's not going to reply now, is he? All five friends who I've been in touch with to discuss his lack of reply agree that he probably won't text back now. Is his lack of response due to the fact he's dying some kind of post-festival death or that, gasp, *he's just not that into me*? Or neither of the above?

Texting. Part 2.

Guys are pretty crap/sporadic/inconsistent/slack when it comes to texting, aren't they? Whatevs, it's still hugely disappointing, and the same thought always nags in the back of my mind when I'm waiting on a response: if he really liked me, he'd text. As always, though, there's the counter-argument, which Angel always pulls out, relating to the early days of her and G's courtship (they're three-years-happy). He often didn't text back and it wound her up no end, but ultimately it didn't mean anything. Well, apart from the fact that he's a bit shit when it comes to texting.

I read in a neuroscience book that there is an actual scientific reason for the post-text lull. When you send a text or email (or whatever), you experience an adrenalin surge in anticipation of what might come to pass. The downside, like any upper, is that when it becomes apparent that there won't be any kind of utopia at the end of this particular SMS rainbow, your dopamine levels plummet. Literally, your mood juices drop. It's scientific fact. I don't know if that makes me feel better or worse, but you know, FYI.

Wednesday, 8 July

'The sky was that dirty violet of a storm coming.' After today's somewhat biblical weather, this is an apt quote, borrowed from the book I'm currently reading, *The Girl's Guide to Hunting and Fishing* by Melissa Bank. It's good – a Lady Jane recommendation and a smart, literary take on the hunt for love. The quote also accurately describes my rather stormy mood today. For why, I'm not sure. Maybe it's the haunting loneliness? Maybe it's the fact I can't seem to drag my ass off the settee to do some work? Maybe it's the fact I've got too much time on my hands to procrastinate over what the fuck is bothering me?

I never did get a text back from Mr Scissors, but I think I'm over that – it only took, ooh, two days of sulking. My friend Pfeiffer is having similar text troubles with, let's call him 'Mr Chicken', and we've been moaning via email about it for the best part of two hours. It's true what they say about the British economy going down the pan. It's not the bankers who are at fault, though, it's all us women whingeing on our work emails about a guy who hasn't texted back.

I've known Pfeiffer – a beauty with cheekbones like Michelle and a retro red pout – for a good few years now. Six? Seven? We did a journalism postgrad together at London College of Fashion and stayed friends. She's the first new friend I made in London all by myself. Lately, we've entered a new phase of our relationship because we're both – shout it loud, ladies – single at the same time! A precious thing. And we're both fond of analysing the shit out of our usually disappointing encounters, like Mr Chicken.

She'd been on an afternoon date with him last week and since then had sent a jovial text in lieu of their next date, arranged for tomorrow. Nada. Nothing. A girl's gotta know what she's doing, though, so she texted him a few minutes ago to find out what the plan was for this pre-arranged meet, suggested by him. He just replied (good of you to respond this time, mate): 'Hello. Hey, I'm really sorry and have messed my dates up. Can we rain check?'

Tosser.

Films with a Romantic Angle. Part 2.

Nick and Norah's Infinite Playlist. A film is often a tonic when faced with emotional stormy weather. This particular movie belongs to one of my favourite movie genres, the indie teen flick, and stars one of my favourite young hotties, Michael Cera, of *Juno* and *Superbad* fame.

Well, hooray for this movie. Not only did I learn some new lingo, such as 'dancewich' (a type of close dancing, not unlike a person sandwich), but I was also able to forget my shitty non-day and drift into the nervous awkward excitement of teenage love. That is not meant to sound creepy. Cera is just so sweet, though – a gent with a knack for language, meaningful-but-shy stares and, apparently, gifted fingers. Yes, he pleasures Norah in NYC's Electric Lady music studio whilst they're, duh, still recording! It's a beautiful moment.

There are other things to learn from this film, too. Witness the following insightful yet witty exchange between Cera's character Nick and his soon-to-be-lady-love:

> Norah: What is it that keeps two people together for so long
> when it's not really going anywhere? (*she is questioning why
> she stayed with her loserville boyf for so long . . .*)
> Nick: Er, I don't know. We could call up my parents and find
> out?

Thursday, 9 July

Watching *Nick and Norah's Infinite Playlist* last night got me thinking about mix tapes, that somewhat retro staple of romantic gesturing. Nick in the movie is fond of making mix CDs. He's a music buff and plays in a band, so he's pretty accomplished at it too. He made them for his girlfriend when they were going out, but his best work came once they'd split. Heartbroken, he keeps on with the love curation, even making special DIY sleeves.

This, I've decided, is the mix tape's true purpose – a post-relationship torture device. We've been conned into thinking they're happy, 'we're-so-in-love-and-we-have-all-this-great-music-in-common' tokens, but in my experience they've always taken on a more sinister meaning. Take the one I received in my early 20s from, let's call him 'Reiki Boy'. He gave it to me when we'd split up, or maybe it was during the horribly drawn out 'we're on a break' period, and contained such gems as 'I Love U, But I Don't Trust U Any More' by Prince and 'Why You Wanna Treat Me So Bad', also by Prince. Yes, it paints me in rather a bad light, doesn't it?

Another significant mix came from the Big Ex, my second-to-last, most painful boyfriend, who I was with for five years. He had great taste and was something of a mentor to me in the ways of credible music (so clichéd, I know). This started out fun but became laborious as my life increasingly became like a game of musical Top Trumps and he'd scold me for mixing up my James Taylors and Neil Youngs.

Anyway, I'd been pestering him for, ooh, about three years to put me some CDs together with stuff I liked. You know, what with him doing fuck all at home apart from downloading music on my computer whilst I brought in the money. Needless to say he never managed to get his act together to complete this task while we were together. He waited until he was desperate and had completely fucked everything up before committing his feelings to CD. By then, it was, of course, too late. He seemed to think, though, that his magic mixing would magic the love back.

I have kept the CDs because he did have fantastic music taste, but I have covered his love message labelling with masking tape (glaringly obvious metaphor, anyone?) and the new titles 'Good Shit 1' and 'Good Shit 2'. That was therapy, of sorts. More on the dismals of my romantic past later, when I can face it.

Friday, 10 July

Oh what a beautiful morn-ing, oh what a beautiful day!

This weekend Angel and I are escaping the cruel metropolis, packing up Alabama, her VW campervan, and heading to the wilds of

Kent for a new-ish, small-ish music festival called Lounge on the Farm. There's nothing like the smell of chemical toilets to make you feel alive!

Tuesday, 14 July

Is this persistent head-wringing I feel swine flu or the after-effects of weird herbal highs? In other predictable news, I have developed another little crush on a very cute young man who we'll call 'Smiler'. He laughed at all my jokes, so he must be all right!

Angel and I are a rather formidable force when we're out together. Some of my best memories come from stupid adventures we've shared. She's also something of a honey trap when it comes to the fellas.

In rather immature fashion, Angel and I decided to clink glasses (if it's possible to clink plastic . . .) with any boys we found cute as we tramped around the festival site. Smiler was one such victim (how could he resist the opening gambit?) and we soon ended up having a little adventure with him, his very cute younger brother and their mate, culminating in a cosy little gathering back at the van with ridiculous conversations over red wine. It was cute because we were all, for some reason, gushing over how much we liked each other and vowed to meet up the next day.

I was getting vibes from Smiler, especially when he whipped off his plimsolls to let me slip them on 'cause I thought I needed to puke outside the van. I didn't, but still, not cool. He also gave me a foot massage – surely a sign of intimacy? I didn't even get one of them from the Big Ex.

When Smiler made his move to leave, I made my move for a kiss. He responded a little before stopping and saying, rather bashfully, 'I can't. I've got a girlfriend.' I was too inebriated to be embarrassed, so responded with a rambling, rather posh-sounding apology: 'Gosh, I didn't realise' – why would I? He didn't mention her – 'I'm ever so sorry.' The next day we meet in the folk tent for a jig and I shrug it off, much cooler this time, with 'Have you recovered from me throwing myself at you?' Laughs all round. And I'm sure

I'm still getting some admiring glances. Or is that just the Pimm's? Hmm.

Today, two days post-fest – the joyful bleep of a text. It's Smiler! 'It was so great hanging out with you. If you're going out on the town soon, give us a shout.' Interesting. Int-er-est-ing. Must forward his text to Angel, so we can give it the full once-over. Surely you wouldn't text the mad woman who nearly puked on your shoes before throwing herself at you unless you quite fancied her, no?

Afterthought of the day: why the fuck am I analysing the texts of a guy who knocked me back *and* has a girlfriend?

Wednesday, 15 July

I knew my mind was not quite my own when I found myself halfway around Sainsbury's putting shopping straight into my canvas bag, having missed out the bit where you pick up a shopping basket. There I was, attempting to squeeze a pack of four baking potatoes into the gap between my *Guardian* and New York Bagels, when I stopped, shocked, and realised what I was doing: shoplifting! Shitballs! Then, as if I was being watched, I started telling anyone who'd listen, 'Gosh, you'll never guess what I've just been doing? I've just been putting everything into my bag! I think I need to get a basket!' You know, just in case anyone did think I was on the rob. Clearly, though, no one gave a shit, so mine were just the rantings of a mad woman in the supermarket of a weekday afternoon. No big deal.

'You probably could've got away with it,' was Mrs Patz's response when I called to tell her en route home, shopping all paid for. I probably could have, since my moves were *Ocean's Eleven*-bold and the security guards are a bit docile, but – and this was the point I made to Mrs Patz – you don't want to get done for nicking a few bagels, do you? How sad is that? Then she told me about her mate who got caught nicking shampoo from the shop where she worked, and got fired for it. Surely, if you're going to steal, steal something good, no?

Anyway, I'm pretty sure my somnambulant circuit of the supermarket is related to the news I'm still trying to process from

Angel. When we were away at her mum's in May, she told me that she and G were planning a trip to South America in January. They'd be away for at least three months and she was going to quit her job. That was a bit of a shock, what with her being next door and like my right arm. But then, at the festival, she dropped a much bigger bombshell – when they get back from their travels, they're going to leave London for good and move to Manchester. Sorry, what?

I feel numb. I actually can't imagine life without her here, which probably explains why I'm sleepwalking through my chores. I need time to process this and work out how much of it is about me knowing I'm going to miss her like crazy and how much of it is about me wondering why *I'm* not embarking on a life journey with a Significant Other. Is my life static while she's moving on? I hate these gremlins, because I know that's what they are, but I can't deny that they're there.

Thursday, 16 July

If in doubt, run home to Mum and Dad. I'm on the train, that familiar journey from King's Cross up the east coast to Leeds. Train journeys are a good time to reflect, gaze dreamily out of the window and generally have a mooch through your brain. Which I totally would do if it wasn't for the fact there's a girl opposite me weaving. Weaving! With a fuck-off wooden frame and threatening-looking needle. The latter is why I'm not asking her to move her shit so I can actually fit my laptop properly on the table. I mean, really. You get all sorts on the train. Especially the ones up north.

Friday, 17 July

Being 'back home' means a number of things:

1. Staying in my old bedroom, complete with the decor I chose when I was 13 and jazzy borders were compulsory.
2. A frantic supply of hot drinks, sandwiches and questions from Mum.
3. Road rage and general grumbling from Dad. Last time I was

home, he called a fellow motorist a cunt. Mum nearly had a
heart attack.

4. Fried egg sandwiches for supper, served at approximately
   11.30 p.m. See no. 2.

5. Bacon sandwiches, my favourite, served for breakfast. See
   no. 2.

6. *Family Guy* – Dad and I always snigger at it together, while
   Mum shakes her head disapprovingly or nods off in the
   chair.

7. Drinking – I always drink a lot when I'm home, either in the
   local pub, which is but a five-minute walk away, or 'down
   town', which is no way as romantic as Petula Clark makes it
   sound in the song.

8. 'Roller Girl' – my old friend from sixth-form college, who I
   always try to catch up with when I'm home. She's a total
   blast.

9. Smoking with Dad in the conservatory and quietly chatting.
   Dad's one cool motherfucker.

10. 'Cartoon Boy'. He broke my heart.

Saturday, 18 July

When I was with Lady Jane and Rockstar a few weeks ago, we sat and
did the Q&A that comes in the front of *Guardian Weekend* magazine.
It's fun to see what answers you'd give if you were a somebody. One
of the questions is 'When were you happiest?' and my answer to that
was 'When I'm having breakfast at Mum and Dad's.' Apart from the
fact that my love of bacon knows no bounds, I always feel content
sitting at the dining-room table eating breakfast with Mum and Dad,
chatting about anything and nothing and topping up my mug of tea
from the teapot. Proper tea, with a strainer. You know you have those
moments where you catch yourself being happy? That's it, for me.
It's the routine and the comfort and the safety. And the pork.

When I'm at home, it's always a lottery as to whether I'll bump
into my most recent and significant ex, Cartoon Boy. This is a total
bummer because home has always been a bit of a haven and now it

resembles some kind of emotional assault course: I never know when I'll get my leg caught in the rope swing and land, shame-faced, in the dirty water trough.

He made quite the impression on me. Still does, really. He was my Nearly Love, in that I think I loved him but we never said the words. He did send me an ambiguous text once, though, saying, 'I luv you!'; the dickish spelling aimed to detract from the true sentiment. I loved him, but he dumped me in that shitty way boys do, by stopping calling or avoiding you until you force them into a corner and practically beg to be dumped. I'm not sure I'm over it even now, more than a year on.

We met 'down town' in a God-awful club. I was with Roller Girl, dancing to 'Dizzy' by Vic Reeves and the Wonderstuff, like you do, in the indie basement. There are three floors at this establishment, each playing a different genre of music – a sign of a rubbish club if ever there was one.

I liked him immediately, standing before me with a massively impish grin and really great style. Unusual in those parts, let me tell you. He stood out. I couldn't believe he'd lived in the same village as me and I'd never seen him before. There was something romantic about that, but then I would say that. Our first date involved a tour of all the 'shit' pubs in our hometown, followed by a hasty check-in to an equally dodgy hotel. It was hilarious – I loved his spontaneity. He bought ten quid's worth of raffle tickets for me to win a giant teddy bear in one pub. In another, a proper rough saloon, hauntingly quiet with a lone gas fire in the middle of the room, this scary-looking guy confronted him at the bar and said, 'What you looking so pleased wi' yerself for? You 'ad knob up?' I nearly spat out my Campari and orange juice at this, but he kept his cool and replied, 'Not yet, but maybe later.' Fair enough. He was right. He didn't get his head kicked in and I enjoyed 'Heartbreaker' by Dionne Warwick on the jukebox. There was a certain pathos to the evening.

He brought me a bright red ukulele on our second date, in London, even though his friends had advised him against it. He ignored them and I, of course, thought it was perfect. It is the single most romantic gesture of my life so far.

Our relationship didn't last long – five months plus one false start – but it was massively significant. Hence the emotional glue I get stuck in every time I'm home. My mum and dad listen patiently when I begin the same loop of exhausting questions. What happened? When did it go wrong? Did I do something? Was there someone else? Was he just too scared to carry on? It doesn't change the fact that we ended and will remain ended, but I still can't shake 'the little fucker' off, as Lady Jane likes to call him.

The last time I saw him was Boxing Day last year. Before that, the last contact we'd had, a few months earlier, was an email I sent in a rage: 'I've given you too much credit, don't ever contact me again.' He'd been contacting me with mixed messages, probably just to preserve his ego, to make sure I was still there. I had to say enough was enough.

I may as well tell you the tragic Boxing Day story since I'm on a roll. I walk into my local pub – it's Donkey Derby day, so it's packed. Everyone comes out of the woodwork for this silly annual pretend horse-race thing. Even though it's not out of the question that I might bump into him, this isn't actually his preferred local of all the locals. It's *my* local. A point that prompted Lady Jane to shriek, 'What's he doing in *your* pub?'

I walk in and bam! There he is, the first impish face I see. That email I sent flashes across my hurt-sodden brain and it's literally all I can do to say hi, pat him on his back like he's a comrade or football teammate and walk on by. On reflection, perhaps this was the epitome of cool, especially since I was wearing my rather fetching fur coat, but it was also residually awful, especially since this time the year before we'd done our tour of the shit pubs.

After doing my weird walk-by, I drained my drink in ten minutes, left the pub without so much as a glance and spent the rest of Boxing Day hunched on my auntie's couch with my little cousin feeling very fucking depressed. There's photographic evidence of this, with me wearing that totem of familial festive misery – the paper party hat. Happy memories.

Sunday, 19 July

Wake up rough at Roller Girl's after a night boozing in town. It's good to go out when I'm home, if only to remind myself why I moved away. In one place last night, this guy said to me, 'You wanna watch somebody doesn't strangle you in that scarf.' That was after he'd licked my face by way of saying hello. I'm not even joking.

My mouth tastes horrific. I've been tossing and turning on the spare futon since God knows what time. Roller Girl's cats Starsky and Charlie keep scraping at the door, trying to get in. Me not being a cat person, it feels like I'm about to become the victim of some kind of horror movie massacre.

I drag myself downstairs to find Roller Girl ligging on her giant couch, watching a shit home-improvements show in her trackie bottoms. This is how the professional classes live, don't you know?

'Morning!!' Roller Girl is the most cheerful person in the world, even when faced with a hangover. Add to this the fact that she's also the most hardcore and that's pretty impressive. She's like the Duracell Bunny – she can go for days. Speaking of bunnies, *Alice in Wonderland*'s White Rabbit was Roller Girl's fancy dress costume of choice at New Year at the party she and her husband, the Chef, throw most years. The costumes, along with the number of days the parties tend to roll on for, are legendary. One year, the Chef 'blacked up' as Mr T, sporting a load of brass bathroom chains slung around his neck and a Mohican. She wore a full rabbit suit, with giant, really heavy head. It was ridiculous because her costume was almost too big for the house and she was absolutely boiling. Sweating. But she's a trouper, so she persevered.

Some of my favourite stories involve Roller Girl. Like the time she was having a mild asthma attack at home after a particularly heavy weekend. This in itself wasn't funny, but what ensued was. The Chef called an ambulance, to be on the safe side. When they arrived, the paramedic put one of those breathing masks on her but said they should go to the hospital, again just to be safe. So they're manoeuvring her into the ambulance, but she's desperately trying to communicate with the Chef, waving her hands, gesturing wildly – but she can't talk because she's beneath the breathing mask. She's in the ambulance and it's too late – she's wearing a flimsy dressing gown and no knickers! It's like a bad dream. The worst of it was, once she'd been given the all-clear in casualty, they discharged her into the dark cold night, leaving her and the Chef to attempt to flag down a cab with no money and no knickers. You've gotta love that girl.

Despite being out in town last night, I've managed to get through the weekend without bumping into Cartoon Boy. Result. Back to Ma and Pa's for the Sunday traditions of roast dinner followed by *Antiques Roadshow*. My dad loves that show, and whereas I used to resent it when I was younger, I now love it. Why? Because it feels like home.

Monday, 20 July

Meet Angel after work for a post-weekend catch-up over a few beers in the Cave. We both sob for the first half hour of seeing each other. It feels like we're counting down.

Tuesday, 21 July

Pasta, pesto, sun-dried tomatoes, cherry tomatoes and mozzarella: standard weeknight dinner. Angel and I have arranged to have a proper conversation about her leaving, rather than our recent avoidance approach, or combusting into tears. It's funny sometimes being the single one in a pair of fast friends because you can't help feeling like the loser who's being left behind. I hate myself for even thinking that, but it's there, chipping away. There's also the fact that she'd rather live in a different city than live in the city she shares with me. At one time we were inseparable.

'I think I'm hurt that you could actually leave me,' I admit, sounding like a jilted lover, as we perch on my sofa, pasta bowls balanced on our knees.

'I can't believe I'm going to leave you,' she replies, swallowing a massive mouthful. 'It's the hardest decision I've ever made, but we just feel ready to have a change and leave London.'

She's filling up. Angel has this habit of crying at the drop of, well, anything.

We've been through a lot together over the years, me and her, helped each other through a lot, which is why this is such a shock. We're like a double act almost (hopefully a good one) and I can't imagine her not being there, next door. You have good friends, best friends even, but how often do you have that person next door? We literally share a life. You can't really beat that. To be fair, her boyfriend, as much as we get on amazingly and I love him, might be ready for a bit of distance. We are weirdos who finish each other's sentences and have silly catchphrases. God, I even hate the sound of us when I write it down. *Change is good, change happens*. I need to try and get my head around it.

'I don't want to become like those friends that meet up for the odd weekend and it's all really unspontaneous and lame,' she says with pleading eyes before offering me a ritualistic, tough-times rollie.

'That will never happen,' I reply, inhaling.

I can't be sure, though, of course. The fact is, I don't want her to be a friend that I go and visit. It's not the same. And we both know it.

Wednesday, 22 July

Lately, I've been considering prostituting myself on the internet. I'm teetering on the edge, thinking about dipping a toe in, but fearful of just how hostile those waters might turn out to be. And the shame. *Ooh, the shame!!!*

The TV ads don't help. One is promising a six-month guarantee – 'Don't wait for cupid,' it warns. 'If you don't find love in six months, we'll give you your money back.' You know what that makes me want to do? *Not* find love just to see how the refund process works.

The one that really grates, though, is eHarmony: 'The relationship site' that is apparently responsible for 2 per cent of all marriages in the US. It makes me want to vom. You know those moments when you're on your own, desperately wishing someone, anyone, was with you to share the unbelievable thing you've just witnessed? Well, seeing that ad for the first time was one of those moments. This particular hammy service is offering something 'unique', indeed something 'serious'. The voice, similar in tone to those adverts for life insurance once you've entered retirement or if your spouse happens to die on you, begins: 'If you're serious about finding love' ... then I got 'deep' and 'lasting' and 'shared values' before switching over in a rage. As if I need another reason *not* to get involved with the devil that is virtual matchmaking.

Thursday, 23 July

I'm in the fashion office today and was greeted first thing with an email from Pfeiffer titled 'Pfeiffer takes action!' Is this some kind of politically themed call to arms, I wonder? Iran, perhaps? Nope, but the action she speaks of is twofold:

1. Daring to call rather than text a current suitor.
2. Sending a direct Facebook message to another conquest rather than continuing to 'poke' him.

Now, don't get me wrong, I'm not criticising my friend here at all because I'd be exactly the same, but it's a sad state of affairs when picking the phone up or being direct (rather than virtually obtuse) is considered affirmative action, no?

But, let's examine the evidence. So she said:

> Hmmm – had a few drinks last night and got a bit brave. Thought why do we sit around analysing texts and messages and not just take action? So I called Boy X to ask him to some film thing next week (he said he was quite into that). Got voicemail and left a message, no response so don't think that's a goer – he prob thinks am a stalker now! On the bright side I also sent a message to fit Boy Y on FB and said look let's stop 'virtual' poking and meet up for a beer next Wed – to which he agreed – so will see ...

My response to this is also twofold:

1. 'You really haven't given Boy X time to respond yet, so let's not be de-throned from our position of power just yet; to text and call once does not a stalker make.'
2. 'You go, girl! Stop virtual poking indeed and yippee for pointing that out to him cos it's kind of pathetic to poke and not follow through.'

Imagine this – they're actually going to meet up. In person. Shit. A. Brick.

Her closing remarks were, 'Well, one out of two ain't bad.' Indeed. And always good to:

1. Skirt dangerously close to a Meatloaf lyric.
2. Remind ourselves every now and then that these flaky good-for-nothings are merely statistics to punctuate the boredom of the daily grind.

Friday, 24 July

Well, she got a response – but by text. Now, personally, I think a call should be returned with a call, not a weedy text. In his defence, Boy X is at a music festival, so could be in a right old state. I hurry to point this out, then Pfeiffer informs me that in said text he called her by the wrong name! Tit.

Texting. Part 3.

Basic text rule no. 1: make sure the person you're addressing is the person you're addressing. *Capiche?* And Pfeiffer was fretting about the lack of a kiss! Cruel, it might seem, but I had to point out to her, at midnight last night when we were, er, texting through the problem, 'Boys are shit with kisses, but he can't even get your name right, so the lack of kiss is neither here nor there.' Tough love.

Saturday, 25 July

A weekend staying in. Goodie! Some people say that weekends for a single person can be lonely or depressing. I think any time can be lonely/depressing whether you're part of a couple or single, and actually some of my most depressed and lonely times have been when I've been in a relationship. At a weekend. There's nothing worse. Give me two days stretching ahead, cable TV, no firm plans, one of my best girl mates (in this case, cousin Rubles), no moaning boyfriend and, well, to my mind, you got yourself a party.

It's all about how you approach every 'task'. And this weekend there were a lot of tasks. It's like my dad has drummed into me: 'You can appreciate relaxing all the more if you do a few jobs.' Now, the ratio of jobs to relaxing is definitely heavily weighted in favour of the latter chez moi, unlike at my parents' house, where the ridiculous work ethic is palpable as soon as you walk through the door. Cross the threshold and you're highly likely to trip over my apron-clad mum on her hands and knees scrubbing the lino. A *little* of this has rubbed off on me, which leads to me to one of my tasks of the weekend:

1. Cleaning the top of the cooker: this really was satisfying because after my porridge had boiled over earlier in the week (I know, get me, making porridge!), it had crème brûléed itself onto the stainless steel. This meant I had to first chisel it off with a palette knife before getting stuck in with the fancy spray. It took some elbow grease, I tell you. But it meant after I'd rinsed my manky cloth out for the 17th time I sat down feeling like I'd achieved something and was content to watch . . .

2. *Diagnosis Murder* followed by *Murder, She Wrote*. Man, I love a murder mystery. It's a passion Rubles and I share, so imagine our glee to discover we were watching The Best Episode of *Diagnosis Murder*, Like, Ever. Now, we love Dick and Barry van Dyke hard, but they outdid themselves this time. The guy whodunnit was pretending to have cerebral palsy in order to cover his crime. This was uncomfortable viewing. The acting was so bad that we were forced to ask, is this a shit actor trying to mimic someone who has cerebral palsy, or does he actually have cerebral palsy? We were kind of put in a position where it was really hard not to laugh, which is obviously really tight. Of course, it turned out that it was a shit actor, not to mention an

absolutely ludicrous plot. I enjoyed it so much from my supine position on the couch, I kept saying over and over, 'I'm so happy right now.' *Murder, She Wrote* was standard: Jessica visits a dear rich friend who lives in a weird American mansion and has a lot of horses. There's a dispute over a will, and the family dog, who stands to inherit millions, is implicated in the murder. Again, ludicrous.

3. Lunch break. Fresh cannelloni with not one but two fresh sauces from Sainsbury's. And a little glass of vino. Rock and roll.

4. Film. Now, Rubles specifically requested something along the lines of *The Holiday*, so a romantic comedy that's not unashamedly shit but is still very easy on the brain. *New in Town* spoiler alert: Renée Zellweger relocates to snowy Minnesota town in ridiculous heels and shags a rugged-looking Harry Connick Junior. This started off a bit silly, if I'm honest, but by the end, when she saves the small town and the factory that glues it together and beats those nasty suits in Miami that she used to be a part of . . . well, there wasn't a dry eye in the house. Oh, and she shags Harry Connick Junior. Did I mention that? He was definitely one of the best things about *Will & Grace* in the end, don't you think?

5. The supermarket. When you're in a good mood, and Saturday was one of those days, the supermarket can be a joyous experience. Rubles and I were specifically shopping for our weekend at home and were cooking up a rather splendid chorizo and chickpea stew concoction and a chocolate cake for our friend Elvis's birthday (hey, keep on the straight and narrow at the weekend and you can move mountains). In a crazy fit of spontaneity, I also bought four and a half quid's worth of feta-filled chilli peppers. Ooh and posh biscuits, and a bottle of Chablis, and stuff to make smoked mackerel pâté, and some of that ridiculous crustless bread. What the heck? Live a little. We also had a hilarious encounter with a young lad who works there, when we realised there weren't any tinned cherry tomatoes. NIGHTMARE. He checked 'out back' and regretted to inform us that there wouldn't be any in store till tomorrow morning but, and this was odd, if we wanted to take him home he'd be our tomato for us to squash. Now, I admit I was showing a bit of cleavage, but that's

weird, no? They always go the extra mile, those lads at Sainsbury's. I'll give them that.

Can you believe all of this fun stuff that took place on Saturday and we're still only at teatime? I can't. Anyway, apart from the cooking, whilst singing along to Craig Charles's Funk and Soul Show on 6 Music (whom Rubles, incidentally, fancies), the rest of the day was spent on TV. It's amazing how much TV you can get through in one weekend if you really put your mind to it. Four episodes of *Without a Trace* back to back. Now, that's what I call a Saturday night.

PS. The chocolate cake, once we'd dabbed the excess oil up with loo roll (classy, I know), was an absolute triumph. Green & Black's is the shit.

Sunday, 26 July

'He has imposed on me, but he has not injured me.' What a great quote, eh? Continuing my lounging weekend, I watched a TV adaptation of *Emma* on ITV3, a true loafers' channel. A pre-Hollywood Kate Beckinsale was playing Emma. That was her line. *Emma* is all about dating manners, etiquette and social acceptability. I was just thinking about it in the shower and my mind wandered to a recent conversation I'd had with Elvis about hair, down there (HDT), a hot topic of modern-day dating etiquette if ever there was one. Anyway, Elvis, who's a lovely lovely boy, so don't judge him on this, said he felt that women's HDT is akin to wire wool and that after sex, when the woman inevitably wraps her legs around his, he, and I quote, 'wishes she'd put some pants on because it's beyond exfoliation'. What a scoundrel! You've gotta laugh, though.

I laughed when I discovered a guy I was seeing, let's call him 'Download Boy', shaved his HDT. I mean, *really*. He was also very interested in my preening habits, which, FYI any boys reading this, is a complete turn-off. I wasn't, shall we say, prepared on our first hook-up. I apologised – why do I do that? It's ridiculous. Though when I have said it, my favourite responses from decent guys have been: 'Ach, I'm a caveman' and 'I don't give a shit about that'. Not

Download Boy, though. He offered to sort it out for me. *As if.* I declined. He also told me it was his ex-girlfriend who instigated his own shaving routine. Again, not appealing. That said, I did go there again (I know, I know) and this time I was prepared. He commented immediately: 'I like what you've done down there.' Eeeew. This is the very same guy who, on our third sleepover date, stayed up whilst I went to bed (who does that?) and downloaded my iTunes AND changed the settings on my computer. I kid you not. Shades of *Sleeping with the Enemy* or what? I still itch now, when I think of him.

Places to Meet Men. Part 1.

'Bars are not the place to meet men' – if I had a drink for every time some bright spark has told me this, I'd be dead. Now, I don't know if it's said because there's some idea that you won't meet the right sort of man in a drinking establishment, but the fact is, I met ALL of my past boyfriends in bars, and as I run through a mental checklist of my friends' relationships they met all their partners in bars, too. And some of them are married. Imagine that!

I don't buy all this meeting men at book clubs, supermarkets or friggin' salsa classes; you look/feel like a weirdo at the best of times, trying to approach people you fancy, but at least in a bar/club or at a festival there is an unspoken level of understanding that romantic fumbles may take place. This, for me, makes it easier. Since getting a bit older, the notion of 'getting off' with someone in a bar or club feels a little less comfortable than it did in my late teens or uni days, but, still, it's not off limits.

I got to thinking about appropriate places to pull because I find myself constantly fancying men on public transport. Before you start bringing to mind freaks in smelly anoraks, bear in mind that in London everybody takes the tube and it's rife with fitties. It's also rife with complications and the potential for high-octane embarrassment.

The thing is, people do check each other out on the tube – have you ever chosen a carriage based on potential talent? I have. I mean, there's jack all else to do. But how do you get to second base? First up, there's the girlfriend issue – do they have one? How painful would it be to ask?! Second, approach anyone on public transport at your peril because they will 99 per cent definitely think you're a freak. Nobody wants to talk, least of all on the way to work. Third, you're in a public cattle carrier crammed with a shitload of people not talking and probably in bad moods. It'd be like some kind of self-sacrificing mission to dare to try and chat up a stranger with the entire carriage staring upon you. And what to say? 'Hi? What's your name? Which stop is yours?' I mean, come on. I cringe at the very thought.

I need to turn this situation around, though, because there's so much untapped potential. For example, one day this week there was this super-hot guy in a pale-grey button-down shirt, rolled-up trousers and cool plimsolls in my tube carriage en route to the fashion office. He had proper green eyes, an ear stud, cropped hair and a deliciously moody face. He was HOT. Sorry, just reliving that for a second . . . Anyway, we checked each other out; I'd like to think there was a shared thought process of 'Yeah, you look like my kinda guy/girl' and I swear I could feel the tension. I didn't do anything – well, beyond burning a hole in his skull with all my meaningful stares. But then – and get this – en route home approximately eight hours later, he only got in the same carriage as me! A sign. Surely?

Of course, this is what my delusionary romantic mind starts thinking. I stare some more and hope that he's as pleasantly freaked as me by our double meet, but alas, nothing happens. So what to do? I'm not exactly shy (and I'm certainly prone to making a tit of myself sometimes), but I can't for the life of me summon up the courage to make a move on the tube. But I say it again – there are hundreds of fit boys all over this goddamn city transport system of ours! And it's so humid and sticky right now. Sigh.

Monday, 27 July

Once more I've left my very moral being at the door and taken the plunge into internet dating. Yep, right now hearts are beating just a little bit faster, thanks to my presence in romantic cyberspace. Or they would be, if the feckin' website hadn't rejected my photo! I can't help but think about those shit bars that don't let blokes in if they're wearing trainers but let manslaughter-hungry style losers through in their droves.

I've enlisted Lady Jane as my wing woman for this cringeworthy virtual journey. She very kindly wrote my recommendation – apparently, if it's your friend waxing lyrical about you, there's less chance of you sounding like a wanker. She's also been rampantly trawling the face-ist website for suitable suitors, depositing them in a cyber box for me to view, with a pithy comment attached, i.e. 'Nice teeth but could be a bit too straight (not the teeth. Him)' and 'I like the fact he laid a patio with his dad'. But my personal favourite: 'Not a recommendation, more an observation. If he's 32, then I'm a foetus.'

This is gonna be FUN.

Wednesday, 29 July

Received the following ode to me from Lady Jane to be approved by me and then posted, all unspontaneous-like, on My Single Friend:

The Sahara Desert, early evening. Two blaggers (aka journalists) on a luxury jeep safari with a group of rich, polite tourists. Most people would behave themselves in the face of such dramatic beauty but not my single friend Alison. As the other tourists posed for photos, she launched herself off the plateau and rolled to the bottom of the dune. She came back roaring with laughter and covered with sand, like a very long, thin, hysterical doughnut.

All the important things are here in this hopefully charming anecdote from my life-so-far with my friend. Al is impulsive, gutsy and original. She is hugely sociable and dazzlingly entertaining company.

Next I must flag up her natural beauty. I don't know anyone else who can wear so little make-up and look so stunning. She wakes up fresh as a daisy . . . And then tucks into a full cooked breakfast. Every day. (NB Non-pork lovers need not apply.) Plus she has still somehow managed to retain the same ass she had when she was 19. Bitch.

Al is bravely working freelance and a very respected and successful journalist she is, too. This is because she is curious, enjoys engaging with

*people and possesses a razor-sharp wit. Laugh? You'll ruin your pants.
She also likes nothing better than skiving on her sofa, watching American
sitcoms with a bowl of her native Yorkshire comfort food. Such as pasta (I
introduced her to pesto at university – it was like the scene where E.T. tries
Reese's Pieces).*

*What else? Well, she's kind, honest, full of the smarts – and (last but
not least) my favourite bad influence.*

Well, wow. What can I say? *I'd* almost want to go out with me. I'm
genuinely left a bit teary-eyed by Lady Jane's overtures. As the
person who's being pimped out, I then have to add some comments of
my own, thus:

*I'll just add a few things – music is a huge passion of mine and I'm
particularly fond of old or dead musicians, like Leonard Cohen and Love.
I'm generally very moved by culture and if I get an assignment to write
about art, music and the like, I'm very happy. I'm not sure if movie-
watching is much fun with me, though, especially if I've already seen it.
I'm always so desperate to share stuff that I love that my enthusiastic
pointing and nodding can be a bit off-putting. I'm working on that.*

*I guess I'm pretty up for it, mostly, and I'm looking for someone else
who's up for it too, but, you know, not in an annoying, shouty, hand-wavy
kind of way. I'm remarkably intolerant for one so liberal. Oh, and I don't
have a fry-up every morning; I think she meant bacon sandwich.*

Give me a shout, before I chicken out.

Now we wait.

Thursday, 30 July

I have a message! Ooh goody, somebody likes me! Even if I don't like
him, it's nice to be liked, eh? So, what's this guy got to say? Well,
once I'd paid some money (no money, no message), here's what I
found:

> Hey – you look cool but beauty is common, you are either born
> with it or can buy it, so I have some important questions in the
> form of a personality quiz. All you have to do is choose 1 of 2
> answers which best applies to you.

Ready . . .

    Lion or tiger?

    Out with friends or out on a date?

    Chinese takeaway or Indian takeaway?

    Blond guy or brunette guy?

    Attractive or funny?

    Vodka or beer?

    Superman or Batman?

    My Little Pony or Care Bears?

    Chocolate or sex?

    DVD or cinema?

    Chick flick or horror?

    Red or blue?

ALL I HAVE TO DO IS CHOOSE 1 OF 2 ANSWERS (that's the thing about a 50/50 . . .) WHICH BEST APPLIES TO ME. What a tool. My favourite insightful dichotomy has to be the chocolate or sex conundrum. Chocolate every time – if you're anywhere near me.

In an email titled 'What a dick', I send the offending quiz to Lady Jane for her appraisal. She replies: 'Oh God. He thinks he's Derren Brown, but he's more like Duncan from Blue. DON'T reply, whatever you do.'

August
Virtual Obsession

Saturday, 1 August

As far as I can tell, internet dating is like a really shit night out. One of those where it's only the weirdo undesirables who darken your door and nobody, repeat nobody, remotely fit or interesting approaches you. Then, to make it worse, there's much less chance you'll be drunk when you're doing it.

This is why I'm disproportionately ecstatic when today I receive an email from 'American Boy', a guy Angel and I met last year in New York and with whom I had a brief dalliance. An unbelievably sexy and mysterious guy who's the lead singer in a band, to be precise. And who's in possession of the best voice and most aloof attitude since the Strokes' Julian Casablancas. In fact, that's a good comparison. He and Julian should form a band, The Brothers Cool. To put this in perspective, he's definitely in the top five of the Fittest Men I've Ever Been With. Hmm, must dig out that list. It's nice to remember such things when your only 'action' is a virtual quiz enquiring after your takeaway preferences.

So, American Boy. Angel and I were out on the Lower East Side rocking 'n' rolling 'n' what not. We were dancing to a rather excellent DJ set in this downstairs dive bar called Mercury Lounge and 'Everyday' by Buddy Holly came on – one of our favourite tracks and too rarely heard out, in my humble opinion. That's when I spotted him. He was brooding around – all indie-meets-preppy floppy hair, a pout and a military jacket – with his super clean-cut mate who looked like Doogie Howser. We got chatting. Can't quite remember how now, but it didn't last that long and I thought I'd not made a particularly good impression. Angel and I had enjoyed a pretty hardcore party session the night before and I seem to remember boring on about that. He was super cool to the point of stand-offish (or so I thought) and then he disappeared, so I figured that was that. Doogie was pleasant enough, though – a real chatterbox. Worst luck.

But then . . . he reappeared – parting the club's crowd to find me. Ha, not quite, but it was verging on definitive. Would we like to join them at Motor City, a sort of biker bar further down the street? Would we ever?! So we went to the bar and then this guy, this beyond cool guy, suddenly turned totally teenage on me. He took my hand and swerved me towards what turned out to be the toilet queue. Then he started kissing me. Did I tell you he was hot? It was all so very unexpected. Then, he's beckoning me into the loo. I agree – I tend to be game when people ask me to do that. In his case, I was thinking this means one of two things – both would be pretty agreeable. So we're in the toilet and it was all getting pretty heated – where the fuck did this come from? He was certainly very dexterous. How very retro.

I think we both realised it was getting a bit ridiculous, so we calmed ourselves down and waited until we got to the more sanitary conditions of the bathroom in my Soho Grand hotel room (is there a theme developing?). Angel, too drunk to get the hint, was smoking joints out of the window with Doogie Howser blissfully unaware that American Boy and I had unfinished business that would have been easier to carry out with the aid of a bed and a bit of privacy. Ah, we laugh about it now. So we're in the bathroom – a gorgeous five-star bathroom, with those chic black and white tiles I would sooo have if I owned my own house – and, well, having sex while Angel's busy attempting some new iPod playlist and getting gradually more stoned. I was fine with it, but I think he started to think maybe this is a bit weird, us being in the bathroom 'n' all, so we wrap things up. Then, the funniest thing – we sheepishly exit

the bathroom and he declares, 'And that's how bills become laws!'
Fucking funny.

We brunched the next day, 'cause that's what you do in New York,
and I, in my usual way, fell a little bit in love. I've given up on the idea
of moving to Brooklyn on a whim and setting up a new life with the
cheeky bonus of dual citizenship, but it's rather interesting that we're
still in touch after what was essentially a rough fingering, a super-
quickie and a morning-after burger. It must be love, no?

Back to present day and the email went something like this:

> Hey Ali,
> How's it going? Haven't heard from you in ages.
> It's hot in NYC. Things are good. Not much new to report.
> Band is well – playing a lot, writing new stuff for new album,
> watching the economy slowly improve.
> What have you been up to? Any NYC trips on the horizon?

I forward it immediately to Lady Jane, who comes back quicker than
you can say nylon with:

> Oh my God – he wants your pants! You have to go to NYC
> asap. I like the way he directly asks you that, actually. And the
> thing he says about the economy.
> xx

I don't know if it's good or dangerous the way my friends whip me up
into a frenzy like this. Still, it's nice to dream, eh? You'd never find
American Boy internet-dating (a verb?). He's way too cool and hot.
Hmph. Still, with him it's always the same conundrum, as I tell Lady
Jane over the phone later:

'There's not enough there for me to hop on a plane to go and see
him. I'd have to be going already for another reason.'

'Wait till I get my book deal, then we'll go!'

She's so can-do. LOVE.

Monday, 3 August

OK, there have been some internet-dating developments that are not altogether un-positive. I have discovered some guys – OK, five – who look all right in their profiles and have set about putting them in my favourites folder. Like you might bookmark a website or pick your friends when you're at junior school. Anyway, as far as I can tell, this is a sort of wimpy first step towards the very big step of actually messaging somebody. Ridic.

I say ridic but then immediately changed my mind when two of the blokes favourite me right back. Glee! I throw caution to the wind and, despite warnings from the website, send them each a witty get-to-know-you message and wait.

One of the guys is a cheese-loving Jew called Saul with antisocial tendencies (tick, tick, tick!) and the other, the front-runner, is a Scouse musician (yep, another one), a spit for LA musician Beck, with natty style. I really do quite like him. That's what happens when you fixate on somebody's profile. You start to feel like you know them.

Later on, I'm relaxing with Jessica Fletcher when, ping! 'You have a message!' Shit, I've got a message! I've got a message! It's him! Let's call him 'Music Man'.

Hi Ali,

And you look lovely in that dress. [because I complimented his lumberjack shirt in my message]

Yes, the covers band was an unfortunate point in my life.

Look, I was a different person back then, it was a long time ago . . .

So, who do you write for?

I'm also massively into Love and Leonard Cohen. They both have/had the power to bring me to tears.

Right now I'm resting after flying to a load of festivals for the last 3 weeks.

Beats working tho :-)

x

OH MY GOD, WE'VE GOT SO MUCH IN COMMON!!!!!

I write my reply so quickly there is smoke rising from my keyboard. Then I forward his message to everyone I know, print it off, frame it and hug myself to sleep with it.

Tuesday, 4 August

Why the fuck hasn't he emailed me back?

Wednesday, 5 August

My email to Pfeiffer went like this:

> You sure it's not too much? His email is cool, isn't it? And I took a risk by taking pee out of him in the first one . . . I guess better to take a few risks than play safe and risk getting boring man! You think he seems keen, then? And not bad sign I haven't heard back yet?

I'm actually exhausted just reading that back again. This must stop! So she said, and rightly so:

> Think you should be yourself as much as poss in messages and good to take p**s cos he'll have to deal with that in real life! X

Good point! So I, yawn, said: 'Just wish I could stick with my convictions rather than doubt them as soon as I've hit send!'

Good point by me. So why do I have to be such a fucking lunatic, then? Be cool. Be cool.

Be cool.

Thursday, 6 August

Broken record (me): 'Why do you think he hasn't messaged me back?'

I'm sulking, smoking and sat, hugging one knee, in Angel's 'rock 'n' roll kitchen' next door. It's kind of sad, but that's what we christened her kitchen after a decision to paint it turquoise and hang black and white prints of rock icons such as the Rolling Stones and Jimmy Hendrix on the walls. Angel's more recent crushes of Pete Doherty and The Streets' Mike Skinner feature on the inside of the pantry door for a bit of romantic light relief. Domestic porn, if you will. All of this was part of the post-break-up healing process when she first moved into the flat after a hideous split from her long-term boyfriend before G.

'When did you email him again?'

She's wrestling with rotating sausages under the grill, taking gulps of wine and being the ever-patient listener. Maybe I should just hold a focus group and be done with it.

'It was Monday afternoon when I heard from him, then I messaged him back on Monday night. I just don't get if he was keen in the first place and messaged me back with a really nice message, why would he suddenly go quiet?'

'Maybe he's away. Didn't you say he's a musician?' She's mashing potato.

'Yeah, he told me he was recuperating after doing loads of festivals for the last three weeks, so he's definitely at home.'

Angel is searching for an answer while adding onions to gravy.

'Give him a chance. I bet he doesn't check it every day.'

I'm nodding, not at all convinced.

'Do you think I might have put him off by replying so quickly? And maybe I said too much. I think I got a bit carried away with the fringe anecdote.'

You see, after he'd complimented my dress I put it in context by telling him I was in California when the picture was taken and that I'd had a run-in with Sweeney Todd of Santa Barbara, who'd feathered my fringe and, quote, 'killed its cool dead'. I then name-dropped hip '60s singer Françoise Hardy as the look I *was* going for. All in all, a melting pot of travel and music references that surely he couldn't fail to resist?

Well, obviously not.

'The fringe anecdote was fine,' Angel reassures me, plating up the sausage and mash in her usual slapdash style, gravy going all over the place. 'It was funny and you were only following up on his message. He said quite a lot in his.'

Angel's so good at making me feel better. And at making sausages and mash.

'Can we go and eat it round at mine?' I say, picking up brown sauce.

The telly's better chez moi. She's not even got digital!

Friday, 7 August

An email, but not the one I want, from My Single Friend: 'You have just been added to someone's favourites . . . go and take a look! GOOD LUCK AND HAVE FUN!'

Er, FUCK OFF! The chipper nature of internet-dating communication really brings out the anger in me.

Today I'm going to Manchester to spread some of my cheer Lady Jane's way.

Texting. Part 4.
Waiting for a reply

The non-reply is the worst scenario of all. Also applies to email (see above).

The non-reply, for a brain like mine anyway, leaves too much room for the mind to make its own story up. Or three stories. Or seven.

You start to hypothesise on the various reasons this person is being rude, whittling away at yourself until you become the equivalent of a wood shaving, a discarded curl of something that was something once. When what you should be doing is thinking, FUCK OFF, YOU DICK. YOU ARE NOT WORTH MY TIME AND WORDS, ETC., ETC.

You're waiting and then 'ping' – a message! And it's a message from Vodafone or, as was the case today, the doctors' surgery with a friendly reminder that my smear test is overdue. Fuck's sake.

Saturday, 8 August

Lady Jane is wearing grey sweats and refusing to move from her position on the sofa. We're supposed to be meeting Angel at Oxford

Road station. We've done the classic – blowing our beans the night before the night we were supposed to blow our beans. I, for once, didn't fully blow my beans. I got some sleep. Lady Jane didn't and she's regretting it now. She's got The Fear. She's only making sounds, not words.

We were in the former public loo bar again last night. I met a guy. A sweet-faced, bearded young man currently writing a novel – let's call him 'Fantasy Boy'. I'm willing to overlook the fact he's a Terry Pratchett nerd because he had beautiful brown eyes and seemed to be fascinated by everything I said. I'm sure it *was* fascinating. We exchanged numbers. I think I might like to tap that Tolkien ass.

Will discuss with Angel over beer and chips. Three pints later and we think it's probably safe to go back to Lady Jane's and wake the beast. Evening is almost upon us – we must shake a tail!

'Ughhhhhhh'

Lady Jane, still in her trackies and talking in grunts, has a very flaccid tail that even Viagra couldn't revive. She will agree only to eat that king of day-after food, Chinese! And maybe, just maybe, she'll have a drink afterwards.

Meanwhile, I've been in textual contact with Fantasy Boy. He says he'll be in town later and we should meet up. Yes! Let's start this thing now!

Fantasy Boy: 'Where will you be later?'

Me: 'Just having Chinese, then be in the Temple at about 9 . . .'

Fantasy Boy: 'See you then x'.

Angel is perhaps more excited than me to meet the current object of my desire. Lady Jane couldn't give a shit. Swallowing is hard for her right now.

10 p.m., the Temple, no sign of Fantasy Boy.

Me: 'Where are you?'

Fantasy Boy: 'Sorry, I'm running late. Be there soon.'

Exciting. I keep looking at the stairs for him to appear. Can't quite believe I've met someone I like and get to hook up again the next night. Such a smooth transition!

10.30 p.m., still no sign.

Me: '???'

Fantasy Boy: 'Nearly there!'

Vokda and ginger ale no. 3. Rollie no. 24 (feels like).

11 p.m. This is getting ridiculous now. I'm miffed/embarrassed/ angry. Angel is desperately trying to find the words to make me feel better. Lady Jane is begging to leave.

Me: 'Where are you? We want to leave soon.'

Fantasy Boy: 'Sorry, I've been held up at my friend's house en route into town. She's having boyfriend troubles. Needs someone to talk to. I don't think I can leave her.'

Who the fuck is this guy?

Sunday, 9 August

It's all kicked off. I'm sitting, alone, in the beer garden of a central Manchester pub after shouting at my two best friends and storming off. Yes, I actually stormed off. I don't think I've ever done that before.

I think I've reached saturation point when it comes to disappointing men. Plus, I don't think the excesses of the weekend have helped either. I'm irritable, to say the least. First of all, there's Fantasy Boy. I mean, what was his game? Why say you're gonna meet up with somebody, text them at least six times on the night indicating that you're en route and then not show? Angel and Lady Jane had no answer to this.

Then Music Man. I'm checking My Single Friend to see if he's replied to my message, now sent almost a week ago. Nada. So rude! Meanwhile, there's this pest who I was too polite to shun who's now getting way too cocky for his own good and emailing me all over the place.

'It's not fair!' I wail. 'I mean, who does this guy think he is? He's so arrogant. And he's 40! I'm way too young for him.'

I know that I'm moaning like a five year old; I also know that our friendships allow me to moan like a five year old (within reason), but for some reason, what they're saying back isn't really cutting it.

Why? Because they don't understand. They're both in

relationships, have been for ages and, well, it's easy for them to say it will be all OK and that I shouldn't take it personally because they're not dealing with these losers every day. And constantly feeling let down. Lady Jane is especially winding me up because she seems to have forgotten what she was like when she was single – and she was way more psycho than me.

'I'm so tired of it all and, I'm sorry, but you just don't understand' were my parting words before slamming the door, jumping in the lift and making my departure into a rainy Manchester Sunday.

I pick up smoking paraphernalia and a paper in the shop, where the guy is actually really nice and reminds me that the world might not be quite as cruel as I think it is. I head to the Briton's Protection, a really old pub with cosy nooks and crannies and, crucially, a sheltered outside smoking area. I'm leafing through one of the supplements, taking it in turns to drag on my fag and sip my pint, and then I see him: Music Man. He's staring back at me from the pages of the magazine. He's in a feature, waxing lyrical about his past relationship with a redhead. It pains me to read it, but I soldier on through. He's clearly madly in love with her, even though he reckons they now go out as friends and find it hilarious when either of them snogs somebody else. Bullshit. Suddenly, Music Man has a strong whiff of ex and his non-reply makes a bit more sense.

This is too fucking weird. I call Lady Jane and Angel – it's time to call a truce.

Monday, 10 August
Internet dating: the end

Yes, it's true. After less than two weeks of peddling my wares in the virtual red-light district I have decided to withdraw my services. It's hardly the work of a fearless romantic out there on the front line now, is it? But I had to. And I'll tell you 4 why:

1. It's worse than being at school. I hated school, by the way. The process of putting someone in your 'favourites' folder and vice versa is excruciating. I felt genuinely hurt when they didn't, well, return the favour. These are people I don't even know! Go figure.

2. You get excruciating, not to mention arrogant, emails from people who you would never normally consider going out with. A particular favourite, apart from the love quiz, was the guy who opened with 'You seem a bit mad, by that I don't mean freaky.' Er, cheers. You seem like a moron. I didn't actually say that – I politely hit the 'thanks but no thanks' button – but I wanted to. (Quite enjoyed the one from the guy who told me I'm 'yummy', though.)

3. It really pissed me off that the majority of men on the site were looking for women younger than them. Why, I ask, if you're 30 is your cut-off rate 26, for example? I raised this with the guy who was confidently emailing me, the one who I regrettably emailed back out of politeness and then opened the floodgates, and he said, 'I guess guys just prefer younger women, but if you actually say that you just sound like a perv. It's biological fact.' He actually said it's biological fact. I felt true rage on getting that email from a 40-year-old bald guy who should be grateful to anyone for going out with him.

4. It makes you crazy. My Single Friend indicates when someone has read your message. So if they don't reply, as was the case with a few guys, you know they've read it and chosen, for whatever reason, not to reply. Note the 'for whatever reason' – for me, the only reason is 'they hate me'. I know it's pathetic, but I can't help taking that shit personally.

So, there we go. I do feel like a quitter, which I'm not. Only recently I forced myself to see that Benjamin Button film through to the end, but not this. I can't do it to myself. I'm not built that way. Ultimately, it's not the place for a soft-hearted romantic to roam.

I will continue to observe the internet-dating business from a critical distance, though. I enjoyed a recent story in *The London Paper* describing a niche dating site devoted to women who want to date guys endowed with a penis of seven inches or larger. The article details how the site doesn't/can't actually prove any measurements; it comes down to trusting its members.

Yes, I think that was a joke.

Wednesday, 12 August

Aghhhh. The excitement really is just too much to bear! I'm almost ashamed to admit it, but I've been having a relationship with Fantasy Boy, the Terry Pratchett-loving Saturday night bailer. I couldn't resist giving him another try. We've been texting upwards of ten times a day since then – chit-chat about our day, food choices and music loves mainly. Today has been a veritable marathon: twice the daily average. At least. It's thrilling! And he sent me a photo (not requested, but to demonstrate a funny anecdote) and, SIGH, he's so hot. You know how you forget because you're pretty far gone when you're chatting? Well, what a bonus! Actually, it's a relief. Shallow, moi?

Me being me, though, I've been questioning the validity of such a vigorous texting relationship with someone I barely know (though I feel like I know him better now – *or do I? Is it real?*). You see? The inner dialogue is killing me! We haven't even kissed. Because my mind is so blown by the crazy amount of texting, I said to him, by text (obvs): 'I'm just not used to texting someone so much who I met for less than an hour and barely know.'

His reply? 'Yes, but it was a nice hour, wasn't it?'

SIGH.

Deadpan as ever, when I update Lady Jane on the developments, she says, 'I bet he'll make you dress up as Hermione.'

Friday, 14 August

Me and Fantasy Boy have climaxed at 50 texts in one day! 50! Each. Yesterday.

We worked it out and, naturally, texted about it. I said to him: 'I think I feel a mixture of exhilaration and embarrassment on learning that.'

His thoughtful and really rather grown-up response was: 'Stop with the embarrassment.'

That's right. Take me in hand, Fantasy Boy.

Later that night, ready for bed, while we were texting our goodbyes, I have a sudden urge and say to him: 'This is cheesy as fuck, but I really wish I could kiss you right now.'

He replies: 'I wish I could kiss you too.'

Before you start wondering if it all went a bit *Red Shoe Diaries* from here, it didn't. Though he did add a little later, 'Kissing is so underrated.'

Saturday, 15 August

It's a gorgeous sunny summer's day and Angel and I are packing up the campervan again – we're going on holiday for a week. First stop Cambridge, then the Norfolk coast for some quality friendship lolling. True to form, Roller Girl is joining us with a bag of semi-legal substances for the latter half of the week. It's all about quality girl time and I cannot wait. I intend to chill out on the texting with Fantasy Boy and my laptop will only be used in case of emergency. Oh, and for iTunes.

Wednesday, 19 August

That thing about not texting Fantasy Boy? I lied. It's all gone nuts. So I thought to myself, this texting madness can't continue when I'm on holiday with my girl Angel. But, goddamn it, it's so addictive! And sweet. How can I resist, at the break of day, 'Good morning, gorgeous, how are you today?' He's been texting me every morning to say hi. Heck, I've never had that much attention from a real-life boyfriend.

So I think, what's the problem? It's romantic! He's so attentive! And thoughtful! And we're just getting to know each other . . .

'Oh how I hope you like Pete Doherty' is one text I sent recently (I was listening to Pete at the time, so it's not *that* random).

'Of course I love Pete, I've seen him live in many forms,' he replies.

We have music in common; I like that when I said I was listening to The White Stripes he mentioned how he likes Jack White's new band, The Dead Weather. Solid music knowledge and enthusiasm? Check!

I'm in the campervan getting more giddy on red wine with Angel. We're lying down on the velour banquettes with our legs dancing in the air. Earlier I sent Fantasy Boy a photo of my feet on the beach. Cute, I know. He says: 'Ha ha love the pic, how was the beach?' With the amount of texting that goes on, it feels like he literally knows every move I'm making. Again, I wonder, is this sad as fuck, or romantic? But, I want to hear from him, and he wants to hear from me. So on we go.

A little later on the same night, more Shiraz consumed, a particularly fantastic playlist on the go and various photos sent of Angel and me air-guitaring (*yes, I know* . . .), I say, 'Sorry, I've gone a bit mad on the picture front!'

'What picture front?! I love all your pics!' he shrills back.

The excitement is through the roof!! I can't help myself – I love that I follow my urges with this boy, so I type, 'Guess what? I think you're ACE.'

Wait. Wait.

'I also think that you are ACE xxxx.'

It's been said before, but . . . SIGH!!!!

Thursday, 20 August

To meet or not to meet, that is the question.

The holiday's over and two weeks into my fabulous textual relationship with Fantasy Boy we are supposed to be meeting up this weekend. This weekend!

The subject of meeting up has come up, tentatively, a few times. My issue with the ridiculous amount of texting is very much based on the fact that there must be some sense that we'll meet up, otherwise what would be the point of it all? I actually said to him, in the early days (that would be day two, but we're working in cat years here), 'It feels like you're some kind of phantom.' He agreed, but I think he was enjoying a superhero fantasy, rather than addressing that particular paranoia of mine.

A particularly cute example of our tiptoeing around meeting up happened on 50 Text Day, when he was in Liverpool enjoying, and I quote, 'noodley-based food'. I said, 'Well, I'm just having cheese on toast, so you win. Save me some?'

He said, 'OK, but come down here now, as it's too gorgeous to save. I will get you some wine xxxx.'

Now, this, me in our beautiful capital city, he on Merseyside, is clearly a logistical impossibility. Well, impossible in terms of the noodles being edible, at least. Plus, I have plans and have to demonstrate some, at least some, restraint. The sentiment, which is all-important at this stage, is very much where I want it to be, though (*He wants me. He wants me now* . . .).

It's also the perfect segue to broach the subject of meeting. I say: 'I would love to come and join you, but alas I have plans. We must put a dinner date in very soon, though.' Cunning!

'We will go out for dinner as soon as possible.'

Is this love? It's definitely culinary love. So many of our texts centre around a mutual love of food and, cutely or inanely, depending on how I'm feeling, what we're each eating or planning to eat.

And so these hints and sweet nothings have continued: 523 messages, seven photos (him), ten photos (me), one virtual kiss, three declarations of like. And we've set a date. It's this weekend.

Texting. Part 5.
Friend or foe?

However much I moan, stress and worry about texting, I can't deny how much I love it. In fact, I'd go as far as to say it's one of my favourite things to do. I'm good at it – yes, and happy to admit it. I pride myself on a quick-witted SMS and like nothing more than sparring back and forth with witty friends and potential lovers – Fantasy Boy, please step up. I'm sure I'm not alone in absolutely relishing that feeling when you receive a text that is just perfect in its execution. When you totally match up in humour, tone and Outlook On Life. If that sounds a bit full-on, well, so be it. But that's what it was like with Cartoon Boy. He was the best text I ever had. He really put the effort in, you know? He was super-sharp, well up for a really good back-and-forth session (we didn't live in the same city, so our communication was key) and just, well, perfect. I fell for him completely – it was thrilling. Before we broke up, I knew something was wrong from – guess what? – his texts. He suddenly got patchy with his responses (before that his reply record was flawless), especially the lovey-dovey ones, and suddenly his words weren't sealed with the all-important 'x'. That hurt.

Herein lies the problem. Texting has become a huge, huge factor in relationships, but the fact is, meaningful as it might be, or seem to you, it could be completely meaningless and insignificant in others (a lot of my male friends maintain that they don't give a text a minute's thought before sending it – imagine that?!). This could never be so for me, being so word-obsessed. With hindsight, my belief in Cartoon Boy's and my complete compatibility based on text was perhaps daunting for him. He did once divulge that texting me was akin to texting a female Stephen Fry. Praise indeed, but maybe he was text-austed!

One thing is definitely true, if all the female friends I know are anything to go by: texting matters. It's changed the fabric of how we do our relationship business and it's here to stay.

Friday, 21 August

Meant to say, in all the Fantasy Boy excitement I forgot to mention that Smiler from the festival has been in touch. Sadly, I didn't get around to checking out his band when he invited me – I had a killer deadline, my mates were dropping like flies with all the swine flu talk and, well, Fantasy Boy has been taking up *a lot* of my time and thoughts. Hey, I'm a monogamous girl at heart, even when no flesh has been bared.

So, earlier in the week I get a text. It was a shock. Mainly because most of my texts are from you know who, but it said: 'All right? How have you been? Did you get your work done on time? I am getting all set for V, was just thinking if you were going?'

OK, now his tenses are all over the place, but that's interesting. Very interesting.

So I said . . . 'Hiya. Yes, got it done on time, thank you for asking! Not going to V, sadly. Away with Angel and another mate in Norfolk. It's bloody boiling, so result! How are you doing? We must hook up soon! Xxx.'

And he said . . . 'Nice one, all is ok.'

This makes me wonder if he's playing . . . 'Defo hook up soon, there must be a party we can drag you along to! Hope you have a well good time away and don't drink too much!'

Interesting. Very interesting.

I *did* drink too much.

Sunday, 23 August

It's Sunday, almost the end of the weekend and, sadly, the much-feted meeting with Fantasy Boy never happened. Now, catch me reflecting on this on Friday night when it was looking doubtful and note my text to Lady Jane: 'He's either got a girlfriend of some kind or is on smack.'

The latter, not a crude joke but a war-weary word of warning. A guy I almost started seeing some years back confessed by – guess what? – text message that the reason he'd been such a flake was because he was struggling with a heroin problem. I was a little relieved, if I'm honest.

Anyway, Fantasy Boy. We'd arranged a northern meeting but hadn't pinned down the day. This was bothering me a little midweek when I was holed up in the campervan with Angel. A girl needs to know what she's doing, innit? I felt he was being evasive, but then I *had* texted him telling him I was gay – it was a joke, a ridiculous one, linked to Manchester Pride, but it caused confusion and acted as an unintentional decoy to the chief subject of Making a Date!

I returned from the wild, looking wild and ready to preen and plan. Two voicemails and one text message later and nada! Unusual. We're supposed to be meeting up tomorrow, aren't we? I get a text just before watershed hour – apologies, he'd left his phone at a friend's and only just 'fetched it' (I do love a northerner), but still no mention of The Date. Hmmm. The soundtrack in my head to this particular text? Elvis, 'Suspicious Minds'. I barely know this guy – what's his game?

I reply, politely, upbeatly actually, bearing news of my pending curry and family drinks (yawn, yes, but typical). Then I press: 'So, what day shall we meet? Friday or Saturday?' Nada.

Nada.

Nada.

Saturday morning comes and I'm incandescent. Wow, I don't think I've ever used that word before. Actually, maybe it's the wrong word: I was upset. Here we were, building up to a date fluffed by three weeks of textual foreplay, and now my phantom lover has completely blanked me. I feel like an idiot.

With Kelis's 'I Hate You So Much Right Now' the new soundtrack in my head, I text 'What's going on? It feels like something has changed in your situation. You seem to be avoiding making a date and, you said it yourself, it's weird to text someone so much who you don't plan to meet.'

Yes, that's right. I quoted him back to himself. In your face, Fantasy Boy! Yes, I know, not cool at all. I'm not actually expecting a reply, so when I get the text I get back, I'm, well, amazed.

'Oh u fool. I haven't been avoiding you at all, I have had the weirdest 24 hours in a long time, basically the flat above me left their bath running and went out, which eventually made the ceiling collapse in on itself, my flat is half ruined and I spent the evening collecting all my stuff and taking it to my dear old uncle's. Sorry for the delay in texts but it was a lot to deal with. Xxxx.'

I actually splutter into my scrambled eggs before replying, heartlessly, with: 'Um, OK, so are we meeting up or what?!'

Unsympathetic, moi?

Also – 'dear old uncle's' – what the fuck? Who talks like that?

Wednesday, 26 August

I've woken up today with a new theory on Fantasy Boy's weirdness: he lives with his parents. You see, I changed our meeting place from London to Manchester due to unforeseen family crap that was going down, at which point he seemed to freak (by freak I mean I detected a very slight change in the tone and frequency of texts that would be undetectable to a normal person). My theory goes that he told a little white lie about having his own place when we first met, thinking he'd have his own place by the time we did meet up in Manc. I threw a me-shaped spanner in the works by forcing him to make up the 'my flat is ruined' sob story.

In the heat of the moment I almost texted him, scathing, 'I can see why you're a fantasy writer.' But I refrained and now I'm kind of glad I did, though my theory just discussed is worthy of at least a hammy detective story, if not fantasy.

Anyway, I've been texting him for updates on the flat situation and he's been pretty good at batting my cloaked accusations away. He's good, I'll give him that. 'Perhaps he's actually telling the truth,' says Lady Jane. Perhaps, yes. But how else would I have kept my rampant mind ticking over this weekend?

To cut a very long story short, I've decided to give him the benefit of the doubt. I admit it; I'm addicted to him. I need my fix.

Films with a Romantic Angle. Part 3.

I know it seems like all I do is think, talk, speak and breathe Fantasy Boy, but I did make time this week to go and see a screening of *Bright Star*, Jane Campion's biopic of John Keats, or, more accurately, the love story of John Keats and Fanny Brawne. I'm writing a small feature on it for *The Guardian* so went armed with Rubles and one of those pens with a light bulb on it, so I could write in the dark (not really).

To my mind, there's no one who manages to portray on film the feelings of love, desire and passion quite like Campion (the sex scenes from *In the Cut* — I rest my case), but apart from that she had some pretty wow-making words to work with, thanks to Mr Keats.

When they were apart, the poet and his love exchanged a series of letters and I can't resist but recount Keats' words:

> My sweet girl,
> I am living today in yesterday. I was in a complete fascination. I feel myself at your mercy. Write me ever so few lines and tell you me will never, forever, be less kind to me than yesterday. You dazzled me. There is nothing in this world so bright, so delicate. You have absorbed me. I have a sensation at the present moment as if I were dissolving . . .

You wouldn't get that in a text. Or, for that matter, from a man of this century.

Thursday, 27 August

I have already received 14 texts from Fantasy Boy and it isn't even lunchtime. I do know, though, that he's already had his lunch – a tuna and red onion sandwich accompanied by a strong coffee. I have to say I find this minutiae over-sharing thrilling. Guys are usually so shit at texting – can't get a word out of them – but not Fantasy Boy; he's relentless. Playing it cool is, like, sooo last month.

As well as sharing lunch suggestions, we trade insults and witticisms. I complimented his humour today – I was moaning about trying to wean myself off pork-based breakfasts in favour of healthy (read boring) cereals. A while later I get a text saying, 'Just bought a sausage muffin, how do you feel about that?'

Tee hee. I like that. Very sweet. And funny. 'Jealous,' I replied. 'Cereal is for pussies and I know it. You're funny. Xxx.'

And he said . . . 'Ha ha how am I funny? Xx.'

The ambiguous nature of texting rears its head at this point – further explanation is required.

So I said . . . 'Amusing. You make me smile. It's a compliment! Xx.'

And he said . . . 'Ha ha, yeah, I know it's a compliment, not going all goodfellas on you xxx.'

Again, funny.

I couldn't resist adding, 'So you were fishing for the specifics of why I like your humour?! It's all about timing, isn't it? Xx.'

'Ha ha yes, impeccable timing is everything xxx,' he said, followed with, 'U also make me laugh a lot xx.'

Aw – sweet. Also, very big of a man to admit that a woman is actually funny.

Funnier than him, I reckon. And he knows it.

Friday, 28 August

Today's texting with Fantasy Boy has been off the hook! So, so many exchanges:

1. I learn that he likes original Irish Guinness – not the kind you find in pubs but that you buy in bottles.

2. He learns that I love Fabrizio from The Strokes' newish band Little Joy.

3. He checks out a flat but doesn't like it as much as the last one (assuming he had one, that is . . .).

4. We have an adorable/gay exchange about our recent sartorial purchases (me a Belstaff jacket, him an American Apparel leather-look hoodie).

After the Little Joy recommendation, it occurs to me, on the train home, I've been texting him so, so much today. It's like a thought comes into my head and my immediate instinct is to share it with him. Now, it's great to be so spontaneous (yes, fits with my ideologies), but then there's the gremlin chipping away at the logical part of my brain, saying, *don't share every goddamn inane thing that comes into your head, woman!*

I compromise (with myself) and add to the Little Joy text, 'OK, texting has gone crazy today. I'm sure I don't need to share my every thought. Feel free to unsubscribe at any time! Xx.'

You see what I did there?

Wait. Eat salad. This is such an unusual dinner choice for me it feels faintly exotic. A rerun of *Location, Location, Location* is on – I know, this is rocking Friday night. I haven't seen it in a while but definitely enjoyed it, even though the couples are always cretins with nowhere near enough appreciation for the amount of funds they have available to them. Tonight they were creaming over a front door. Seriously. It would make the right impression at dinner parties apparently. Dicks.

Wait.

Bleep! It's him!

'Ha ha aww I wouldn't ever think of unsubscribing, you are just very lovely xxx.'

I've said it before, but SIGH.

Saturday, 29 August

It's bank holiday weekend and I'm heading to Mum and Dad's again.
I'm flying off to a private island off Ireland (make sense?) with Lady
Jane on Thursday. We've blagged onto the same press trip. Do you
know what else I'm gonna do?

Meet Fantasy Boy.

I know.

It's finally happening.

AUTUMN, 2009

autumn *(n)* the third season of the year, when crops and fruits are gathered, and leaves fall

autumn *(n)* the time when summer's flings linger, fade, then eventually fall; traditionally a time to let go of old habits and then pick them up again – one's new school pencil case never stays unblemished for long

Guest list:
1. Fantasy Boy
2. Music Man
3. Bar Man
4. Mr Scissors
5. The Big Ex
6. Smiler
7. Cartoon Boy

September
Back on the Stallion

Tuesday, 1 September

Email from Mrs Patz:

> Hey hun,
> How are you feeling today after yesterday's events?
> Any word from the shyster?
> x

I write this with a shrill chorus of the 'I told you so' overture ringing in my wilting ears. My brain is sore, my heart smarting. The date with Fantasy Boy hasn't happened. Again. We should've been 'dating' now. I'd said to him, way back last week (bear in mind we've had about a million texts since Friday), 'I'm family tied Monday, can we do Tuesday?' He'd said, 'Tuesday is fine, darling.' The 'darling' part makes me just want to vom now. I said, 'Cool, I'll let you work out what we'll do.' Then I waited. And waited.

So, darling, Tuesday it isn't. I got up yesterday, bank holiday Monday, the day before our date, from my nephew's single bed at home and kind of expected to have a text from my beloved. Nada. Not suspicious, perhaps, to anyone else, but with 'us' (ugh, how sad is that – the 'us' that I so blithely use . . .) I'd usually have a wake-up text. Not on this day. My mind started to whirr, but I remained cool. Well, as cool as a person with my overactive brain can remain.

12.30 p.m. Still nothing. Now this is definitely strange. I start thinking – we're supposed to be going out tomorrow and he's not arranged it yet. The part of my brain that occasionally engages with stupid 'rules' type dating-etiquette guides thinks it really is an OUTRAGE that he's not confirmed plans with me. I need to know what I'm doing! It's only right. There are wardrobe choices to be made, transport times to be researched and the like.

I send him a breezy text, asking how he is, then, 'What time shall I come over tomorrow?' I'll make the short journey to him, you see. Nothing. Nothing. Then I call Mrs Patz to workshop, so that I don't go out of my tiny mind with worry, predictions and inevitable doom scenarios. She thinks it's totally legitimate that I should need to know what our plans are and advises me to wait until 3 p.m. before calling to find out.

I make it until 2.45 p.m. Now, it really is unusual that he hasn't got back to my text. I've always heard from him by now. He's avoiding. WHAT KIND OF WEIRDO TEXTS SOMEONE LIKE A LOVESICK MOFO AND THEN DOESN'T WANT TO MEET UP???

I ask myself, as I have done before, is he:

a. Deaf? This is a little out there as a theory, but a while back when I called Fantasy Boy he failed to call me back, making all manner of lame excuses, including that he was watching his 'guilty pleasure' *Ugly Betty*. I should've written him off right there, but there you go, I'm clearly a sucker for this shit. Anyway, the unwillingness to call back was definitely suspect and Mrs Patz's reasoning was: 'He must be deaf.' This was very funny at the time. Well, you know, funny but kind of sick.

b. Gay? Apart from the fact he seems terrified to meet me in person, he loves fashion and *Ugly Betty*. I asked him when he gave me the *Ugly Betty* excuse (which, let's face it, most men would rather die than own up to) if he identified with Betty's nephew. He said no, but that he was fond of musicals. Hmm.

c. Already spoken for? This is an obvious 'conclusion' to come to. He wants a bit of an ego boost, a bit of texting fun (like those joyous people you see on late-night chatline ads) but isn't actually in a position to meet.

d. A virgin? He lives at home with his parents and has woven a web of deceit to the contrary which he now feels he can't get out of.

So many possibilities. Let's call to clear this matter up. I ring him. It's his answerphone. What a surprise . . .

'Hey, just calling about tomorrow. Let me know what time you'd like to meet up. I might be meeting my friend for lunch, but apart from that I'm free. Maybe we could meet mid-afternoon-ish?'

Our plan was always to have a daytime date. You know, what with the fact he lives with his parents (joke, sort of). NB He has never once answered his phone. Every Goddamn Time I Have Called Him. Suspicious? Yes.

A few minutes later, I get a text. 'Looks like tomorrow might have to be an evening affair. How do you like them apples?'

Is that or is that not irritating? He's still not confirming and why could he not call me back to discuss? I hate phone calls replied to by text. It's for pussies. OK, actually I'll modify that slightly with, it's OK if you say something along lines of 'Can't talk now, will call you later.'

I call him again – will be easier to work out a plan via an actual conversation, no? He doesn't answer AGAIN. Perhaps he *is* deaf.

Now, this is the point where I possibly lose it. Just possibly. But, your honour, please bear in mind that he blew me out last weekend too. I give him 20 minutes or so to get back to me before texting something along the lines of: 'Enough is enough . . . you're being evasive again . . . can't be bothered . . . know you'll come back with some bullshit or other . . . DON'T BOTHER BECAUSE I DON'T WANT TO GO OUT WITH YOU NOW AND DON'T CONTACT ME AGAIN.'

I didn't text in capitals (only losers do that), but I felt like it, you know?

I sort of feel like this might've been a teensy weensy bit of an over-reaction now, but after last week's leaving his phone at a friend's, then his flat getting flooded BS, the not answering my calls, like, ever, and the inability to answer texts when we're due to go on a date whereas the rest of the time he's surgically attached to his phone . . . Deep breaths . . . Well, it's got too much.

His reply — very speedy, of course, when he's pressed: 'What? I texted you! I'm with a friend showing me around a flat, but if that's how you feel, well, fine by me.'

Oh, goodie, another flat-and-friend-related excuse. My first point, if you're with 'a friend' (your psychologist, perhaps?) why could you not just quickly answer the phone? You clearly have time to text . . .

I decide not to reply. I've genuinely had enough. About ten minutes later I get another message. (Just pick up the phone, dufus!!!!) Now, this one is UNBELIEVABLE. Let's take a close look. Note my comments in CAPS.

'I am sorry for what's going on at your end.' PASSIVE AGGRESSIVE FUCK.

'But I really think you had no right to send me such a text.' BOO HOO. DON'T LIKE IT WHEN SOMEONE IS ACTUALLY DIRECT, DO YOU?

'I had a lot on today.' AGAIN, BOO HOO.

'And, like I said, I planned to ring you in the evening.' NO, YOU DIDN'T.

'Missing your phone calls wasn't deliberate, but, to be honest, I am in the company of friends trying to show me their flat and the surrounding area.' I SMELL BS AGAIN. IF INDEED HE DOES LIVE IN CENTRAL MANCHESTER, AS STATED IN EARLIER CORRESPONDENCE, WHY THE FUCK DOES HE NEED SHOWING AROUND THE 'SURROUNDING AREA'? THE NORTHERN QUARTER IS NOT THAT BIG.

'I will honestly not txt you again after this.' YEAH, YOU WILL.

'But what you said was a complete over-reaction and I didn't really know how to reply to something so bloody judgemental.' YEAH, YOU DID, COS YOU JUST DID.

'I hope everything gets better for you.' PATRONISING, PASSIVE AGGRESSIVE FUCK.

So there we have it. The judgemental part did push my buttons somewhat, but I leave it unanswered. This took some restraint, but, as we know, sometimes not to reply at all is the only way. Mwah ha ha!

I head out for a family meal, leaving my toxic phone at home (You go, girl! That'll show him!), and actually have a nice time despite my acute case of text rage and rising disappointment at my doomed romance. We take the pee out of him and I feel a bit better. My no-nonsense younger cousin 'the Nurse' brands him a 'freak' (said with a strong Yorkshire accent, it's all the more satisfying).

I get back home to discover another text. You know, the text he was never going to send . . .

'Is that it, then, or can we brush the little barney we just had under the carpet?' WHAT??!

I don't reply again. Later, another bleep.

'OK, I get the message. If you want to react like this just because I didn't reply to two of your phone calls when you wanted me to, then there's nothing else I can do. All the best x.'

'All the best' – I ask you! AGAIN, PASSIVE AGGRESSIVE. If I'm honest, that did kind of hurt. My inner gremlins and annoying ability to turn everything around to be My Fault got me thinking, have I been too hasty? Did I, as he points out, completely over-react? I didn't give him long to get back to me, really, did I? And, worst question in the world ever coming up, what if? Aghhhhhhhhhhhhhhhhhhhhhhhhhhhh!

Even though he deserved my blanking him, it's not really my style, so I do the mature and polite thing . . . I call. Again. For the third time that day. He seems to want to sort this out; I'll give him the chance to explain.

Guess what? He doesn't answer.

And herein ends the story of a Love Fool and a Fantasy Boy.

Wednesday, 2 September

Manchester. I'm walking, talking and generally incredulating with Lady Jane over Fantasy Boygate, as it will now be known. We're en route to review a restaurant (well, she's reviewing, I'm along for the free booze and food). It's pissing it down. Love the place but, boy, is it grey and rainy.

We had a pre-dinner drink in the public loo bar and we're walking, Chinatown-wards, link-armed against the rain. That's when I see him.

Holy fuck! What? Is that who I think it is? I think all this in a nanosecond – my brain is good at it. I recognise that colourful psychedelic T-shirt and that grey American Apparel-ish cardie and THAT FACE. Shitting hell, it's only Fantasy Boy!!!!

'Hi,' I say, with the most meaning I've ever put into such a short, oft-used word.

'Er, hi,' he replies, with the tone of voice of the pussy he is.

His face is going red. Like ridiculously red.

I'm holding him in the kind of steely stare Anne Robinson would be proud of.

'You remember Lady Jane, don't you?' I shrill. Forcing him to be re-introduced to my wing woman whom he first met on The Night I Wish I'd Never Met Him.

'Um, yes.' (Shit! Now I'm forced to talk to her as well, he thinks.)

Lady Jane, being the picture of poise, politeness and polish that she is, proceeds to inform him of our pending restaurant appraisal and asks what he's been up to.

What? Apart from fucking with my mind?

I continue to stare. I am the victor in a staring competition of my own creation.

'Er, I've just been . . . mutter, mutter . . . flat, friend . . . mutter . . . bar, er . . . mutter, mutter, stammer.'

I think I'm enjoying this, but I'm not sure. I'm in Major Shock. More shock than when I met Mark Owen back in the days of Take That The First Time Around, I think. Actually, that reminds me, Fantasy Boy has quite a squeaky Mark Oweny voice that isn't that sexy at all. Maybe that's why he never wanted to talk to me on the phone. Hmm.

Anyway, *back in the room*, we're still stood getting wet on the pavement. I am wearing a bloody marvellous, recently purchased Chloé dress, my new Belstaff coat and some brogues. Thank you, Universe, for this gift of brilliant dressing for such an important occasion.

Lady Jane is now rambling, I'm still giving the death stare (with a hint of irony) and he pipes up, 'Right, we'd better get going.'

Yes, run while you still can, Fantasy Boy! I soften my look slightly and hold out my arm for a handshake. He looks surprised and shakes my hand. I smile.

Walk away.

Cool. As. Fuck.

Thursday, 3 September

'He really did blush up, didn't he?'

Lady Jane's securing her Pre-Raphaelite mane into a bun and (still) marvelling over the Fantasy Boy accidental meet-up. We're wet again. Not in the Manchester rain this time but a bubbling hot tub, on the deck of the posh house we're calling home for the weekend, on the Irish island.

What a difference a day makes.

'This is the life, eh?'

Hair secured, she holds out her champagne glass to clink mine, with a daft expression on her face.

'A toast: to Fantasy Boy. What a fucking lunatic.'

I'll drink to that.

Friday, 4 September

Today I've ridden a horse for the first time, had an exquisite buffet lunch prepared by a dedicated in-house chef, I'm about to go sailing on the Atlantic (another first) . . . yet I'm still thinking *why has he not been in touch?*

Now who's the lunatic?

Later on, back from the exhilarating boat ride, so fast and windswept I nearly drop my camera in the water like a total goon, I get an email from my wise journo friend 'Elfie', kindly offering up her own recent boyfriend woes in an attempt to help me:

> He genuinely had to be re-educated into understanding that what he had done was wrong. He sees it now, but he didn't to begin with. Guys just aren't built like us. Or they are seriously about ten years behind us on the emotional maturity scale.

> They're not assholes – I mean 'Kit' isn't a bad person – but look what he did? However, it does completely beggar belief.
>
> But please don't let it get you down. It's not worth it. It's ridiculous that we let guys damage our self-esteem when they're basically blundering bears. Just hold your own and strengthen yourself.

She's right. I'm gonna pull myself together. I will repeat over and over again, like I'm practising my times tables, that he was a total weirdo and allow myself some time to heal from the experience. I need a week off. From myself.

'She's taking a break, she needs a break.'

Mrs Patz and I once laughed for an hour after she pulled this amazing joke that only *Dirty Dancing* fans would get. So, she was in the fashion office, when it was in its old location before the big move to the swish new place, and she was crouched beneath her desk, unplugging wires and fishing out old sandwiches and the like. I walked past and peered under before asking her what she was doing. Stupid question, I know. It was pretty obvious. But she came out with, 'I'm taking a break, I need a break.' If you need a little nudge on this, it's the bit where Johnny is sticking up for Penny because she's been working too much (and had a dodgy abortion).

Anyway, there's a life lesson in here somewhere: the importance of taking time off from whatever your current obsession is, or, even better, trying to take a break from your thoughts (when your thoughts aren't doing you any good, anyway – I'm not talking about a lobotomy). Taking a break from your thoughts isn't that easy. It involves a lot of distractions, filling/feeding your mind with other things (a great novel?), and eventually something in your brain will switch; breaking a chain of actions/habits is easier, in that you just have to stop fucking doing it. For example, if you've been having a text/email/Facebook stalking 'relationship' with somebody and you notice yourself start to obsess, force yourself to stop doing it for a bit and you will suddenly have perspective on the matter, not to mention more hours in the day to do something useful. It's like taking time to cool off after a row; you really do make a lot more sense once you've done that.

If you catch yourself droning on to your mates about the same situation, force yourself not to when you next speak to them – I once asked Lady Jane to sing Fleetwood Mac's 'The Chain' (with a view to breaking it – get it?) to me when I was spinning out on Cartoon Boy for the zillionth time. There's only so much you can dwell on something before you become a crazy ol' lady in the manner of Miss Havisham. I'm not saying this always works, and it's like you have to make yourself (like with Brussels sprouts at Christmas), but when it does work, it really does work. You know? It's the 'wh' questions that fuck you up – *Why did this happen? What does it mean?* The fact is, you can never really know what's going on in somebody's head or, if it's someone you don't know very well, you can't ever truly know their situation. You can guess – I do that a lot – but what I'm saying is, sometimes it doesn't pay to predict. Take a break. Somebody give me a publishing deal NOW for a self-help book. *Dirty Dancing* really was an important film, you see.

Places to Meet Men. Part 2.
The post office, apparently. Well, in my little corner of London it's actually a newsagent/post office/deli combined – many joys under one roof. Buy a paper, scratch card, samosa and post a letter all in one go!

Anyway, I'm in the hideously long queue (this is the un-fun thing about post offices), waiting to post Lady Jane's phone charger back to her. This is a matter of some urgency, as you can imagine. I'm idling, looking at the funny greetings cards and picking up essential Bestival supplies (yippee! I leave in a couple of hours . . .) – safety pins and sticky stars, for fancy dress purposes. There's this guy behind me, like, really close behind me, coughing loudly (without using correct swine flu prevention methods), sighing, tutting. This is NOT the hot guy, by the way. I just had to tell you about him. He was in his 50s and, frankly, getting on my tits. Why he insisted on sharing every piece of antisocial body language and function with me in that queue, I do not know. But I was getting agitated; *he* was making me agitated!

Then, ugh, he talks to me! I didn't even make eye contact with the guy. (Well, apart from the fact he was practically dry humping me from behind.) 'You could die standing in these queues, couldn't you?' he mused. I reckon I could have died from his shit breath.

Finally, I get my parcel sorted and move on to the newspaper counter . . . AND THERE HE IS! One of my favourite types of men: The Man With The Conflicting Image. You want to put him in a box, but you can't, there's too much going on: a feast for the senses and the imagination. The guys who run the newspaper part of the enterprise are Indian, and this guy's Indian. I definitely haven't seen him before. He's got the slim build of the romantic lead in an indie romance film, like the guy out of *(500) Days of Summer*, with the same kind of laid-back confidence, wry but friendly smile and twinkly up-for-it eyes. Then he's got glasses like a graphic designer would wear. Like, classic. Or Scandinavian-looking. But then he's got long flowing hair, with a nice wave – very period drama. Then, and this is what really blows my mind, he's wearing a Motörhead T-shirt! Rad combo. Oh, and he was soooo polite and smiley and responsive and keen to make sure that he selected exactly the right scratch card for me. I likey.

Sadly, I only saw his top half from my side of the counter. I intend to investigate his bottom half at a later date.

Friday, 11 September
'Have you got beers for the train?'

That's Angel's hello when we meet under the clock in Waterloo station.

'I have beers, pork pies and everything else we need to have fun this weekend,' I deadpan, before we both drop our bags and do an excited jumping-up-and-down hug.

Rubles runs over five minutes later, off the tube from Vauxhall from work, and our trio is complete. It's Bestival weekend and it's going to be BIG.

Monday, 14 September
We arrived, raucous and triumphant, in a taxi with 'It's Raining Men'

blasting from the stereo and left, today, in a moody silence, part of one of the worst conspiracies known to the modern reveller, the queue to *leave* a festival. Queuing to get in somewhere is one thing, queuing to leave is quite another, especially when you've barely slept for three nights, are nursing a wicked sunburn (Rubles) and feel like your insides have been hollowed out.

I actually want to punch Rubles for her moody non-compliance by the time we touch down in Waterloo just shy of 11 p.m. (Yep, it's taken us that long to get back.)

I want to die.

Thursday, 17 September

Last night I slept with a very hairy young man – a bear, to be exact. My Harrods bear of 1994. You know how the popular store 'releases' a bear every year at Christmas with the date stamped (well, stitched) onto its paw? Well, I got into this blatantly exploitative marketing ploy and bought Mr Harrods Bear 1992 (christened Rodney, God knows why – I don't think it was *Only Fools and Horses* related) and Mr Harrods Bear 1994 (christened Douglas – again, go figure). I think it's because I thought it was super-impressive to own something with 'Harrods' on it.

Whatever, I'm glad of my ill-thought-out teenage purchases now, with a furry friend to cuddle up to, as the nights are getting colder. Is this rock bottom? Possibly. It's definitely in the 'sad' ballpark. On the plus side, though, it provided an amusing picture message to send to Angel and Lady Jane. They thought me very cute indeed.

Sunday, 20 September

Lady Jane is in Mull, on a writing retreat. She's not supposed to be online, but, whaddya know, an email from the very lady:

> Hello Gorgeous,
> Happy Sunday!
>   Well, would you Adam and Eve it, I have internet access on
> Mull!

Beautiful here, not that I can really go out with the amount I've got to do. Still, what a view. Highland beauty. Me and Rockstar gonna get on case re: Music Man too . . .

xxxx

I ping back, with a view of the telly:

Happy Sunday to you too – bet it's beautiful there. I'd love to go. Looking forward to seeing what happens with Music Man. Hopefully something good! What's Rockstar plotting?!

Good luck with the writing, hun xxx

Yes, Music Man. He's back. And it just gets weirder, as I tell Angel over a pint in the pub later.

'So, Rockstar is gonna set you up?' She takes change from Elvis and hands me a vase of Kronenbourg.

'Yep!' I take a tentative first sip and end up with a froth moustache. 'Mental.'

We head to the beer garden while it's still just about warm enough to do so.

She's right. The Music Man script is mental. After the Redhead In The Magazine incident, fate has once again intervened.

'So, they were all at the wedding? And he was playing in the band as well?' Angel's gone all high-pitched on me.

'I know it's hard to get your head around, but yeah. Both Rockstar and Music Man were in the wedding band.'

Back in August, Lady Jane and Rockstar were at the same high-profile music wedding as Music Man. I get a covert call from Lady Jane, who's crouching behind the buffet table, along the lines of 'Guess who's here, guess who's here?' They resolve to set us up on their return. Apparently, Music Man entered the dance floor knees first, like young lads do at family parties, and this was met with Lady Jane's approval.

'He's spontaneous, like you,' she announced proudly when she got back, as if she'd found my soulmate. 'Fun.'

'So when will you find out?' Angel asks, draining her pint.

'Apparently Rockstar is on the case, speaking to their mutual friend, so it's a waiting game.'

'I've got a good feeling about this.' She's rubbing her hands together in that excited way she does.

'Oh God, don't have one of them. You'll jinx it,' I tease. 'Another pint?'

Monday, 21 September

The Arctic Monkeys' new album *Humbug* (great sweet, great name) has got me hooked. I always had a soft spot for Alex Turner, but now, as he matures and his hair and lyrics get more wayward, my love just grows stronger. 'Cornerstone', track seven on the album – all about lost love, longing and dark obsession – has been on repeat for a week now.

Thursday, 24 September

Brave Heart. No, not the Mel Gibson movie, but my good self, two days ago. Acts of bravery are often spurred by moments of high pressure (you know, burning buildings, random acts of violence). Well, I was drinking at a pub in Spitalfields, a favourite, though not local, watering hole with Angel and Mrs Patz and found myself under extreme pressure . . . to give, let's call him 'Bar Man', my number. I dared to note to my faithful friends that Bar Man was cute. If memory serves, he looked like a younger, less pumped version of Matthew Fox, that bloke from *Lost* and the cheesy-as-fuck Gillette ads. He was also too young and a bit Emo. You know? He had a lip piercing.

Anyway, we'd had a nice little exchange when I was ordering drinks, due to the fact that he screwed up my order by pouring a large glass of white for Mrs Patz instead of red. He seemed nervous, so I had a change of heart on my pint and offered to keep the white for myself. He was very twinkly-eyed and we definitely had a bit of an over-the-bar moment before I delivered the drinks to my soon-to-be imbecilic friends. We were chatting about Mrs Patz's recent good fortune in the romance department (a super-hot long-standing teenage crush that finally came to fruition!). I was aware of Bar Man, though. I kept catching his eye and he did seem to be hovering a bit. Didn't he?

He was certainly looking over when Mrs Patz thought it funny to do the symbol for lady oral sex to wind me up about my new, new crush.

'Just give him your number,' she says, pulling her tongue back into her mouth, with Angel shouting, 'Yes, yes' like she's Meg Ryan in a deli.

'No, I can't,' I say. 'It's too embarrassing. I daren't.' I genuinely daren't. Is it not a horrible cliché, cracking on to the barman? Also, I'm having a real bad case of 'can't be arsed'. I feel like I've been pretty good at making moves in my single career – why can't he ask me for my number? Oh yeah, because I'm with two screaming banshees who think it's funny to simulate sex with their tongue and fingers. Whilst this game of yes–no tennis is taking place, the two nice young men sharing our large table pipe up, 'Just give him your number, what have you got to lose?' Jesus, it's getting like *Trisha* in here.

It's time for us to leave and despite the fact Mrs Patz has gone to the trouble of writing my number down on a Fabric flyer (as in the super-club – I know, classy), I head straight for the door, the nice young men shaking their heads in disappointment. But then something great happens – he follows me!

We end up nudging shoulders at the door, then making close-up eye contact.

'Helloow,' I say, doing my best sheepish impression, tucking my hair behind my ear.

'Hello,' he replies, looking quickly at me and then at his Vans.

Time for me to fess up: 'Er, you've probably noticed my friends goading me all night to give you my number. It's actually really embarrassing.' More hair fiddling.

He manoeuvres me to a quiet bit outside, which is handy for my shame levels. I'm nervous too, because I don't give him time to respond before blurting out: 'Are you single?'

'Yes.'

Now, normally I'd think, ooh goody, but I've been told that before when they're not single at all. Shocking, I know.

We exchange names and bashful how are yous. He's lovely close up and increasingly calm next to my rampant mortification.

'Er, would you like my number?' I flirt, keeping the bashful thing going.

'Yes, I would,' he says. I give him the rave flyer caked in make-up and start my away.

'I've got to get to a gig now,' I say, 'but it was really nice meeting you.' Better.

Mrs Patz and Angel are looking at me all expectant and silly-eyed. We walk off and wait, ooh, at least ten metres, before letting out a huge squeal. Not cool at all.

'He went straight back into the pub. He went straight back in!' Mrs Patz is practically hyperventilating, telling me this news.

'Er, and?'

'Well, that means he came out solely to see you, not for any other reason.'

Is that romance? Perhaps it is.

'Do you think he'll call?' I love the utter pointlessness of this question and also the fact that my friends pretty much always answer me seriously, rather than quipping something heinous like, 'Er, let me just look into my crystal ball . . . ' like a guy would.

'YES!' they chime in unison.

At bedtime, a bleep. 'Did you enjoy the gig? The barman, in case you've forgotten.'

'Of course I've not forgotten . . . '

Monday, 28 September

I'm twitchy. Eating has helped a little bit, but there's only so much a girl can eat when she's wearing a pencil skirt and wide leather belt with non-adjustable hook-and-eye fastening.

Bar Man kicked off a texting to-and-fro four days ago now, with a view, I think, to 'make contact'. No mention of a date yet, which is fine because he was slaving at the bar all weekend and I was otherwise engaged. Our 'chat' focused around a polite how-are-you-what-you-up-to-at-the-weekend dialogue, ending at the rather late hour, for an early textual relationship, of 12.40 a.m.

'Twenty minutes till the end of my shift. Need my bed!' he exclaims.

I let that one lie, literally. Since then, nada.

The question is, do I now text him, since he was the one to first get in touch, or leave it to him? But then I was the one who did the brave approaching in the first place, so he knows I'm interested, right? Plus, I want him to chase me, really. But what if he's waiting for me?

I'm bored, aren't I? I need to get a hobby, or work harder.

Tuesday, 29 September

In a case of severe boredom in the fashion office today – there are A LOT of hours to fill – I texted Bar Man. The funny thing is, I wasn't even that bothered. Genuinely, I wasn't. It was fun to bar-stalk him, and he *was* cute, if a little young and short, but I couldn't quite put two and two together and make a date.

That said, I still texted him – a breezy little number, informing him of my boring day and would he like to hook up for a beer some time? Not too chatty, 'cause I don't want to get into a whole Fantasy Boy nightmare again (false levels of intimacy generated by obsessive texting), but, you know, why not? Send. Send, but with nagging feeling that actually it would potentially be weird to meet this stranger. But then isn't that what you have to do? Take a leap and all that. And so it goes on . . . be still, stupid head.

He hasn't replied. I'd like to say it's a shame, but I really don't think it is. I need to give less of a shit about the nobodies. That's no reflection on Bar Man, though I do think he could do with finding a backbone and some manners when he grows up. It's just that I can't judge them by my own emotionally rampant standards. Just because my somewhat pronounced fuck-it gene means I'm likely to take a risk on something that's probably nothing in case it could be a something doesn't mean they will. You know? But it's disappointing how many wimps there are out there, I must say.

I should add, I think it was probably less a case of venturing into a possible something and more a case of potentially *getting* a bit of something. Something I haven't had in a while. And that's not fraught with complications for a thoughtful girl like me at all, is it?

I'm writing this watching, as I tend to if I'm in at 10 p.m., *Sex and the City* on the Comedy Channel (yep, give me a bar of Galaxy and a glass of Ernest & Julio and the cliché is complete). It's the one where Big goes to Napa and Miranda has her baby. Carrie rushes off to try to catch Big before his plane takes off, but it's too late. In the apartment, she finds the *Breakfast at Tiffany's* 'Moon River' record with a note reading 'If you ever feel lonely', and a plane ticket to Napa with a note reading 'If *I* ever feel lonely.'

Nice that.

Wednesday, 30 September

I've been indulging myself in a lot of song lyrics lately. It's what I do in the absence of any real emotional engagement with the opposite sex. I'm searching for something – answers? I never did have a teenage angst-ridden, lock-myself-in-my-bedroom-for-hours-on-end-listening-to-Nirvana phase, so maybe this is it.

I'm listening to 'Music When the Lights Go Out' by The Libertines on my bed, with headphones on. Deviant, I know, using earphones when you don't have to. In the song, Pete (Doherty – love him or loathe him, you can't argue with his lyrics) likens the deterioration of a relationship to not feeling the music any more. I'm sure this is ravingly cheesy, but I really do take a lot from that sentiment. Is it not just a perfect way to describe that feeling of knowing you've fallen out of love? That sinking, sorry feeling? I know I recognise it and the emotional deceit that inevitably follows. And who actually says it? Who actually fesses up that they no longer feel the music? Not many people, I reckon. It's too hard. Better to dress it up in bullshit.

Anyway, without making this too depressing, I know I've been moping a bit lately, but I emerge feeling positive tonight – an epiphany, if you will. The fact is, it's important to feel the music and if you don't, it's not worth it. That's why I left my last big relationship, why I'm not with anyone right now and why I won't be until the tune is right.

October
Detox, Retox, Ex, Wax

Thursday, 1 October

I've just had an epiphany with a fox. Before you start thinking I'm talking about another wildly unsuitable man or, worse, bestiality, it's actually quite a beautiful thing that happened.

I'm stretched out on the couch when it appears at the French doors, illuminated by a half moon. He – I assumed he was a he, for some reason – nudges his nose on the glass pane and peers into my living room. Actually no, not my living room – me. He totally eyeballed me. This is not an exaggeration; the fox's and my eyes were locked for at least eight seconds before he made his exit. I was *this* close to asking him in for a cup of tea. Me and my mate, Mr Fox. It would've been cool.

Joking aside, it was an amazing moment. Magical, really. I think foxes are beautiful and this gorgeous wild thing was totally having a moment with me. Like he was watching over me, or something. I know, cheesy. I text Mum with that particular theory and she comes back with, 'What a load of bullshit!' Cheers, Ma – but I really did feel something. If nothing else, it whipped me out of my fug.

'The fox is your muse!' says Lady Jane by text. I knew somebody would understand.

'I am the fox and the fox is me,' I reply, somewhat mystically. I don't really know what that means, but it sounds fucking cool.

Friday, 2 October

My hairdresser Mr Scissors is doing his acid house night tomorrow at a bar in West London. This is not to be confused with acid jazz, a very different genre of music, which I thought was the musical theme last time he did this night. Wasn't expecting the strobes, smoke machines and gurning ravers. This time I'll be better prepared.

Monday, 5 October

It all went wrong when the Middle Man came round during the Barbra Streisand programme Rubles, Angel and I were watching on Friday. What was meant to be a sedate night turned into me not surfacing till Saturday at 2.30 p.m. Then I had the real night out to deal with. You know, the acid house night?

Despite ourselves, Angel and I round up the troops, go and see a man about a dog in Halfords car park in Brixton (like you do), eat some Mexican food on Westbourne Grove, then descend on the party about ten.

I introduce Mr Scissors to the troops.

'Er, he's not usually wearing a bandanna,' I explain, baffled. He *doesn't* usually wear a bandanna.

'I wanted to look a bit acid house without looking like a total cock,' he says, before planting his usual kiss on my lips. Hmm. The party's taking a while to get started upstairs, so we're dancing to Kelis's 'Milkshake' downstairs – a great tune to shake your ass in a possible suitor's direction if ever there was one. I'm wearing a very tight black American Apparel dress – kind of low-fi sexy. My male friend 'Mr C' has already noted my arse.

'I never really noticed it before, but it kind of, well, sticks out, doesn't it?' He means this as a compliment. I can tell by the way he's licking his lips.

Anyway, I know I'm working it pretty good. But what is Mr Scissors thinking? Well, I don't know. And I still don't because it all got very misty/messy after Kelis – partly due to the crazy strobes and smoke machines (*Tonight, Matthew* . . .) but mainly due to the party fuel. My so-called friends told a whole crowd of strangers that I dance like Ian Curtis at one juncture. Not funny.

We had a right laugh, up until the point we got back to Mr C's, who lives nearby, and I suddenly start violently puking (thank God I didn't take Mr Scissors up on his offer to go to the after party). I swear to God someone Rohypnoled me. Now, I know that reeks of 'it must've been something I ate', but truly, I don't know what the fuck happened. I'm in Mr C's spare room and Mrs Patz has left me with a bag – a sort of laminated gift bag – to be sick into should I need it. I did. I need the bag because I literally can't lift my totally limp body off the bed. My head is spinning out to the point of explosion. It feels like my eyes are gonna pop out.

Next thing, Angel pops her head round the door and gasps. It's as much as I can do to raise an eyebrow back, much less speak. The gift bag has leaked a rather gross present of puke all over Mr C's beige carpet. Angel is now gagging too. I'm mortified beneath my complete immobility. It's like I'm trapped in my own body. Angel is very good in a crisis, so she sets to work, cleaning my sick, all the while gagging and telling me, 'It's fine, it's fine, it's coming off.'

The party continues downstairs; I'm still a prisoner in my own body upstairs. Now it's Mrs Patz's turn to care for me. This time with a proper bowl. She lies next to me, strokes my hair and congratulates me when I manage to 'get some more up'. A lot of the time, you see, I'm just convulsing without actually being sick. It's the worst I've felt. Ever.

Enough puke talk now, you get the picture. Angel and her mate have to leave me and Mrs Patz at Mr C's because I'm not capable of getting in a cab all the way across town when they leave at 8 a.m. We wait it out till about 11, leaving Mr C still downing straight vodka 'with fresh lime' (which makes it infinitely more classy) and singing along to Womack and Womack. You know when it's time to leave? It was *sooo* time to leave.

We get back to mine about noon and I breathe a huge sigh of relief. Home at last. It's like I've been to war and back (not that I know what that feels like, but, you know). Mrs Patz and I sink into my sofa, drink tea and giggle – don't know what about . . . relief that I came through this alive, I think. I neck a couple of vallies about 2 p.m. to make sure I get a good sleep. Mrs Patz gets her head down, too – she's heading to her sister's later.

I'm in bed and Mrs Patz is stood over me. I shift my eye mask, pause and realise, thank fuck, I don't feel like total shit any more. Nice one.

'What time is it?' I ask her.

'It's eight.' She's dressed to go – damp hair, bag thrown over shoulder.

'You gonna go to your sister's or are you just gonna go home?' I'm peeking out from my duvet.

'It's 8 a.m. Monday morning,' she says. 'I'm going to work.'

Holy fuck.

Wednesday, 7 October

Dinner with Mrs Jones. She's my very beautiful, very-caring-and-excellent-with-straight-talking-advice friend from uni. She also happened to marry the best friend of my Big Ex, the one who I lived with for five years. We met on the same night at the Vibe Bar on Brick Lane. She succeeded where I failed. No, hold on, that's not right. I didn't fail. He failed. Or maybe we both failed. Anyway, tonight Mrs Jones and I are going to Automat, that posh American diner in Mayfair, so I'll no doubt tap her up for information on him. It's weird when your mate has a connection with your ex and you don't. That's kind of what happens when there's a restraining order involved, though. Not really, but almost. Let's just say it got ugly.

We're eating tapenade. I always feel smug eating this gravelly paste now that I know what it is and have discovered it doesn't taste half as disgusting as it looks.

'So, how is he, then?' I ask, administering a healthy black slick onto the crusty bread.

Mrs Jones shoots me a *do you really want to know?* look. She's trying to protect me. As much as I obviously do care how my biggest love is doing, the facts are he's not in good shape. His problems were what broke us apart in the end. His many problems.

'He looks awful,' she says, with a knowing shake of the head. 'You wouldn't recognise him.'

I've been getting this impression the last few times we've met, though she's held back until now. Without me in his life, the Big Ex has spiralled further into a bad place. He's not looking after himself, still doesn't have a job and is, by all accounts, making less and less sense holed up in his bedsit.

'He's started doing paintings on his walls.' Her brow couldn't be more arched. She looks like Sarah Jessica Parker.

Mrs Jones, a successful and hard-working career woman, doesn't have much time for flimsy creative aspirations – the kind of flimsy creative aspirations I tolerated for far too long with the Big Ex and which meant I was the provider in our relationship because he was pissing about thinking he could be a photographer without actually doing any work.

'It's really sad,' she continues, surveying the massive steak that's just appeared in front of her. 'You definitely did the right thing, though. He's never gonna change.'

She's right. And, as much as it pains me to hear what bad shape he's in, I do know that I was right to leave. It was the hardest decision I've ever made, too. How do you ever know when to leave?

That was over three years ago now, yet I still feel like I gave up on him.

Reading my mind, Mrs Jones looks me squarely in the eye and says, 'You couldn't have stayed with him. You tried to help him, but he just kept fucking it up.'

I still feel very sad.

Saturday, 10 October

After last weekend's near-death experience, this one has to be about R & R. That's how it tends to be with me: retox or detox. That said, I did manage to squeeze in a couple of gigs and one small crush last night. It was Elvis's birthday and his skiffle band played in one of those time-warp jazz clubs, Peter Parker's, in Soho. But I was on the night bus at one and in bed by two. Practically an early night.

Before going to see Elvis, I had some review tickets for another gig, Man Like Me, at one of my favourite London music venues, the

Roundhouse. I went with Rubles and Angel, but also invited Smiler along. We've been in touch a bit since I threw myself at him at that festival over the summer and have attempted to meet up, but it hadn't happened until last night. I was intrigued to see him and was feeling a bit *Ooh, I wonder, what does it mean? Does he still have a girlfriend? Why would he want to meet me if he didn't fancy me?* You know, that kind of shit.

Anyway, we met up before the gig. He brought his lovely mate along, who was wearing a spectacularly bad shirt unbuttoned to the navel. Weird, but, like I say, nice guy. It was great to see Smiler – and he *is* handsome. A bit like Liam off *Coronation Street*. He was wearing a mod-style Harrington jacket and tartan scarf, in the manner of Bay City Rollers, as he pointed out. But I didn't fancy him. He's too meek. I don't mean that badly, but he said he'd described me and Angel to his mate as 'mad'. This has been said before, but I don't think it's so much that we're mad as he just couldn't handle me.

I felt sorry for him in the end. His friend started banging on about the hot tub Smiler has at his place, which is a bit odd for someone living in South London who's not particularly rich. We were laughing (kindly) and reminiscing about the episode of *Come Dine With Me* where a woman took everyone to the hot tub in the back garden of her three-bedroom semi. Smiler was trying to get off the subject, but we were prying for more details.

'So, what's your place like, then, if you've got a hot tub? Is the hot tub outdoors or indoors?'

I'm imagining some kind of pimped-up shag palace. Intriguing, I must say. Smiler looked uncomfortable with the questions, then his mate cleared it up. 'It's his parents' house.' Ahh. He was gutted about that revelation. Poor thing.

The night was fun and we did have an intimate cheek kiss on departure. He is cute, but I think not re: further action. But still I go through the inner dialogue motions: *Nothing was mentioned of the girlfriend. Again. We did get on and he was sweet and making an effort. But, more to the point, did he like me?! Obviously, this is crucial.*

I discuss it with Angel on the night bus, scoffing a burger – did she think he would've made a move after last time? Did she think there was any kind of romantic vibe? Then a funny thing happened. Maybe it's because we were on the night bus and knackered, but you know what? We couldn't even be arsed to come up with any hypothetical theories. I was just going through the post-mortem motions. If me and my best mate can't even be bothered to chat about a cute boy with multiple vodka ginger ales in our bellies, then, really, it's a non-starter. RIP Smiler. I'll have to get my hot tub experience elsewhere.

Sunday, 11 October

Me, Angel, G and Rubles are having Sunday lunch at mine (Jamie Oliver's roast chicken) and G, as is often the case, is pissing about with his iPhone. He's geeking out, saying something about how he nests his apps (*sorry, what?*). Meanwhile Angel, who's practically a Luddite, is rolling her eyes and giving me an all-too-familiar yawn face. I take a gulp of wine, then look at G and suggest: 'Maybe you could use that time you spend nesting your apps to pleasure your lady?'

'Is there an app for that?'

Credit where credit's due. That's fucking genius.

Tuesday, 13 October

Going braless has its downfalls:

1. When tradesmen drop by unannounced (Southern Electric – you know who you are), they get all starey and weird. Thank God it's me who's braless, though, and not Rubles. They really wouldn't be able to handle her without armour. It's all in the cup size.

2. Contorting yourself to remove your bra in moments of too-tightness is a vaguely erotic act that only serves to remind you that you aren't getting any sex at all.

Any.

Want.

Some.

Jesus, I must want some if I'm writing about taking my bra off.

Wednesday, 14 October

'I threw a pen at Rockstar today and it hit him in the face. Not a good look.'

Lady Jane's tone is breathy. Breathy, yet she's barely pausing to draw breath.

'Shit, man, that doesn't sound good. Is he OK? Any visible scarring?'

'No. He was furious with me, though.'

'I'm not surprised. Are you OK, hun? You sound stressed.'

I know when Lady Jane is anxious. Her voice can't hide it. You can practically feel the tension crackling through the phone.

'I've just got so much to do. I'm worried I won't have much time when you come up. I threw that pen at him today because he was talking too loud – what the fuck's that about? Something's got to give.'

'Aw, hun. Don't worry, it's totally fine.' I'm doing my best slow and soothing voice in contrast to her mile-a-minute. 'It doesn't matter what we do or don't do. I'm around, so I'll do whatever I can to support you. OK? Now, stay away from sharp objects and I'll see you early next week.'

'Love you.'

'Love you, too.'

Friday, 16 October

I'm heading up north for a week to spend a bit of time at Mum and Dad's before heading to Manc to see Lady Jane and Rockstar and potentially do some In The City stuff. In The City is a music conference, akin to South by Southwest or Miami, except not as good. But I'm thinking chock-full of fit music types. My types, in other words. As a single girl, it's always good to try and put yourself in situations where fit men will be.

Tonight, though, in contrast, I'm going out in town, where I'm predicting there will be no fit men. But if there are, I'll stand corrected.

Saturday, 17 October

I've slumped. Last night, me and Roller Girl bumped into a mate in the only bar in town that's any good and the first thing he said, chipper as anything, was, 'I was just with your ex half an hour ago.' Boom! It put a strain on the evening from then on. I hate that I desperately want to see him and desperately don't want to see him at the same time. I tried and failed to put a brave face on it.

Now I'm not even trying. I'm wearing a shitty old and holey pair of grey marl leggings that I refuse to throw out, my pyjama top and my dad's argyle cardigan. I'm thinking about Him and the fact that he's just a bus ride away.

Am I over-romanticising again because I'm sitting on my own, having watched *Good Will Hunting*, and it's got me all misty-eyed? Maybe he watched *Good Will Hunting* too?

It doesn't change the fact that we ended and will remain ended, but I still can't shake him off.

He's a bus ride away.

I haven't seen him since The Curious Incident of Boxing Day in the Local Pub. We'd been split up for months at that point, but it still hurt. A lot. Oh God, this is bad. It's practically Boxing Day again (well, the Christmas ads have started on the telly) and I'm *still* thinking about him. Why can't I get him out of my head, even now?

I bring to mind the strap line from *(500) Days of Summer*:

> *Boy meets girl*
> *Boy falls in love*
> *Girl doesn't*

In this case, I'm the boy.

I hate that I deleted his number from my phone.

I hate that it's for the best that I deleted his number from my phone.

I hate that he's just a bus ride away. And that I still have his email address.

Monday, 19 October

So while I've been brooding over Cartoon Boy, Pfeiffer has been getting busy with it. I love Monday's emails because there's always boy news:

> Met quite a nice guy on Fri eve – friend of my mate's, she was trying to hook me up with. He is a singer in a band (we watched their gig – not brilliant, but he is pretty fit!) and has a day job, so reckon OK! He called me yest and we had a grand old chat – we have a hot date on Tues. He didn't mess around either, texted me on the Sat morning and said he wanted to meet me again cos he fancied me – straight to the point, eh? And rang me on Sun after a text or two, rather than messing around with texting. Too good to be true?!!!!

So I said . . . 'I think that sounds promising, yes. And I like the fact that he actually – shock horror – called you! Why are we so thrilled for such small mercies?'

Tuesday, 20 October

It's Pfeiffer's big date tonight and I have to say, this guy actually sounds OK. She's been keeping me abreast of the developments – i.e. forwarding every single piece of email correspondence – and what he's done is give her three restaurant choices, complete with a link to either the website or a review (Giles Coren, *The Times*) and left the final decision up to her. The top three were picked on the basis that, and I quote, 'They're all in and around London Bridge, as that's kind of halfway between the two of us.' They're going to the Anchor and Hope in Waterloo.

Meanwhile, I'm heading to Manchester to have dinner and drinks with Lady Jane, Rockstar and an eminent author who's doing a talk at In The City. I'm very much looking forward to making his acquaintance because I hear he's quite the bon viveur. 'He's outrageous,' Lady Jane keeps telling me. Outrageous will do nicely. I learn an important lesson from the author later on, something I suspect carries him through his exploits. 'Alison,' he said as we knocked back whiskies late into the night, 'never worry, never apologise, never explain.' I'll have to remember that.

Wednesday, 21 October

As is customary whenever I go out with Lady Jane and Rockstar, I'm feeling delicate, to say the least. I'm on the train at Piccadilly by 10 a.m. because I've got to get back to London for a photoshoot for this women's network thing I've been invited to join. I feel like a bit of an impostor amongst all these high achievers, these polished women tucking into granola and yoghurt, when I rock up, unwashed, in a battered leather jacket, stinking of booze. Imagine Keith Richards at a WI meeting. Deep breaths.

Later on, back at the flat in my scruffy leggings again, hair still very 'bouffy' from the shoot, an email comes through from Pfeiffer on The Big Date. I'd describe her tone as orgasmic.

> We had such a lovely date – he was the perfect gent, bought me an amazing dinner (ace food – I had full crab for first time ever and he helped me and even politely said I had crab in my hair at one point and pulled it out – nice!), walked me along the river then we got ciders and went down onto the riverbank and chatted and then he deposited me at the station with no angling to come back. We got on really well – I like him!
>
> He sent me a really nice text on the way home too – 'tonight was perfect x' – I was quite excited and couldn't sleep for about an hour!

On a more random note, there's also an email from Yorkshire in New York just saying, 'For some reason I've got one armpit that smells like crayons.'

Thursday, 22 October

As it stands at the moment, my future beau could be:

a. A northern policeman
b. A globetrotting musician, or
c. The son of my parents' friends.

Er, can I phone a friend?

At various points throughout my single life, I've moaned to my friends (in an adorably cute and funny way, of course), 'Don't you know *anyone* you can set me up with?' I got a bit excited once when I watched a programme where an over-zealous woman was doing matchmaking Indian stylee – via family connections. She'd get a hopeless single person's friends and family to write lists of all the people they know (and all the people *they* know) who have two legs, two arms and their own free will to go out with said sad, single person.

Why aren't my mates sitting down and writing lists for me, I cried?

'There's nobody I would want to set you up with' is the stock response.

I take this to mean that they don't think anyone is good enough rather than that I'm too loopy for them to risk breeding with their square mates. Anyway, the times, it seems, are a-changing.

Just last week there was a text from my brother-in-law, a member of our beleaguered police force. For the sake of originality, let's call him Mr Vice.

'I think you should meet one of my cop friends – he looks just like the guy from Maroon 5!'

'Wow,' I say, thinking, *that guy from Maroon 5 is a bit of a tool* but I suppose he is quite good-looking, in a *Guys Go Wild in Vegas* kinda way. 'Perhaps you could set up a dinner party?'

'He's more of a night out in Manchester kind of guy,' says Mr Vice.

'Is he clever? Funny?' I say. A girl's got standards, after all . . .

'He's really smart, and the funniest guy I know. Can I give him your number?'

I must say at this point, in my whole 13-plus years of knowing Mr

Vice, he has never once put forward a possible suitor for me, so this is a real novelty. He must be good, surely?

'OK, then. Yeah, give him my number. Tell him to give me a call.' Am now shitting it.

'What do you think of policemen?' I ask Mrs Patz the next day. I'm not sure, you see.

'Sex bags in hats,' she says without hesitation.

She actually said that.

Friday, 23 October

After the Policeman, now the globetrotting musician.

'I've got Music Man's email address and mobile number. Love me?' goes Lady Jane's lunchtime email. Her Rockstar, who's a romantic soul as well as being very well connected, has made a call and come back with the digits. Apparently, Music Man remembered me from our brief cyberspace encounter and has urged me to get in touch. Eeeeeek!

I drop him a mail without delay (well, it's already taken nearly four months):

> How are you? Hope all's well in your world . . . the small world
> that it is! Be great to meet up for a drink sometime. Fancy it?

Within the hour – the hour! – I get:

> Hey,
> Great to hear from you.
>   Yeah, [Rockstar] asked about passing on my details.
>   Drinks would be lovely.
>   I'm on tour just now, but I'll be back in a few weeks if you're
> around?
>   x

On Rockstar's drunkenly delivered advice to play it cool (well, he actually told me to throw him a line and leave 'my bait' dangling enticingly), I resist the urge to tell Music Man my life story this time and reply simply with: 'Yes, I'll be around. Give me a shout when you're back in town x.'

Cool as, no?

'Will do! x,' he comes back with. Now, as I pointed out to Lady Jane, Angel, Rubles, Mrs Patz, Pfeiffer and my mum, he didn't need to send that last email, did he? No. But he did. And it was very polite, and affirmative. I like. Now we wait.

Saturday, 24 October

Mum and Dad are down staying with me and they bring with them, figuratively speaking, the third possible set-up to complete the trio: the curveball. 'Timothy' is the son of the couple my mum and dad go ballroom dancing with. I call him Timothy because of that TV sitcom *Sorry!* where Ronnie Corbett plays a henpecked mummy's boy.

I'm pouring tea in my living room and Dad's smoking his pipe when the subject of Timothy comes up.

Mum: Can I give him your email address?

Me: Why? [I have literally no clue why she would give him my email address and, crucially, why he'd even want it.] Did he actually ask for my email address?

Mum: Yes, he'd like to get to know you.

Me: Why? [I repeat what I think is a perfectly viable question.]

Mum: Well, why not? How else do people meet people?

Me: Er, by actually meeting them and not just because their parents go dancing together and because they happen to share a decade of birth.

Mum: It's no different to that internet dating, is it?

Me: Are you trying to sell this to me, Mum?

Mum: Well, what have you got to lose? He might be really nice.

Me: Is he good-looking?

Mum: He's very tall.

Fucking hell. That's almost as bad as *he's got a great personality*.

I'm laughing uncontrollably at this point, while shoving a biscuit in my mouth, and my mum's getting annoyed. It's time to push it further.

Me: What kind of clothes does he wear? [You know, to get a sense of whether we might have anything in common . . .]

Mum: Well, in the photo I saw of him he had his holiday clothes on.

Now, I don't know if this is a northern thing, but my parents have 'holiday clothes' – a ready-made wardrobe, so that if, say, you decided on a whim to book a last-minute holiday on Teletext, you could just literally pick up your suitcase and go (they don't have it packed for this reason, because they'd never book a holiday on Teletext, but, you know). They've even got toilet bags packed and ready. When we were kids, we had 'holiday clothes'. But surely no self-respecting 30-year-old men living in 2009 have holiday clothes. Do they?

Me: Who was he on holiday with?

Mum: His mum and dad.

I rest my case.

Sunday, 26 October

I've just seen Mum and Dad off to the station, as is customary, two hours ahead of their scheduled departure time from King's Cross. I don't know if it's adorable or infuriating, their obsession with 'leaving enough time'.

I get back to the flat and, by way of release, burst into tears. Every single time they go, I do this. Why? What's wrong with me? Why am I such a baby? I love spending time with them – infuriating or not, I do. And I think, *whisper it*, when you don't have a partner, you still need to suckle on the parental teat, so to speak. I know I do. I'm lucky that I like them in that respect. I've got my friends too, of course, who are brilliant, but Mum and Dad are still my first and main port of call; my go-to in times of need. Maybe as well, because I'm so totally myself and so totally relaxed when I see them, I do feel an immediate sense of loss as soon as they leave.

If this all sounds a bit rose-tinted, I should point out that despite the fact I put a lot of thought into planning the perfect weekend doing 'authentic London things', I know deep down my dad would quite happily sit in my flat, smoking his pipe and nipping to the local pub for a couple of pints. He's not one for walking too far and London inevitably involves a lot of schlepping around. When I do tempt them out, it's like role reversal, with me being the nagging parent, insisting, 'No, you'll love this antiques market' and 'It's just down here. It's the oldest pie-and-mash shop in London!'

'We just come to see you, love. That's all we're bothered about' is what Mum always says when I'm getting all white-knuckled about my itinerary.

They did enjoy the pie-and-mash shop experience, as it goes. We went to the one down Tower Bridge Road – all wooden benches and white-tiled walls – after browsing round Bermondsey antiques market. Always game once you've managed to persuade him out of the house, Dad dove straight in with some jellied eels. 'Too much jelly,' he said, stuffing the disgusting frogspawn into his mouth regardless.

Being in that part of town became a bit of a trip down memory lane, too, because it's near where I used to live with the Big Ex. After the pie shop, we decamped to a pub and I ended up telling Mum and Dad a bit more about how I felt towards the end of that relationship. How miserable I was, how difficult he was and how sad I still feel when I look back. It's hard, after you invest so much time and love in a relationship, when it goes bad. Where does the love go? It has to go somewhere. If you're careless with something for long enough, though, it breaks.

I used to hide how miserable I was from my parents, partly because I was ashamed of how badly things had turned out and also because I didn't want them to judge him too harshly; I was still trying to make it work and protect him in the process. At the time, say if we'd had a huge shouting match in the street and he'd be yelling at me in public or I'd scream and cry out of sheer frustration, I'd sometimes think to myself, God, if my mum and dad could see me now. They wouldn't recognise me. *I* didn't recognise me.

Talking to them about it this weekend, sharing some of the memories, good and bad, I feel like I've moved on a bit more from it. Also, I feel proud that I have. They're certainly glad I'm not in that situation any more. It also serves as a bit of a reminder to myself that you just don't get over things like that so quickly. It takes time. I thought I would probably have met someone else a bit quicker than the three and a half years it's been, but I guess that's just the way it is. The right relationship is not easy to come by and I should know: I was in the wrong one for long enough.

Later on, a text from Mum:

'Hi love, back safe. Got Cornish pasty to eat on train. £4! Thanks for having us to stay – we've had brill time. Love you. M+D. xxx.'

Tuesday, 27 October

It started innocently enough. I was doing some picture research for an upcoming project, which involved looking up photos of Kate Moss. There were a few from her Johnny days (sigh), which 'forced' me to type 'Kate Moss and Johnny Depp' into Google's image search.

I've entered a dark hole of longing and relationship envy. They're not even together any more. And it's just a photo.

Wednesday, 28 October

I'm seeing Mr Scissors later for my, ooh-I-dunno, four-monthly haircut. It's weird with him because we've clearly got a hairdresser/client relationship, but then we're also sort-of friends. We've got loads in common – we're always chatting about films and music – and we've seen each other socially a few times, like the debauched acid house night earlier this month. Then there was the Curious Incident of the Wimbledon Text Exchange – surely he was flirting with me?

Anyway, this is the crap I'm carrying around in my unkempt head as I arrive at the salon and tuck into *Tatler* in the waiting area. This was a great discovery, incidentally. I'm so not a *Tatler* reader; in fact, I'd admit to being something of an inverted snob, but actually that mag had some great pieces in it. One such article was written by the actress Emily Mortimer about her dad, the late John Mortimer, who I love(d). A wise, wise man with a great wit, brains and a huge capacity for fun. That's how I imagine him, anyway – the perfect afternoon G&T drinking partner.

I'm tucking into this article when Mr Scissors arrives to greet me.

I've kind of shot myself in the foot a bit by being so engrossed because we usually start proceedings with an *is-he-or-is-he-not-interested* kiss on the lips. Because I was slow to get up from my magazine trance we end up having an *is-he-or-is-he-not-interested* awkward half-hug.

Him: You can bring that magazine with you, if you like?

Me: Oh, great. Yes, I will. [Cue one-minute blabber from me about how I don't usually read *Tatler* but actually the articles are quite good . . . blah, blah.]

We decide that my hair, although definitely straggly and in need of care, is looking pretty good long-ish, so opt for a trim after he unwittingly (or wittingly?) seduces me with lots of tousling into the mirror. Apparently the dye in the ends gives it much-needed texture. I'm sent off to have it washed. He tells me not to worry, he'll keep my page.

Then the cut begins and we're chatting about the usual stuff: gigs, places we've visited. He really is after my heart when he tells me about his recent jaunt to a Derbyshire country house for a murder mystery weekend. He shows me pictures of him lying dead (with self-administered bullet wound) on his phone, while resting one hand on my shoulder (meaningful or not?). I can't see any pics of a girlfriend. Hmm. This is one of the ridiculous things – we know each other pretty well, but I actually don't know whether or not he has a girlfriend and can't bring myself to ask.

Then an interesting thing happens. I read to him from the John Mortimer article while he's administering the fancy whipped cream stuff into my hair (yeah, baby) and notice there will be a 'Remembering John Mortimer' evening at the Royal Court theatre soon and express an interest in going.

He pipes up: 'Maybe you'll meet your future husband there.'

What? At first I'm a bit put off, thinking rapidly that he: a) has realised I'm in love with him and is trying to gently put me off and b) has no interest, therefore is quite happy to mention a future husband that is clearly not him. I dust myself off and carry on being as charming and breezy as ever.

We're done, my hair's done and it's time to leave. I part with 16 quid on the whipped cream stuff. *Hey, I'll always have the memories.* He walks me to the counter, gets my tweed jacket and then starts really mumbling; it's quite hard for me to concentrate on what he's saying with the gorgeously camp receptionist guy cooing over my hair and me going, 'Yes, it is great, isn't it?' while fumbling for funds in my purse.

He's helping me on with my jacket: 'Er, so I'll text you then . . . if anything good's going on . . . '

Why is he telling me he'll text me? He never does that. 'Do, do,' I say cutely, being spazzy trying to get my arm in the hole.

'Yeah, so I'll text you, see you soon?'

'Yeah, it'd be great to see you.'

OK, now I'm confused. He had mentioned that his favourite DJ was playing mid-November; perhaps he wants to let me know about that. But why? I might've been to a couple of his gigs, but it's not like we're mates. He definitely sounded a little bit fumbly, nervous almost . . . interesting, very interesting. Or am I just being my usual fantasist self? Ach, who knows? In all the years I've known him, I can't figure him out. Imagine if we've always both fancied each other but neither of us dared do anything about it. OR he doesn't fancy me at all and if I'm not careful I could quite easily make a right tit of myself. It really could go either way.

Because it's good to get all hair removal jobs done at the same time, next stop, waxing. Some bikini waxing, to be exact. *Why?* I hear you cry, *you're not seeing anyone!* Well, I know, but you never can tell, can you? Plus I was doing a review for a website, so it was free. Can't argue with that and it really was needed. I was grossing myself out, never mind anyone else.

So, I was persuaded into having a Brazilian. I've had a Brazilian only once before and, believe me, it wasn't pretty. The woman really didn't know what she was doing and took absolutely ages, getting stuck, if you know what I mean, all the way round. Horrendous. Torture. I was sceptical, to say the least, but this place specialises in waxing, it's all they do, so they *should* know what they're doing. Plus, they use liquid wax and actually strip off the wax rather than using the strips. They cut out the middle man and go straight to the source.

It works too, goddamn it! I'm like a baby in no time and, have to say, LOVE it. Now I just need to find someone else to love it before it starts growing back, otherwise *what* a waste!

After the somewhat humiliating but ultimately satisfying experience of the Brazilian, I'm sent downstairs to test out the new i-bar, for some brow grooming. I'm gonna be threaded. My lady sizes me up and soon whips my eyebrows into a sexy new shape and I'm thrilled. It's true what they say – having your eyebrows shaped really does give you an instant facelift.

I'm on a high. My lady parts are completely bare and my face looks attractively surprised. Excellent. The therapist interrupts my mirror gazing and daydreaming with:

'Hope you don't mind me saying this, but I think I should do your top lip.'

Winter, 2009

winter *(n)* the coldest season of the year; a bleak or lifeless period

winter *(n)* the coldest season of the year; a bleak or lifeless period save for Christmas time when parties elicit ill-fated liaisons and exes rear their ugly heads; traditionally a time for breaking resolutions

Guest list:
1. Mr Bale
2. Ant
3. Cartoon Boy
4. Music Man
5. Geezer Boy
6. The Big Ex
7. Model Man

November
Finally, a Guy with Balls?

Sunday, 1 November

When did Halloween become such a big deal? Last night, Angel and I went out in Shoreditch, which had morphed into some kind of *Dawn of the Dead* meets God-awful hen-do, with ghouled-up revellers everywhere. As is tradition, we had a few drinks in the Griffin, one of our favourite haunts – a shabby-chic old man's pub full of people who look like they went out in the '90s and never made it home – before meeting her boyfriend G and our mate J at another pub of similar ilk, with red walls and singalong jukebox (at one point, the whole place joined in with 'Maggie May').

We head for the bar and I spot a guy with a nice, open, smiley face, longish, fairish hair and cool preppy-style clothes. Angel will tell me later that she and G thought he looked a little like Christian Bale, the actor with psycho tendencies. That didn't occur to me at the time.

I smile at him, he smiles back, then, as the next hour or so progresses, we make eye contact several times. I think I might even raise one or two newly arched brows to him, too. The boys arrive and although I'm definitely flirting on some level with this mystery man I'm not fully committed to it, you know? Also, what's the charming phrase for when you go out with male friends? Cock block, that's it.

Two drinks later I notice him get up to leave, putting on his jacket and gathering his boys-only posse. I'm having a laugh with my three and, pretty much without thinking, wave at him as he leaves. Angel looks at me and laughs. I'm laughing too, at my own cheesiness. What was the point of that move? We're continuing to joke – I've gathered the tapered end of my jumpsuit's pussy bow and fashioned a moustache across my face, when . . . wait! Who's that? It's *him*, coming back in. Wait, what's he doing? Ooh, he's coming over!

He appears at my side and says, 'Can I just ask, are either of these two guys your boyfriend?'

Me: 'No, no, they're the thorn in my side! [Funny, I think . . .]'

Him: 'I've got to go now, but I was wondering if maybe you fancied going out for a drink some time?'

Me: 'Yes, I would like to do that. [Blimey!]'

Him: 'Do you want to put your number in? I don't want any disasters. [Presumably by disaster he means he might get my number wrong if left to his own devices. I like this neurotica very much.]'

Me: 'Sure.'

As a non-iPhone user, I set about typing my digits into his handset with the trepidation and pointy finger of E.T. Then we have a farcical misunderstanding where he's trying to tell me his name and I'm mishearing it, like seven times. We clear that up eventually and I tell him my name, which I also have to repeat more than once. This is what happens when an entire pub is singing along to the Black Eyed Peas' 'I Gotta Feeling' and you're on the wrong side of too many vodkas.

I've finally finished with the spasmodic typing.

Him: 'OK, well, I've got to go now, but, yeah, er, random Halloween thing . . . '

He's smiling sheepishly. I like his wry acknowledgement of the slightly bizarre, not to mention brief, nature of our exchange.

Me: 'Yeah, give me a call. Bye, have a good night. [He was off to a friend of a friend's house party.]'

Well, no one is more shocked than me by this encounter. I can't believe this guy actually came back in to get my number based on very little indeed. I'm impressed! He had guts.

'It's romantic,' gushes Angel.

'He looks like Christian Bale,' adds G. J just shakes my hand – 'Nice work.'

Angel and I discuss it on the way home and realise this has never actually happened to me before – a guy, let's call him 'Mr Bale', making the move to get my number (I usually beat them to it). This temporarily makes me feel like a bit of a loser, but then I resolve to feel chuffed that it's happened.

'Finally, a guy with balls,' says Angel. Well, quite. Will he have the balls to actually call, though? I do hope so.

Monday, 2 November

I can't stop crying. Correction, *we* can't stop crying. Angel and I are having a post-cinema drink in Brixton at a bar called the Rest is Noise, a name that couldn't be more apt right now as we sit and sob into our pints of lager.

'I . . . just . . . can't . . . believe that you're leaving . . .'

I can barely speak for crying. My face has become a log flume.

'I know, I know . . .' She's rubbing my knee. 'I don't know what I'll do without you.'

I'm doing that thing where you have a wobbly smile and cry at the same time.

'I love you so much,' I say, looking her straight in the eye whilst rescuing a strip of her blonde hair that's dipping into her glass.

'I love you, Al. I don't know what I'm doing, really. I don't . . .'

'You'll be fine.' I'm switching to rallying mode. 'You'll have an amazing time . . .'

It's so difficult because I know you shouldn't hold your friends back, make them feel bad for their decisions. I know I'd move for love. I get it. But I'm still hurt that she's leaving me. I am. Part of me doesn't get it and I know that's why we've been avoiding the subject.

'I just can't believe we won't be able to meet up like this any more, on a Monday night. For a pint.'

I hate that that's gone for ever. Precious pints and chats.

'I know.' She takes a deep breath and sucks back tears. 'I know. It's going to be so weird.'

'I'll miss you so much. But we'll just have to make the effort . . .'

I'm blagging it now.

'We will . . . ' She's wiping her face, trying to smile.

For me, *An Education* will always be the film where afterwards I bawled my eyes out for an hour straight.

Tuesday, 3 November

Guess who's got a hot date on Friday night? Yes, it seems – until he proves otherwise, anyway – that Mr Bale does indeed have balls. Sorry, I'm gonna stop using that word now; it's making me feel a bit nauseous.

He texted me yesterday, at 5 p.m., saying, 'Hey, shame we didn't really get to chat but good to meet u on Sat night. How do u fancy a drink sometime and perhaps we can get a little further past hi my name is . . . ?'

WHAT A GREAT TEXT!! Keen but funny and not cheesy. I likey. Actually, given that he texted on a Monday, just two days after our meet, I'd say *very* keen.

So I said . . . 'Ha. Yes, it was a rather brief encounter. Be great to meet up and attempt actual dialogue. I struggled with your name, if I remember rightly. Duh! When you free?'

Then I went to the cinema, you know, the precursor to the sob-fest with Angel, and had a minor wobble about whether I sounded too flippant with the struggling with his name chat but then I pulled myself together and came out of the cinema to find:

'Timing might be a bit difficult as I'm off to Argentina for a bit next week but could do a controversial cheeky couple on Friday or else when I get back in a couple of weeks' time?'

Must admit, when I read the 'timing might be difficult' I had an instant rush of blood to the head, but then read the whole thing and was, well, delighted! Argentina, eh? Very adventurous. And the 'controversial' – witty and just the right side of paranoia.

So I said . . . 'Well, I'm all for controversial, so Friday it is, then. Shall we arrange the specifics later in the week? Argentina – exciting! x'.

Pretty cool, no? Panic is setting in via slow release, a bit like what happens when you eat porridge. Keep thinking, I'M MEETING A STRANGER ON FRIDAY!

Thursday, 5 November

'It's nine o'clock, the night before our so-called date, and I still haven't heard from him.'

'You will.' Lady Jane is unwaveringly confident, as ever.

'Do you not think, though, that it's polite to make arrangements the day before?'

'He's— '

I cut her off. 'I mean, I'm working tomorrow, I need to know what I'm doing, don't I?'

She tries again. 'He's a bloke. He'll probably text you tomorrow when he gets up.'

I'm not convinced. I think it's because I've got so used to flaky blokes that act interested one minute and then disappear the next.

'You think he'll definitely get in touch, then?' Oh God, I've turned.

'You made a plan, didn't you? For Friday night? He'll get in touch tomorrow.' Lady Jane's tone indicates it's the last she'll say on the matter.

'Okaaaayeeee.' I sulk off the phone and drop him a 'casual' text, asking if we're still on for tomorrow and what does he fancy doing.

Friday, 6 November

Wake up to no word from Mr Bale and feel a mixture of anger and disappointment. In that order. What a dick. Why bother going to the trouble of going up to somebody you don't know in a bar, risking humiliation, asking her out, texting her two days later to arrange a date and then fucking it off.

'Why? I just don't get it.' I'm bending Mrs Patz's ear in the kitchen at the fashion office. She's loading up the coffee machine.

'You might still hear from him,' she says, looking unconvinced.

'Even if I do, I think I've been put off now,' I say, grabbing milk from the fridge.

'I mean, I didn't know what to wear today because I don't know what we'll be doing. It's just not romantic, is it?'

Mrs Patz raises her eyebrows and presses her lips together. It's one of those moments where she thinks I'm over-reacting, which I probably am. 'I still think you'll hear from him. He was well keen.' She stirs our drinks. I mope back to my desk and check to see if anything's happened to my phone in the past six minutes.

An apologetic text arrives at 1.10 p.m. 'Sorry I didn't get back to you last night. Went to a gig and it got a bit messy. Shall we meet in the Bricklayers later?'

Mixed emotions. Glad he texted, underwhelmed by his cavalier attitude and fact he's suggesting we meet in the same pub I saw him in last weekend. Talk about lack of imagination.

I suggest the Griffin, just to be awkward, I think, more than anything, since it's much of a muchness.

Mrs Patz raises her eyebrows again. This time she's saying *I told you so. You dick*.

I get home, get dressed and set off to meet him. I thought dating was meant to be fun? All those people giggling over coffee, teasing each other with their eyes on those eHarmony adverts, the thrill of the early days that people who've been in relationships lament so often . . . so why do I feel, well, full of dread? I'm trying to picture the moment where we meet. What will I say? I literally can't see it. 'I don't want to go,' I text Angel, who's the third person to send a good luck text.

'You'll be fine. Just have fun.'

Hmph. Fun? Easy for you to say. You're not the one in the fur coat in the pissing-down rain.

Saturday, 7 November
It started with pissing-down rain . . .

This was upsetting, mainly because I was wearing my (fake) fur coat and, generally speaking, you can't help but look like a bit of a knob dressed as a drowned rabbit.

That said, I did have an umbrella, so when I turned up at the pub – before him, I hasten to add – my hair at least wasn't slapped to my head. His was when he arrived, but he actually looked quite cute for it. The Baleness of Bale turned out to be not quite as Baley as I'd imagined. For a start, 'my' Bale is slighter and shorter. I actually don't think his face has that much in common either. I can't imagine him pulling off *American Psycho*, put it that way. He's cute, though – smiley and boyish.

His first move is pretty cool, too. I'm already ordering a pint whilst simultaneously texting him to see what he wants, given that he's not arrived yet, when he appears all smiles, apologies and drips. I ask him what he wants. Cider (hmm), but then he insists on buying, which is nice.

To say I was nervous leading up to this date is a massive understatement. I was, to use one of my favourite phrases, shitting it. 'You'll be fine once you get there,' cried all my well-wishing friends. Turns out, I was more than fine. I was cocky. Nice, but cocky. Was this my defence mechanism?

Now, this nice-but-cocky thing is fine when you're out with your mates, talking nonsense very fast and taking jokes a bit far, etc. It's perhaps not, however, the sort of behaviour to unleash on an unsuspecting suitor. Not to say I was offensive or anything . . . the only thing that bordered on offensive, and this was entirely a joke, was when he was telling me about the voluntary work he's been doing for a children's Aids charity to fill some time while he's not working (alarm bells!). 'I'd go for Aids too if I did charity work' was my response.

What the fuck? I don't know what came over me. Now, I think that's funny, but it's a bit risky at this stage and I certainly didn't mean to cause offence, to either him or the cause. Long pause. He looks at me and . . . laughs! Thank God for that. Am I pushing him on purpose? I'm honestly not sure, even now, retrospectively.

So this stands out as a rather ludicrous thing that I said, along with the next thing, which Angel literally could not stop laughing about when I told her. Context is everything, I know, but I can't quite remember it. Damn you, Amaretto Sours! We were talking about hair. Can't remember why. And he said he always used to have short hair, or was it long? Can't remember. Anyway, his hair now, or on our date at least, was kind of ear length and floppy. It was also, unfortunately for him, looking a bit shit. Like a bob. I think the rain was punishing him for being late. Anyway, it wasn't super shit but it certainly wasn't how I remembered his hair looking when we met. Now with all the hair history chat that had been going on, I said, 'So, what's your plan with your hair?'

Another pause.

Him: 'Er, I don't know. Why? Do you think my hair's terrible?'

Me: 'Gosh no, no, that's not what I meant – it's just cos you said you were growing it [or something like that]. No no . . . '

Sweet Jesus! What. An. Idiot.

I played that one back to Angel and she roared with laughter so hard I thought my phone might give up the ghost. Bless him, though, he took it in his stride and I promise I wasn't being mean to him. It's just a bad case of foot-in-mouth.

The date progressed along much the same lines. He bought nearly all the drinks – very sweet, especially considering he's currently, and I quote, 'a man of leisure'. (PS. I've been out with enough men of leisure to know that I don't intend to go out with another, so that's something definitely stacked against him.)

We had lots of open, funny chats. My problem is that I'm too open for my own good. Always searching for the holy grail of no-armbands conversation. This is definitely a problem sometimes, in that it gets me in trouble.

Bumps aside, we did have a laugh. He was pretty hardy to my thunder-and-lightning company; you know, rumbling along for a bit, gathering momentum, then – BAM! – ridiculous/inappropriate comment number 57. Despite this, five hours went by, so I must've done something right. We 'shared' quite a lot, I think. I, again inexplicably, told him something pretty personal about a member of my family – something that's been on my mind – and was relevant, I think. Not to him, of course, to me. But still. He told me about his family – an interesting bunch, I must say. We were both bullied at school, which is nice. Him boarding, me comp.

We also, thrillingly, given the fact that I write about relationships, talked about dating etiquette. Again, can't remember how it came up exactly (though I expect I had something to do with it), but I was moaning about the fact that nobody calls any more. It's all texting. Interestingly, he agreed, but was under the impression from his friends (er, what do *they* know?) that the correct etiquette is to text because someone, particularly a someone you don't know very well, might not want to speak on the phone. Int-er-est-ing.

Then I said, because I couldn't resist, 'Well, I didn't even know if we were going out on this date since you didn't actually confirm until lunchtime.' I said this jokingly, but still. I know it is date suicide going in with such a 'womany' statement, but this was the thing about the date – I genuinely didn't give a shit what I said. I was uncensored.

His response was excellent, though, I must say. 'Aw no, gosh, sorry, it's just because I was at the gig and it all got a bit messy and I wasn't up till lunchtime. I hope you don't think I was playing games because I really wasn't.'

I mean, that is quite an admission. You see, he'd texted me as much when he finally did confirm at lunchtime and I was satisfied with his text. Why I had to bring it up, I don't know! Anyway, he rose to the challenge, so to speak.

The date ended in charming fashion. It was my fault because I hadn't eaten earlier and we drank a lot. I needed to eat and fast. So he's walking me to the tube station and we stop at a little bagel place en route. I've had a pint, two cocktails and about four vodkas, so though I'm holding it perfectly well together (actually, really well for me) I'm starving and in need of sustenance. I get my favourite bagel combo, bacon and cream cheese, and set about stuffing it into my mouth. I feel pretty comfortable with Bale; we've had a nice date, a lengthy date (five hours of sustained chatting and laughing), so I don't mind so much stuffing said bagel into my mouth enthusiastically.

So I'm eating the bagel as we near the tube, and I'm thinking, shit, we're nearly there, I should probably give him an end-of-date kiss, but there's no way I've got the chance to clear my mouth by then. You know how adhesive a half-chewed bagel can be. Oh God. We're at the barriers, the last chunk of bagel has just gone in and I'm frantically chewing, attempting to clear my teeth with my tongue and trying to be smiley and witty at the same time. This is extreme multitasking with a high risk of jaw lock.

Him: 'I've had a really nice time. I'd like to do this again some time – would you?'

Me: '[Swallow.] Er, yes. [Gulp.] Give me a shout once you're back from Argentina.'

I should point out that although the date's been good, and lengthy, and we certainly got on, I'm not fully feeling it. I'm sort of attracted to him, but had I been fully enamoured I would've blatantly jumped on him before now. That said, I feel a kiss is in order and might also serve as useful research for the viability of a future date. BUT I'VE GOT BITS OF BACON FLOATING AROUND MY MOUTH!!

Fuck it. I move my head towards his and opt for an 'extended peck' – open mouthed but not full-on snog. Despite my floating bacon worries, I think I got away with it. Of course, Mr Bale might well be blogging as we speak about the terrible oral manners of the drunk girl he went out with.

A note on kissing etiquette

I only wanted a half-snog; it seemed appropriate to:

- a. My levels of desire.
- b. The fact we were hovering by the tube station barrier.
- c. It really was the only way to go given that I still had half-chewed bagel bits stuck to my teeth.

My plan only went slightly awry in that Bale decided to stick his tongue in my mouth. Eew! Eew for him potentially, but definitely eew for me. Personally, I don't think it was that kind of kiss. I'm screwing my face up now as I write this.

I relay this to Lady Jane, who says, with the tone of my mum when she thinks I'm moaning disproportionately, 'Well, *that's* a snog, isn't it? You put your tongue in each other's mouths.' She might as well have added 'duh!!!' to the end of that statement.

It wasn't that the kiss was wholly unpleasurable; it just took me by surprise. I think if you're not in full-on snog mode (i.e. passionately, gropingly . . .), then why the tongue?

Mrs Patz sheds some light on this for me: 'Sometimes they just can't resist sticking in the tongue. He'll have been wanting to do that all night.'

'Really?' Thankfully, she did agree with my objections.

'I wholeheartedly agree. There's a time for tongue, and standing at the tube barrier isn't one of them.'

Yes! Yes!

Now, Mrs Patz is definitely of the, shall we say, restrained variety, and we don't always see eye-to-eye on matters of the heart or pleasures of the carnal (in that I would on a first date and she definitely wouldn't), but we do see eye-to-eye on this. It's important in these situations to pick the right friend to moan to, after all. We extend the tongue debate further:

Mrs Patz: 'The tongue should only really happen in private.'

Me: 'Er, yes. Actually, I'm not sure I fully agree with that – you can be in public but in a suitably dark and dingy corner somewhere maybe or really off your head, in which case anything goes.'

Mrs Patz: 'The tongue should come as part of a sequence of open-mouth kissing that builds up to a full-on pash, not straight away.'

Me: 'Yes! There's nothing elegant about sticking your tongue in straight away! Especially not on a first date.'

Ha Ha Ha!! Sorry, I realised what I just said! What a load of BS . . .

Me: 'On a first date, it's either an extended peck or full sex, there's no in between. The tongue is definitely a precursor to a penis.'

THANK YOU!!! I love it when a theory comes together.

I should add that I do feel a bit mean now, because Bale *was* really nice. On the date, it was me who needed nicing up.

I guess that's why, when he asked to see me again, before the horror snog, I said I would. I need to 'give him another go', as my mum put it. It wasn't fireworks, but there's something quietly cool about him, especially given what a wanker I was at certain points.

So we parted at the tube, and he said he'd call once he got back from his trip to Argentina. Before I'd even arrived home, a text: 'Hope your journey back wasn't too painful. Enjoyed tonight, although have to apologise for my zombie-like state. Will give you a call when I'm back, if you fancy another outing?'

Now my initial thoughts on getting that were:

1. Bloody typical – you sit for days waiting on a text from some idiot who you fancy whereas the one you're absolutely not sure about texts before you've even got home.

2. What's he on about – zombie? I felt that was a bit feeble of him. Is he saying 'I'll do better next time'? I don't get it. Then I relented and thought, OK, he was on it last night so maybe he wasn't firing on all cylinders. And how could I possibly know that? In the end I decided all kudos to him because I reckon if I'd been on it the night before there'd be a good chance I'd still be out and wouldn't have made the date at all.

3. Go out again? Hmm . . .

Me: 'Almost home. Tonight was much fun. I don't think you were zombie-like at all [note the polite but firm approach]. Have a great time in Argentina and, yes, give me a shout when you get back.'

Now, I know that that text isn't exactly fully affirmative, but you know what? Fuck it.

Shoe. Other. Foot.

Wednesday, 11 November

Email is just pissing me off today. First there's Pfeiffer's woes. That bloke who rescued crab out of her hair, the one with three dinner choices, has gone completely quiet. Like he's dead. They had another three dates (two sleepovers) and now the goon won't answer her texts. How rude. Maybe he *is* dead? The situation is further complicated by the fact that it was her mate who set them up. And now the mate is going quiet too. How rude.

'It's all just so weird.' I can hear her 'steeling herself' voice as I read the email. 'Am determined to take a step back from it all, but just really want to know what has gone on – I think I prob could email my friend again but don't want to look like a weirdo stalker and make her feel more awkward. I thought he might at least email today – even if not good news, but guess only early!'

What a prick. Guy ignores texts, girl feels like she's a stalker. It's bullshit.

In other news, I get a chirpy invite from one of Angel's school colleagues, asking me and G to Angel's leaving do next month. She's lovely, this girl, don't get me wrong, but it feels weird to be invited to my best mate's leaving drinks. G replies to all: 'I'll be there with bells on!' I feel ever so slightly resentful. Enough to make me reach for a beer and roll-up at 3.30 p.m.

Friday, 13 November

What with Angel leaving, my love life not even on a downward spiral so much as completely stagnant, my main joy of the last few days has been some rather hilarious email exchanges with Yorkshire. We're in touch a lot anyway, as mates – truly as mates – but I do wonder if I enjoy our encounters that little bit more when there's nothing else giving. A little trip down memory lane never harmed anyone. Hmm. The thing about Yorkshire, though, is he's so damned funny and original, it does make me wonder sometimes. Especially in light of all the duds.

So, we're emailing and transported back to the '90s. And arm cuffs. I've been asked to write about a teenage experience for a Sunday supplement and have decided to recount Yorkshire's and my trip to Cyprus the summer after my A levels: the summer the Spice Girls first came out, the summer I was fond of wearing a spiral gold-plated arm cuff.

I look through the photos from the trip and get a pang of nostalgia. I email Yorkshire:

> I've got the Cyprus photos with me today. So funny! We're so young! And soooo '90s! I'm wearing mules, an arm cuff and a fucking crop top in one photo!!! And you look well gay in a lot of them.

He looks gay mainly because he's wearing my Body Shop sarong in most of the daytime pictures. He's not proud. That's what I love about him still: his ability to not give a fuck.

'My editor says you're, quote, "very good-looking",' I say later. Flirting? Flattering, certainly.

'Hmm . . . yeah' is his reply, just as I'm packing myself off to bed. 'Maybe because I was about nine and a half stone then, scary! Anyway, sarong beats arm cuff but not too sure about suede halterneck . . . '

Oh yeah, my backless suede halterneck top. And I thought my memory was good.

Sunday, 15 November

'I'd go out with him. He's fit.'

Lady Jane is in London and encouraging me to stalk some guy on Facebook.

'Who is he again?' I'm leaning over her shoulder, trying to decide if he's quirky or a knob for the fact that his profile picture shows him doing a '70s-style catalogue pose, complete with ribbed polo neck.

'You know Louise? It's her mate's brother. He was at a party we were at recently and everybody was commenting on how gorgeous he was.'

'Fucking hell. That's a bit tenuous. Does Louise actually know him, then?'

'No but she knows his sister and reckons he's really nice. And he's looking for a relationship.'

She's browsing his other photos now and I must admit he does look pretty hot. And, crucially, doesn't seem to have bad dress sense.

'OK,' I relent. 'How will this work, then? Is Louise gonna pimp me out?'

'Yeah. She'll big you up and see what happens.'

'What does he do?'

'He's a teacher. A history teacher.' Lady Jane breaks her gaze from the screen to look at me. She knows she's got me with that.

'OK. I'm up for it.'

She smiles a smug smile. I'll give her that. She's a trier. Let's hope he doesn't turn up in full cycling Lycra like the last guy she tried to set me up with. That was awkward.

Monday, 16 November

I've realised tonight who my male equivalent is when it comes to relationship maudlin: Simon Amstell. Angel and I went to Shepherd's Bush Empire to see his stand-up show. He is so funny, and angst-ridden. And gay. What a shame, we'd make such a good match.

Wednesday, 18 November

I recognise the name; the subject header is a simple: 'Hello'. It's the History Teacher suggesting we meet up next time he's in London. He's keen but not too keen and manages to nod to the crudeness of our set-up in his prose. I like. I like very much. What to reply?

Thursday, 19 November

'Shit shit shit! What should I do?' I'm wailing down the phone to Lady Jane.

'Just leave it. He probably won't even notice.' I can hear she's stuffing her face while we're talking.

'Of course he'll notice. I don't want him thinking I don't know the difference between the two words.'

'Mmm . . . ' I can tell Lady Jane is nodding, whilst chewing.

I've sent my response to 'Ant', the History Teacher, and used *complementary* instead of *complimentary* in my witty but cool response. *Zut alors!* So what do you do? Leave it and hope he doesn't notice or acknowledge it so he doesn't think you're a total dufe but risk coming off as a bit neurotic? As this is what they call a blind-ish date, to my mind the written communication is all the more key.

I opt to acknowledge my mistake with what I think is a light-hearted follow-up.

'The complimentary/complementary mix-up happens to the best of us' is his reply later.

Phew.

Friday, 20 November

It's my birthday in four days' time. I'll be 32. 32!!! Geez. It's funny, when I was in my mid to late 20s I was in a relationship and couldn't really conceive of not being in one in my 30s. Now, I can't conceive of being in a relationship at all. Like it's an alien concept. Birthdays don't half have a habit of creeping up and making you think about where you are with your life and other unanswerable questions, such as:

1. Why am I still renting?
2. Why do I still live in my overdraft?
3. Why am I still being sick after a night out?
4. Why do I not have a pension?
5. Or savings?
6. How on earth did I get to 32?
7. Where is he?
8. Why hasn't he texted me back?

Just threw the last one in there for good measure. What can I say? It's a theme.

I have a feeling Angel and cousin Rubles are plotting something for my celebrations. This pleases me because even though I genuinely don't feel like dancing for this particular milestone, I know that deep down I want someone to make a fuss and do something. Anything. It's so unbecoming organising your own bash. I did it for my 30th and never again. I nearly had a nervous breakdown.

I'm taking my mind off the big 3-2 tonight with a gig-date with Angel. We're seeing an eight-strong band of cosmic disco New Yorkers called the Phenomenal Handclap Band. It will be an uplifting experience – think Sly and the Family Stone meets Beck and the Doors. In jumpsuits. Waving.

Sunday, 22 November

Friday's gig was as funky as I'd hoped it would be. No cute men, though. I think more girls like this band because it's so unashamedly disco and glitter-filled. The girls go to dance and admire the dancing girls. I know we did. Those lead women – louche, lean and glossy-lipped – are so cool. Like, *I want to be you* cool. Bet they don't fret over an unreplied-to text. It's good to put yourself in front of greatness every now and then to remind you to stop being such a sap.

Friday was also tinged with sadness. Another 'last time we'll do this for a while' occasion with Angel.

Monday, 23 November

I spoke to the nicest guy in the world today. Well, the nicest guy in the world apart from my dad. I did a phone interview with the man who invented the Post-it note. I know! He's called Art Fry and is a true gent. He's retired now, but I imagine him pottering about in his inventions shed in deepest, frostiest Minnesota in between looking after the grandkids and being lovely to his wife.

'It's a huge satisfaction seeing something that you've done being used by people over the world,' he said to me in the softest Midwest accent. 'It's a connection to the world. I made them, you use them, that brings us together.' How romantic. It's true. My relationships with Post-it pads are some of the most satisfying I've had. In case you're wondering, the clinching factor in the invention of the Post-it was devising an adhesive that sticks to paper with less force than the paper fibres stick to each other, to avoid tearing whatever you're sticking the note to. It's on days like today that I love my job and appreciate the fact that I get to shoot the breeze with guys like Art. The kind of man that in my head I'd like to grow old with.

Tuesday, 24 November

Happy Birthday to me! Feel a little sad to be waking alone on this supposedly special day but cheered to discover prezzies from Angel and Rubles and a load of cards that Angel has clearly been squirrelling away from her position next door. She's stuck a, yep, Post-it to the pile, saying, 'Happy Birthday, gorgeous girl. See you later probably!'

I love the fact that she's still pretending there might not be anything happening later, even though several friends have already let slip that they will be schlepping over to my corner of South London for a gathering. Before that, though, work. I'm in the fashion office. Must get a move on.

One year, on my birthday, when I was still with the Big Ex, I was working, he wasn't (not unusual) and he didn't even open his eyes to say Happy Birthday to me as I skulked around in the dark getting ready, let alone get me a card, make me a nice breakfast, anything. Then I spoke to him on the phone at noon when he'd finally roused himself and we had a row. I cried during my lunch break, then we went out for dinner later that night with money I had to lend him. It's good to remind myself of this when I'm feeling the lonely pangs. There's nothing more lonely than that.

Wednesday, 25 November

Ugh. Ouch. Hmph.

My phone is ringing, but I've no idea where it is. I've no idea what time it is. Day it is. Where I am.

Still ringing.

Found it. 'Hello?' My voice is feeble and questioning.

'Hello, love. Did you have a nice birthday?' My mum's voice is strong, loud and northern.

'Yeah, yes . . . It was lovely.' I'm desperately trying to piece it together and ignore the mounting feeling of nausea.

'Did I wake you up?' She's clocked my shady, husky demeanour. 'It's four o'clock.'

Oh God. Is it really? Mrs Patz is lying next to me in bed. It's starting to come back to me now. It was a civilised party in my local, which Angel and Rubles had catered with pork pie and mushy peas, then the 9-to-5 crowd left and the remaining stronghold carried on until it came light.

'I was just dozing,' I lie. But she knows what I'm like. I feel guilty.

'OK, love. Well, just wanted to check you're all right and you had a good time. Did you have pie and peas?'

Rubles must've reported back to the family.

'Yeah, it was a surprise. It was great. Everyone seemed to like it.'

I got a Marc Jacobs bag too. Everyone clubbed together to buy the black leather beauty.

If I didn't feel so rough, I could almost be happy.

'Speak later, then, love.'

'Bye, Mum. Love you.'

'Love you, too.'

I'm such a loser. My mum's so lovely and I'm a loser. Happy 32nd birthday. Loser.

Saturday, 28 November

The post-birthday fear and loathing has now subsided, I've done two days of hard(ish) graft in the fashion office and I'm on a train back up north to see Mum and show her that I am a good person and not a lush who can't seem to say no. Not that she's asking me for such displays. I'm more than capable of putting that pressure on myself.

I'm keeping myself distracted, pissing about with a new-to-me phone due to mine being totally fucked. My brother, who changes his phone more times than I change my knickers (which is more than every 18 months), has furnished me with a rather snazzy brushed silver number but, and there's always a but, it doesn't seem to want to save my sent text messages. Imagine that? I know, rad. There is probably a sensible reason for this that can be easily rectified and the universe can return to normal, but for now it's a useful distraction.

For a start, when I've composed the Wittiest Text in the World Ever, I won't be able to keep revisiting it to congratulate myself. Then there's the art of sharing text conversations with my mates. That thrilling yet tedious (for them) process of relaying a text conversation word by painful word while dexterously traversing between in and sent boxes – 'And I said that', 'Then he said that' . . . It's important, during the analysis stage, that you relay EVERY SINGLE WORD. You never know how much hidden meaning there could be lurking in a 'the', do you? I think a lot of guys would be alarmed at how many women forward their personal texts to their girl-mates. I know Angel's boyfriend was horrified when he got wind of us.

Anyway, as it stands, I can kiss goodbye to sent items. I'm trying to put a positive spin on it: this could be an important lesson in letting go. Two words that thus far I have failed to build into my psyche. Imagine this: you send a text message and it's gone. Pow! Gone and forgotten? Hmm. Well, we can wish, but I venture it'll make that 'maybe he didn't get it?' urge all the more virulent.

The guy opposite me is three-quarters cute and drinking a beer. My boy interest levels have been pretty dry since the big birthday bash, but I'm feeling them coming back, along with the urge for booze (groundbreaking scientific research topic unearthed?). So, the boy. He's wearing a T-shirt that says 'Tokyo' on it. It's average, but not offensive, like a logo T-shirt I saw recently on a waitress in a posh fish restaurant in Whitstable that said: 'Ketamine: Just say neigh'. He has a sweet upturned nose, tanned skin, tired eyes and a sort of pissed-off expression.

I enjoy having travel fantasies. Not necessarily in the pervy *Risky Business* sense; rather the 'wouldn't it be crazy/nice/romantic to meet a future lover on the journey I've done about a million times' sense? One to tell the grandkids, eh? How Granny was flashing her new hot-pink bra at the shy-looking bloke opposite, quietly going about his journey. Oh, how we laughed!

Which brings me to my final comment of the day: how much of my life is lived out in some kind of fantasy sequence in my head? I can confidently say 65 per cent. I'll be telling the story of how our eyes met, we kissed, chatted, dated, married, moved to the country, procreated and called our first kid . . . Tokyo.

I'm nearly at Wakefield. I can see the familiar buildings, the outlet stores just on the edge of the city, the moody church spire coming into view and, finally, the start of the platform and Mum and Dad in their winter coats waiting, rapidly scanning the train for sight of me. I wave, but they don't see me. Mum's informed me by text that we're going for fish and chips. Result.

'Have you got enough stuff with you?' Dad's opening gambit is always the same. I have long since given up on the idea of travelling light. I like to have options. Lots of options. Dad takes my enormous bag from me and I look at his swollen arthritic wrist and think he shouldn't be carrying it.

'Let me, Dad.' I'm trying to take it back off him.

'Don't be daft.' He hoists it up higher onto his shoulder, knocking his flat cap slightly askew.

I feel a deep pang, which is love mixed with an undeniable trace of fear. I know my parents are getting older and the thought of them not being around does not bear thinking about. I love them so much.

December
Broken Dates, Open Dates

Tuesday, 1 December

I dreamed last night that I had a boyfriend. I was snogging him and everything. How sad is that? It's like the plot of one of those straight-to-TV movies they're fond of showing on the Hallmark channel in the run-up to Christmas. I swear to God I've seen the same film each year for the past three years, where this slightly frumpy, unlucky-in-love woman asks Father Christmas for a husband. Admittedly, she made this wish when she was a kid (which is flashed back in soft focus), but she's still haunted by it all those years later when she's 30, desperately lonely (that's the subtext, anyway) and doing a bit of charity work at a homeless shelter or something. I really must watch it again to firm up on the details.

Anyway, my point is I'm becoming the star of my own cheesy B-movie fantasy. This is not good. The guy, though, was an interesting specimen. For a start, he really was a MAN. Built like a warrior, like a Scandinavian warrior – a bit like the villains in the *Die Hard* movies but without the thirst for blood, or gold bullion. Actually, the gold bullion I could handle.

Now, I never go for strapping lustrous-haired men like this. I like my men skinny to the point of ill. You know, Pete Doherty when he's not trying to give up the crack. I don't know what this means, but maybe changes are afoot, ready for a brand-new year of . . . disappointments.

Films with a Romantic Angle. Part 4.

Anyone currently angling to get off with a friend could learn something from the advice of Ben Kingsley's crazy character Jeffrey in the hip-hop-loving COA* movie *The Wackness*. I like it because it's about throwing yourself into love.

Luke, the school-leaver protagonist, deals weed to therapist Ben Kingsley in exchange for cock-eyed but ultimately bad-ass romantic counsel of this nature . . .

> Luke: But she just wants to be friends.
> Jeffrey: Make her like you – that's what I did with my wife.
> Luke: How'd you do that?
> Jeffrey: Be her friend, confide in her, earn her trust, then when you're at your least threatening to her, grab her and stick your tongue so far down her throat she starts to get some pleasure.
> Luke: Can I grab her tits, too?
> Jeffrey: Baby steps, Luke, baby steps.

Oh, and is this not the best walk-away line ever? Spoiler alert: Luke ultimately gets his heart broken by the sexy girl but definitely has the last laugh, plus my favourite super hero, emotional honesty, wins out.

So after she's blanked him a good few times (after heartlessly boinking him for an entire weekend) he bumps into her by chance and she tries to talk to him (her conscience is obviously kicking in). He interrupts her when she's trying to lame an apology and says:

'Do us a favour and don't say anything. Just stand there until I leave. I wanna remember this because I've never done it before.'

The 'it' is getting his heart broken. Fucking excellent.

PS. The movie's tag line is 'Sometimes it's right to do the wrong things'. Say no more.

* Coming of Age (yep, another one of them, which begs the question, why does a thirtysomething woman take so much from teenage love stories? Hmm).

Wednesday, 2 December

Since I'm up home I've decided to drop Ant, the History Teacher, an email to see if he fancies meeting up. He said he'd get in touch when he was down in London next and I said the same if I was up north. He's living in Manchester at the moment, with his mum and dad. I'm willing to overlook this on the basis that, if I'm honest with myself, I'd probably quite like to live with my folks too and, according to my sources, he's having a career change hence the living-in-limbo. Anyway, the email:

> Hi Ant,
> How's it going? Hope all's well . . .
> I'm up north to see my folks and Primal Scream (!), amongst other things/people. If you're free at all next week, it'd be great to meet up. Perhaps you could show me your Manchester haunts?
> Ali x

Approximately 10 hours and 37 minutes later, he comes back with:

> Hiya,
> I'm fine, thanks. Should be free one night – pick the day.
> Where are you seeing Primal Scream?
> Ant

I can't quite put my finger on why, but I feel underwhelmed by his response. He doesn't seem that enthusiastic and there's no 'x'. Hmm.

I forward his reply to Lady Jane, Mrs Patz and – OK, I admit it – a new friend I've made in the fashion office, too. She says:

> Not overly woop-de-do but if he's stressed at work that would probably explain it. Remember, men are simple creatures . . .
> And he's basically saying he'll make himself free whenever you are, which is incredibly promising!

AND asking you a question at the end. This is good, Ali! x

We agree to meet up on Friday, before I go back to London on Saturday and after Primal Scream, which is tomorrow! His tone has definitely gone up a notch. 'Oh, that'll be fun. Transported back to the early '90s. I've got fond memories' is what he says about the band, which makes me think three things, all good:

1. He knows who Primal Scream are and seems to like them.
2. He can't be boring (surely?) if he likes/liked Primal Scream.
3. He must be in his mid-30s at least, which is probably a sensible age.

Thursday, 3 December

I've said it before but what a difference a day makes. I'm waiting for the Primal Scream gig to start, stood in Manchester's Apollo with Angel and, of all people to be going to an acid-house-tinged night with, her mum and dad. They are pretty cool, though. An email, from Ant, comes through on my BlackBerry. I get an excited flutter in my tummy, thinking he's probably gonna be telling me where we're going to meet up, then I read it:

> Hi Alison
> Really sorry, but think I'm going to have to cancel. Work's really hectic, so it's just gonna be too much of a rush. You must have me down as a total flake by now. I would still like to meet up. Here's what I suggest. I'll be in London in January a few times. I'm also hoping to restore my work–life balance. How about meeting then?
>
> Hope you're having fun at Primal Scream – maybe you're even getting your rocks off.
>
> Sorry again x

I know the email is nice enough, but I can't help thinking, what a cunt.

Friday, 4 December

So, no date for me tonight, but I've calmed down on the cunt vibes and composed the following super-understanding reply to the History Teacher.

> Hey,
>
> No worries, I understand. When you're really busy with work, it's not the best time to be having a blind date (!). Primal Scream were ace last night. Both generations enjoyed it without any kind of chemical aid. I particularly like Bobby's dancing and the crazy strobes.
>
> Give me a shout in January.
>
> X

How fucking reasonable am I? I think my initial reaction was because you just get so fed up of the culmination of disappointments, however big or small. Why, for once, can't somebody just come through on a promise? Impress you? Woo you? The rational side of me knows his reasons for postponing are fair enough, but, yes, it's still a bit of a let-down.

He does claw it back somewhat when he replies later with:

> Glad you had fun at the gig. You're more rock and roll than me, parents or no parents. At the moment I'm listening to Abba on Spotify while reading online news in my pyjamas. Speak soon x

I'm wondering, is this the new timeline of dating? Waiting months rather than days or even weeks to actually pin down a date? It's quicker to get a referral on the NHS.

Sunday, 6 December

Happy happy happy – that's me today. It's Sunday, I'm not hung-over (shock horror) and having a rather brilliant day (go figure). So, I get up, have work to do and actually get on with it (shock horror). Then I take a little break to go for a run (shock horror). Then I get back and listen to a bit of Kim Wilde's Secret Songs show on Magic FM.

There are certain times when Magic is the only way to go. Late night/early morning minicab journeys is the obvious one, but I also favour cooking by Magic and showering by Magic. Now, Kim, star of the '80s, is a nostalgic sort, so you get gems such as Phil Collins' 'Two Hearts' (living in just one mind – aw), 'Your Song' by Elton (really find it hard to decide whether to sing high or low with that one), 'I Think We're Alone Now' by Tiffany (never can more fun be had in the shower without a boy) and, just finished, 'A Little Time' by The Beautiful South.

Ahh, The Beautiful South. LOVED them back in the day; they were my semi-credible teen music love – not quite as cringey as Jamiroquai now, when I look back. Every time I hear them on the radio I feel so happy.

Anyway, 'A Little Time'. The lyrics are just brilliant and we ladies should take heed. The scenario reminds me too, too much of the predicament some of my gorgeous girlfriends have been in with cowardly boys asking for an agonising amount of time/space. Ring any bells??

Monday, 7 December

Another datee following the long timeline trend is Music Man. He's been in touch. We have been exchanging rather exhilarating emails, which is nicely timed since the History Teacher has written himself out of my present narrative.

Music Man is in the States doing exciting musician-on-the-road stuff. I, on the other hand, am re-watching *Look Who's Talking* and really, *really* enjoying it.

Anyway, he's started a trend for sending photos. The first one is a picture of a truck he saw when his tour bus was stuck in that snowstorm in Texas. The huge lorry was emblazoned with the slogan 'Jesus Christ is Lord'. Ha ha ha.

You know what this makes me think? Correct, that we're on a wavelength! Uh-oh. Never a good sign. We'll be married soon and living an adventurous life touring the world, cool boho kid in tow, me writing on the road.

Then, his next email had, brace yourself, a photo of him in it! And OMG, does he look fit? Definitely very, very, very cute. And all my friends, who I immediately forwarded his mail to, agree. He's wearing one of those furry hats with the earflaps and an appealing cosy plaid shirt and cardigan combo (from what I can tell) in pleasing shades of grey. He looks cool.

But what do I reply? And do I now send a photo of me back? Don't wanna get into the realms of the Fantasy Boy 'we'll email/text-but-never-meet-up' nightmare but equally am enjoying this burgeoning pen pal relationship. Especially given that I have no chance of seeing him until his return, mid-Jan, from the southern hemisphere.

What do I reply? I *want* to say: 'You look FIT in that picture – makes me wanna grab and squeeze your little face like my grandma does to me and then give you a big kiss right on your lips.'

Would that work?

Saturday, 12 December

You know when couples on TV and films do that thing when they're on the phone: 'You hang up', 'No, you hang up!', 'No, you hang up!!!!!'

Well, surprisingly, I've taken some comfort from that this week. You see, I replied to Music Man's last picture-adorned email and he hasn't, as yet, replied. It's been six days. Or is it five?

Now, because he sent me such a sweet, funny and clever email with a photo of him attached, I thought it's only fair that I send a photo of me back to him. Right? So I did. By the way, I didn't say anything about wanting to grab his face and kiss it (though I still do).

My email was funny – hey, that's how I roll – and informative. He wanted to know more about what I do, so I told him a bit. I told him his emails made me want to travel (to see him – no, only joking). Lady Jane told me the email was perfect – 'Oh I love it, I love you! It's perfect – just the right tone' (*all right, don't gush, love*). And the photo, one from a set I had done by Yorkshire (who, incidentally, had taken me at my word with the grandma comment and urged me not to say it), was pretty cool – me sort of staring into the middle distance, looking pensive. I took the piss out of the fact that it's potentially a bit posy, so I think that's fine. Plus, I look quite good. You're not gonna send a photo of yourself looking like a munter, are you?

Anyway, that was the email and, like I said, I sent it about five days ago. Now, I guess I thought he would reply. I definitely hoped he'd reply, especially since I sent a photo. What I wanted him to say, I'm not sure . . . 'Wow, you are SO FIT' would've been nice. 'Marry me, I've never known anyone as pretty/funny/interesting as you' would've been a surprise, but nice. Not replying is a bit rubbish.

HOWEVER, and I do mean this, we can't get into emailing every day or every other day at this stage, can we? That would be weird. It's nice that we've had the exchanges we've had; now there's a little break. All my friends have said this. I don't want another ridiculously involved technology-dependent relationship without actually having met in the flesh, do I? Also, he's a musician on tour, for fuck's sake. He should be taking loads of drugs and having a good time, not writing to some strange girl at home, shouldn't he? It's not the Second World War.

This is why the 'You hang up', 'No, you hang up!' comparison is relevant. At some point, one of the parties has got to hang the fuck up. I just wish it'd been me. But hey, shit happens.

Right, time to shake this one off and get ready to go out. It's Elvis's brother's 30th at our local, the Cave. See you on the other side.

Reasons why they might not reply: a true insight

I've been thinking about this with my brain firmly fixed into rational gear. The fact is, guys don't always reply straight away (duh, so what's new?), but I think I know at least one reason why, which might well apply to Music Man (I know I said before not to hypothesise on the why, but just hear me out . . .). He doesn't want to just rush something off. He always sends something quite thought out and thoughtful. So at first I was a bit, like, why isn't he replying? I'd write quite a lot, send a picture and then not hear but, as I pointed out to Mrs Patz, I think we forget that not everyone's as witty as we are off-the-cuff! I'll just think, write and send, but not everyone's like that, eh?

PS. I have no clue, of course, whether any of this is true, like all the best theories.

Sunday, 13 December

Oh God, I think I've got a stalker and I'm not entirely blameless. On the plus side, he is thus far a friendly stalker, not violent or too weird. Yet. I met this guy, let's call him 'Geezer Boy', about a month ago in the Cave and got on with him like long-lost friends. I'm fond of cheeky chappy types, and young types. He's both – a gift-of-the-gab, Barbour jacket-wearing painter-decorator who's only 22. That's ten years younger than me. Now, I have been known to go there with the younger end (my motto being they stay fitter for longer), but my research (and there's been quite a bit) tells me that the youngsters, fit as they may be, are a bloody nightmare to go out with.

On the first night I met Geezer Boy, we chatted and smoked with Elvis, who was manning the bar, and had a situation that threw us together a wee bit. This obnoxious-ridiculous guy from the pub was attempting to drunkenly chat me up and I needed a get-out because he doesn't take no for an answer. I said I was with Geezer Boy and he played along. We didn't do anything to consummate this relationship, you understand, but maybe in hindsight it was a bit of a tease on my part. When I left for the evening, Geezer Boy swooped in to ask me out, which took me aback because I'd not thought for a minute that we'd be a romantic pairing. I wasn't sure what to say, so I decided to give him my number and cross that bridge when I came to it.

I collided with that particular bridge last night at the party. He collared me to say I'd given him the wrong number. I insisted I hadn't – not my style. Anyway, somehow, and I honestly don't know how this happened, I ended up kissing him. I know, I know! He kind of tripped up and landed on my face. Then, under duress, I agreed to go out for a drink with him. I did say to him, though, and I was proud of this, that I wasn't sure how I felt about going out with him, but we could go out for a matey drink and see what happened.

Famous last words. From that point on, he was like a boy obsessed. There I was, trying to have a laugh at my mate's 30th and suddenly I've got a hyperactive little boy virtually hanging off my thighs. He kept prodding me, grabbing me, trying to drag me off. Seriously, it was ridiculous. Then he was constantly asking me questions – what was I doing later? DON'T KNOW. Could he come back to mine? NO. Would I like to dance? NO. Would I like a cig? YES, BUT NOT FIVE MINUTES AFTER I'VE JUST HAD ONE. God help me, he was full on. In the end I managed to shake him off and went back to mine with my inner circle. A few hours later, at God-knows-what-time-o'-clock, a text from him:

'Soz if I acted like a bit of a idiot 2nite. I hope we can still go out for drink. I'll call you in week. x.'

This juvenile text speak is not my thing, so can't actually recount exactly how it went but you get the gist. Then I deleted the text, which shows how interested I am.

Oh good God. Why did I deign to kiss this oik?

Monday, 14 December

Continuing with the young men theme, Rubles and I bumped into one of the boys from the flat downstairs on the bus tonight – he looks a bit like Withnail, crossed with Kurt Cobain, and constantly has a guitar strapped to his back.

We walked back to the house with him, patiently listening to his woes, The Woes of a 20-Year-Old Student. If that sounds patronising, well, it probably is, but it made me chuckle to myself and cemented the fact that dating (much) younger guys is maybe not the best idea.

Withnail is an excellent lesson in Just Saying No. For why? The constant whining about his life and struggles, for a start. He actually complained about how he'd 'literally passed out for 14 hours', which to my mind is a delicious luxury. Then there's the fact that college is so difficult, how nobody understands him in all his complexity, and his dilemma – should he do a Masters or focus on his music? Ahem.

Despite the clichédom, I do like him; he's a sweetie, really. And herein lies the potential problem. These young 'uns have an uncanny knack of whining like fuck but still being cute and full of youth and making you want to look after them. Witness the following bit of dialogue in response to his raft of moans, as we neared the house:

> Me: Aw, you're a heavy soul, aren't you?
>
> Withnail: Yes, I should be wandering the street like some kind of urchin.
>
> Me (trying to withhold the sniggers): What you need is a nice cup of tea and a piece of cake . . .
>
> Withnail: No, what I need is a line of coke and a blowjob.

And, for that line alone, I'd almost be tempted to give him one, or both.

Tuesday, 15 December

Hooray! So Music Man has been back in touch. A week later. But back and proving my earlier theory that it doesn't always happen straight away. They wait until there's news to share and there's time to be all witty and charming with it.

So he said . . . [note my comments in *italics*]

> Hola,
>
> Nice pic. You look quite Parisian in your mac. (*OK, I'll take Parisian. He could've said gorgeous/fit, but he's holding back.*)
>
> We're now halfway to Detroit. Some of the crowds so far have been pretty wild but they seem to be enjoying the gigs.
>
> This tour's been great but it's also been knackering. Endless drives and little sleep but we're doing a good job of keeping one another entertained.
>
> How's the ankle? (*Caring, attentive . . . I mentioned I'd hurt my ankle running.*)
>
> I had the best intentions of exercising on this tour but of course it hasn't happened.
>
> I'm now looking forward to my first full night's sleep in a while!

Oh yeah, saw the White House the other day. It was like *West Wing* coming alive before my very eyes! We walked past it about six in the morning. Trippy.

Saw a phone-in on the environment yesterday. This place is full of scary flat earth people. The funniest was the woman who said that thermometers have only been around for 100-odd years, so how could they tell the temperature before that . . . (*Nicely topical, though it did take a while for the 'flat earth' penny to drop.*)

We're in New York at the weekend! Bring it on!

(*Cosmopolitan!*)

See ya, (*When?! Only joking.*)

xx (*Right back at ya!*)

How exciting! 'Ooh, he's sharing the minutiae of his life with you,' squealed Lady Jane, once I'd forwarded the mail to her. He also attached a rather hilarious photo (at least I decided it was hilarious after a bit of thinking) of himself wearing a – gasp – vest and what can be only described as a medallion – a dollar-shaped, fake-jewel-encrusted pendant lolling around his hair-sprinkled chest.

The subject line of the email was 'Making it Rain'. Now, I must admit, until I'd discussed it with Mrs Patz, my hip-hop loving friend, the meaning had completely passed me by. I'd been looking up the weather report for Detroit, thinking, it's not even warm, why does he want it to rain?

Thank God for Mrs Patz, though. I would have been ruminating on the weather in my reply to him had she not consulted the Urban Dictionary to discover that on da street Making it Rain refers to, and I quote, 'when you have a wad of cash and throw it in the air in a strip club'. OR, and this is the explicit definition, 'when a man ejaculates all over a woman'.

Something to mention in my reply?

'It's a bit early for ejaculation,' scolded Lady Jane later over the phone.

She's got a point.

Wednesday, 16 December

So, despite being a total pain, prodding, poking and generally annoying the fuck out of me last Saturday night, Geezer Boy is still wondering if I want to go out with him and still worrying about his behaviour. In some ways, it's quite refreshing.

I reply to his text: 'Don't worry about Saturday night, everyone was wasted. Sorry, but I'm going to change my mind about that drink.'

I agonised over this for hours, hovering on the send button. Do I then follow it up with a jaunty 'See you soon!' or is that too flippant? Despite him acting like a dufus and me knowing I definitely don't want to go out with him, I'm still worrying how to let him down.

I needn't have worried. He texted back straight away with: 'Don't worry about it. I didn't fink I was too smooth.'

Aw. And, yes, he did say 'fink'.

Friday, 18 December

The time has come for Angel's leaving drinks. Correction, her work leaving drinks that I have been invited to as a sort of VIP. I am a surprise guest for the latter portion of the evening. The fun part. The part that goes on into the morning. I'm putting a brave face on it, but it's so hard to be jolly when I'm so gutted that she's leaving. G and I are already ensconced in the Hoxton Pony bar in Shoreditch when she arrives, all smiley and sparkly, with her work crowd. She sees me, her face lights up and she runs over and we do a jumping-up-and-down hug. Man, I love this girl.

Monday, 21 December

'Ready?' I'm doing a balancing act with five bags, my Christmas loot.

'Yep. Let's go!' Angel is doing the same, wearing a woolly hat and a massive grin.

We slam the big red door – our communal front door – and enter the crisp, eye-blue day to get a cab to King's Cross. She's coming to my mum and dad's for a couple of days, pre-Christmas, pre her leaving, next month. It's another landmark event. I love it and hate it at the same time.

The taxi driver is listening to talkSPORT – lots of irate men calling in to chat about ill-advised transfers and crooked chairmen. We've just gone through Brixton and are approaching Stockwell and the weird MI5 building that commands the bridge from south to north. We're both looking out of the window at London. I look at her and take her hand. She presses her fingers into my palm.

Here we go.

Tuesday, 22 December

My mum thinks Angel and I are weird because we always want to sleep in my bed together, rather than for Angel to be in the spare room. I think it's because of the time Mum came in one morning with bacon sandwiches after we'd been out the night before and we were taking pictures of ourselves. We were in hysterics because I, no shit, looked like Michael Jackson. I guess you had to be there, but Mum looked at us like we were total weirdos. She's suspicious. In a way, she should be, the stuff we've got up to over the years. Partners in silliness.

Today, though, despite a jolly night out last night with Roller Girl, we're not *that* hung-over and have elected to have a civilised day doing last-minute Christmas shopping in town. Mum's coming with us. Compared to London, it's so stress-free shopping up home because there are only, like, three shops you'd actually want to buy anything from. Easy.

Wednesday, 23 December

Said bye to Angel today. Mum, Dad and I dropped her off at her mum and dad's, in the snow-filled north-eastern countryside. We had a lovely day, our folks hanging out together, like we're a couple or something. Her dad is a keen potter and Mum and Dad threw pots! How exciting! The next time I see her will be new year, when there will be literally a couple of weeks before she goes to South America. I think it's sinking in now. I guess it's about time.

Boxing Day

Christmas is a time for exes. For me it is, anyway. The last time I saw Cartoon Boy, the Nearly Love, was Boxing Day last year. It's now Boxing Day this year and I saw him two days ago, on Christmas Eve.

I was in what had been described to me, before I had experienced it for myself, as a wine bar. *A wine bar.* That in itself isn't that shocking, but put in context, i.e. my northern village and the fact that it used to be a right dive of a pub, it's like sticking the pyramids on the M1. Also, wine bars – do they still exist? Last I knew was that one where Del Boy fell through the bar hatch when he was trying to act cool in front of them yuppie birds.

It was in this yuppie wine bar – which actually looks like an alpine ski lodge – that I bumped into Cartoon Boy and had my own Del Boy moment. I'm on my way back from the toilets when my brother collars me and says, 'Top of the stairs,' in a really conspiratorial manner.

'Cartoon Boy,' he says, without moving his lips. My tummy flips. Oh God, *not this again*.

'In a Christmas jumper.' Four words that instantly add a farcical element to the scene.

It's not like I won't recognise the guy I nearly loved – OK, probably did love – without that visual cue, is it? But still, I'm walking up the stairs, slowly, looking out for a ludicrous jumper with the object of my continued heartbreak attached to it.

And there he is. His face lights up. Now, is that happiness, or nerves, or fear? I don't know. Actually, it's probably surprise, mixed with fear. I've done a brilliant job of misreading this little fucker for years. Whatever that face (which is super cute) means, I'm going in. I have to. For my own sanity. Whenever I go home, I think about him and bumping into him. It's ridiculous. And debilitating. So here I am, facing my fears and, er, doing it anyway. Must read that book.

Last time I saw him, this time last year, it was a similarly impromptu affair, but the hurt was still so palpable. A year has gone by now, though, and I'm determined not to replicate that scenario. I need to make a new, happier memory, where I am the smiley, confident, breezy heroine who is totally comfortable chatting to her ex as if he and she are long-lost friends; where I am 'over him'. What a load of shit. I don't get over anything that easily. It's not how I'm built, so even though I did a bloody brilliant job of acting cool, funny, a bit flirty, and I know I looked all right in my new dress with lace inserts, now, in the comedown period, I feel shit about it. Again. Damn you, Boxing Day.

This was always the problem and what I think is always the problem with exes. How can you have once had this really intense, passionate, rewarding love affair and then suddenly, with no explanation, be dumped and have to make small talk about a ludicrous new wine bar that has sprung up, tumour-like, in your homestead?

I think I could've handled the Christmas Eve rendezvous. Like I said, it needed to happen, this shiny new memory with me as the breezy lead girl, but what's really thrown me is the text he sent me on Christmas Day. It's from a number I don't recognise but a voice that I do. It goes like this: 'Merry Christmas, great to see you last night. Have a great day. Sure I'll bump into you again before you leave x.'

What does this mean? My stomach lurches in that way it does when you really like someone. I'm trying to approach with caution. Like when the tabloids peddle the government's anti-drug agenda, this should come with a written warning. Instead of 'Don't mix cocaine with ketamine and/or alcohol', it should say 'Don't mistake friendliness for romanticness [if that's a word] and, whatever you do, don't bring hope into the mix.'

Lady Jane and my ever tactful/fearful mother have told me in no uncertain terms to banish this and him from memory. As I look at it for the 35th time, I feel like it must read like a supremely average text. I suppose to a normal brain it probably is. Roller Girl, who is mad in most ways but very sane when it comes to love (probably because she is genuinely happily married), read it straight up. I spoke to her earlier today when she was regaling me with tales of how she 'slapped it' on the ice, walking home drunk from her mother-in-law's last night. Her take on it? 'He's just following up on seeing you, wanting to check everything's still OK and saying he might bump into you again. He's probably just glad you were OK with him and wanted to send a nice text to make sure you're still OK with him.'

Lady Jane said practically the same thing. 'He's doing what he always does and checking his reputation is still intact. Don't take anything from it. It's what he always does. If you follow up on it, he'll be flaky and avoid you.'

Do you know how much I didn't want to hear that? But that's what makes me pathetic. I read so much more into it on Christmas Day. Don't you just hate the way your mind tricks you into believing exactly what you want it to? What you hope? Hope is a very powerful thing and is generally thought of as being positive. If you have hope, then good things will happen. In my case, or in this case, hope is like a noose that is slowly strangling me. It holds you back and makes you gasp for air. Misguided hope is even worse because, like now for me, you can feel like a right idiot for having flirted with it in the first place. Or the 17th place, when it comes to me and Cartoon Boy.

My thought process was, why is he contacting me on Christmas Day? He must be thinking about me. Is that meaningful? It must be, no? He thought it was great to see me – does that mean he's regretting dumping me? Did I reignite some kind of flame in him last night when I was being all charming and gesticulating in that endearing way that I do? And the 'bump into me' bit. Is that a half-arsed way of seeing how the land lies? Does he want me to go back to him with 'Yes, well, why don't we meet up?' Is he too afraid to actually ask in case I say no?

'No,' Lady Jane says in no uncertain terms. 'It's just a sign-off, like "see you soon" because he had to sign off with something, otherwise it would've been too meaningful to just say "It was great to see you last night" and leave it hanging.'

Ugh, I hate that she's probably right. I happily skipped through yesterday, thinking *I've won, I've won! He wants me again! He misses me, he was thinking of me on Christmas Day*. Now I'm a twat who's endlessly analysing a text that I'm sure he spent no time at all constructing and was probably just a symptom of his relief that I'm now at least talking to him.

You know what the worst part is? That's fair enough on his part. Despite my mum saying, 'It's out of order' (she always turns into Mo from *EastEnders* when she thinks she's got my back), perhaps what he was doing was actually thoughtful: following up on seeing me and acknowledging that it was nice, wishing me a Merry Christmas. He was doing his bit. I totally fooled him into thinking that I was fine, with my friendly-friendly act. Now, the hapless idiot that he is, he probably thinks we're forever friends happily able to drink casually in ghastly local drinking joints. I should be able to do that too, shouldn't I? But I can't. That's why I'm here, in my old bedroom, writing this, and not out meeting friends and family in one of the two establishments where he's highly likely to be.

Boxing Day sucks.

Sunday, 27 December

In other love-related news, Music Man and I exchanged cute emails on Christmas Eve and I still have my stalker, who also texted me on Christmas Day with 'Merry Christmas Gorgous [*sic*]'.

Fuck's sake – why me? Even with Christmas spirit supposedly abounding, I still had to slag him off for his spelling mistake to cousin Rubles. I didn't text him back – he needs no encouragement. Despite the fact I've knocked him back twice, he still texted me the Friday before Christmas asking if he could take me out for dinner and then the following Sunday inviting me to a local quiz night. I mean, how very dare he?

It's hard to feel positive when an ex comes back and whacks you in the face with his cheery act-like-nothing-happened ways, but Music Man is actually a positive thing that should bring at least some Christmas cheer to my dreary bones. He seems very cool, funny and thoughtful. Just not very present, given that he's back in the country for three days before buggering off again. Bet he's not hanging around in pseudo wine bars. Hmph. Anyway, I emailed him on Christmas Eve to wish him a merry Christmas while I was sitting wrapping presents with Mum, and attached a photo of Boney M singing 'Mary's Boy Child'. I took a photo of the telly – it was one of those Christmas song countdown programmes. I think that kind of thing is funny and decided to take a risk that he might think so too.

Luckily, he does and comes back with this:

> Hello hello,
> That's a lovely image you captured there – brings back a lot of happy memories. Hope you're having a good time back home. I'm in London, then off to Oz! Can't wait! Hope Santa is good to you and it would be lovely to meet up when I get back.
> Merry christmas.
> xxx

Well, that's nice, isn't it? Hopefully, I'll meet him at some point and he won't turn out to be a total fucking weirdo.

Roll on January.

January
New Year, Same Shit

Sunday, 3 January

A text exchange:

> Me: 'Am I saying happy new year to Music Man or hanging fire?'
>
> Lady Jane: 'I would hang fire a week. You did the happy Christmas.'
>
> Me: 'Yes, I suspect you're right, Jeeves. Just bored. As good an excuse for romantic encounters as any!'
>
> Lady Jane: 'Write your blog! No, stay off the blasted internet. Drink some wine and watch a film! I am just starting *The Devil's Advocate* – bit of Keanu action never goes amiss. He is so stupid you could keep him in the wardrobe and get him out once a week for silent sex.'

Ha ha ha! Crisis averted.

Monday, 4 January

I think my stalker might finally have got the message. I didn't reply to his Christmas text message, deciding a wide berth was the best course of action. I don't usually ignore text messages – after all, don't do to others that which you don't want done to yourself (or whatever that saying is) – but in this instance I had an ex to torture myself over. I was busy. Plus he can't spell for shit. That's a turn-off.

New Year's Eve he strikes again. Why all the special occasions? That's usually when men fail to perform. Do I want to go to our local pub to celebrate the birth of a new year? This is easy enough to deflect – I'm larging it in Dalston with Mrs Patz. 'Have a good one,' I politely reply. He comes back, like a gremlin, with: 'U want 2 hava drink in the new year how woz ur christmas hava gud night x.'

Umm, what?

I leave it and get on with taking several taxis around East London in celebration of the end of a decade.

It's Saturday, 2nd, and I'm finally dragging myself home. Another text (heart sinks when I see it's him):

'I'm going in the pub wiv a few m8z do u fancy a drink?'

Good God, man, will you ever let it lie? And what the fuck is 'm8z' all about?! That's what I'm thinking, but I reply:

'No, I'm en route home after the excesses of New Year. I'm staying in.'

And he said . . . 'Ur always turning me down should i get the msg.'

Well, yes! I thought I'd already given him the message. Last year.

So I said . . . 'I've told you what I think already. We're mates! I genuinely haven't been able to go when you've asked, though. I'm not dicking about.'

You see, I *have* told him, via text *and* face to face, that we're better off as mates. He knows this and yet here he is, not dying: 'I no I don't meen it in a horrible way I was just wondering if u wna do something in the week. I'm around.'

WHAT?! I can't even be arsed to reply to this. It's like Groundhog Day. Twenty minutes later, he's back, and this is really quite revelatory:

'I notice the "!" after mates i'm sorry but i really don't give up easily nd no usually just means a challenge 2 me so wot i mean is i'd ratha no if ur really not interested I won't bother texting again.'

WOW! Is this the male of the species, albeit a male with a slovenly grasp of the English language, analysing a text message? For that, I thank him. Alas, he's got to go. So I say: 'I'm not interested beyond being friends, no.'

To be honest, even the friends bit seems slightly alarming now. I guess by 'friends' what I really mean is: 'I have no option but to see you in *my* pub, so I need to keep things civil, for your sake.'

'Thatz good wiv me,' he replies, before picking up his chimney broom and skipping off with Dick Van Dyke. That's how it plays out in my mind's eye, anyway.

Wednesday, 6 January

There is good news and there is bad news. Ant, the History Teacher, has been in touch. He's coming to London and wants to meet up. The bad news? He goes swing dancing with his mum.

So we were emailing about what we'd been up to at the weekend. His Saturday night involved going swing dancing. I asked him if it was a throwback to watching *Swingers* in the '90s. He didn't see the funny side and said no, he goes with his mum because his dad isn't interested. Hmm.

Anyway, after I'd told him that I was enjoying the naked wrestling between Oliver Reed and Alan Bates in *Women In Love*, he said he'd give me a call to arrange when and where to meet. 'I'm not sure I would enjoy naked men wrestling as much as you' was his PS. Fair enough. And *I'm* not sure I would enjoy swing dancing as much as *you*, but horses for courses and all that.

Thursday, 7 January

I'm really struggling to get to grips with this new year. I need to drag myself away from the Universal Channel and do some freakin' work! In a bid to kick-start proceedings, I've come up with some winning motivational tips.

How to be a winner

1. Get up at a reasonable hour (standard).
2. Wash hair, dry it like you're going out and definitely use

product (it works for Cat Deeley . . .).

3. Apply blusher – it's good to at least look healthy.
4. Brew up a cafetière of coffee (thanks, American Boy, for that tip).
5. Disengage TweetDeck!
6. DISENGAGE TWEETDECK!

Saturday, 9 January

Because I've failed to get anything productive done this week I've imposed a going-out ban for this weekend in a bid to tackle the workload deadlines looming for next week.

'You used to be so good when you were younger,' says Mum helpfully over the phone at lunchtime. She's right, I did. I was a total swot. I never left things to the last minute, I always put 150 per cent effort in and I didn't even know the meaning of procrastination. What changed?

Today's verbs of procrastination

1. Hunted . . . for a Phillips screwdriver.
2. Washed . . . three duvet covers, one load of whites, four pillow cases, one duvet, two bath mats.
3. Made . . . smoked mackerel pâté.
4. Scrubbed . . . my body all over with a facecloth. A retro bath, as it shall now be known.
5. Hoovered . . . my entire flat, and even did the skirting boards with the nozzley bit.
6. Dusted . . . the cobwebs from my bedroom ceiling (this is not a metaphor).
7. Watched . . . a double episode of *Diagnosis Murder* and a True Movie of Judy Garland's life.
8. Bought . . . an extortionate train ticket to go up north.

Monday, 11 January

Me, in bed on phone, fully clothed: 'So, we've arranged to go out this Wednesday.'

Lady Jane, in bed in Manchester (not sure of her state of dress): 'Where you going?'

Me: 'One of my drinking haunts in East London.'

Lady Jane: 'What did you say to each other?'

Me: 'He said he didn't mind coming to me because he didn't have anything he needed to do the next day, so I joked, "Oh, so we can get leathered, then?" He said, "No, that's not what I meant" and didn't seem to laugh.'

Lady Jane: 'Do you think he might be a bit square?'

Me: 'Maybe. But maybe he just didn't get my sense of humour.'

Lady Jane: 'Well, you'll soon find out when he orders a fucking bitter shandy and then nurses it all night.'

Texting. Part 6.

My communication with Ant has got me thinking about how much you should censor yourself in the early stages of courtship: the Art of Holding Back. I think it's safe to say he virtually flinched at mentions of naked wrestling, getting leathered and, in an earlier nod to *Women in Love*, when I shared: 'Jesus, I'm squirming. It's difficult to watch someone's face being bitten, then be rammed repeatedly in the eye with the butt of a Zippo lighter. Eesh.'

That was me telling him exactly what I was doing at the time of his incoming email. It's honest. And I don't think you could level boring at it. But how much should you say in an email or text? Chatting to Rubles earlier, she'd had a text from an occasional lover of hers and was planning to do nothing about it. Nothing! We couldn't be more different. I'm that person who always runs straight into the sea whatever the conditions versus Rubles, the tentative toe-tipper (Rubles isn't like this in other areas of her life, I hasten to add, but she's a tactically reserved texter).

So, my technique, if you could label something so recklessly delivered thus, basically involves a thought coming into my head, the more ludicrous or inappropriate the better, and, hey presto – press send, usually on the basis that I think it's funny. Then, wait 30 minutes or so for it to cook before entering the Deep Regret phase.

This can last hours, days, or as long as it takes for them to reply.

Rubles, on the other hand, just doesn't bother and her weary advice to me, if I ask her about the validity of sending a particular text, is always don't bother if you'll worry about it afterwards. 'What kind of way to live is that, though?' I cry, all grandiose, wounded at her character assassination. Then I send it. Feel the fear and do it anyway! Out of fear of no reply, fear of putting herself out there and, definitely, self-preservation, Rubles would never send that text. And she would definitely never discuss, at great length, the pros and cons of sending that text.

I'm a Text Person, you see. A card-carrying, thrill-seeking, no-holds-barred Text Person. I'm not an idiot, though, am I? There must be a reason for this often-miserable state of being. Yes! It's about connecting (umm, duh!). No, I mean *really connecting*. If you have it, you just can't beat it. And I have had it. Thinking about it, though, maybe it's only the slightly autistic (am I allowed to say that?) and emotionally retarded (am I allowed to say that?) ones who do good text? They sparkle, from a safe SMS distance. And then, when they withdraw their texting affections, you feel utterly starved. Cartoon Boy, you know who you are.

All I'm trying to say is, if you're thinking about sending someone you really quite like a text message or email, bear in mind that your idea of funny might be their idea of sick. Rubles says, don't do it. I say, fuck it. You only live once, and if they can't handle you, that's their problem.

Thursday, 14 January
The date with the History Teacher

7 p.m. I arrive at the East London pub by black cab to be sure to be on time. Walk in, look around to see if I can recognise the tall, dark, handsome guy (a touch of the young Paul McCartney, if you will) I've been checking out via Lady Jane's Facebook.

No sign.

Get a pint. No seats, so stand at bar trying not to look like a terrified person waiting for a blind date.

Check phone for time/text/sign of life. He's ten minutes late.

Call Mrs Patz. 'Do you think I'm being stood up?'

Laugh nervously.

'No, definitely no. He's probably stuck on tube. Shall I check TFL for you?' Ever helpful, Mrs Patz.

Victoria line delays apparently. OK, that must be it.

'Give it until twenty past, then call him.'

Fag outside.

7.20. Phone his phone. Straight to voicemail. OK, he must be stuck on tube. Fine.

Back inside. Drink more.

7.30. ANGRY but trying not to be.

7.35. Text. It's him: 'Just emerging from Old Street tube.'

Hmm. Where's the apology? Grovel? How fucking casual is that?

7.40. Man resembling Facebook guy walks in. Looking like a right miserable bastard.

'Hello, hi,' I smile, almost gushing, trying to pre-empt the massive apology that's about to come.

'Hi.' No smile. Then he grunts his name, pointing towards his chest, like an ape.

'Were we supposed to meet at 7 or 7.30?' Still no smile.

'7.' Grimace.

'Oh, I thought it was 7.30 and I didn't have a record because we arranged it verbally.'

Eh, what? My mind flashes back to our, yes, verbal conversation two days earlier when we made the date. For 7. It also flashes back to the text I sent him to confirm the time and venue. A record, I believe.

'So, what have you been up to today?' I say, trying to start afresh.

'I met my ex-girlfriend.'

Is this guy a fucking knobhead or what?

It carries on in similarly dismal fashion. You'd think he might be keen to make up for the fact he was so late, grumpy and clearly hungover from spending the afternoon with his ex, but no. The whole thing was a struggle, a tiring struggle. Like when you're playing tennis with someone shit and hit the ball over the net, not too hard, easy enough for them to stroke it back, but nope, they fuck it up every time.

This guy was clearly unhappy or even angry with the world. He argued with everything I said, moaned A LOT, had a rant about me smoking (before asking for a drag) and was generally unpleasant company.

A few more gems:

Me: 'So where you staying while you're in London?'
Him: 'My rich parents' flat.'
Me: 'Well, you're very lucky, aren't you?'

Then he tells me he's been busy putting a photo of his mate's face on beer mats ready for a stag do. I comment on how silly stag and hen dos are generally, all these daft things one has to do, yada yada. He gets super defensive, as if I'm criticising him, before telling me how he's got a game of rounders planned using an onion instead of a ball. Woo-pee-do! Hold me back, that will be a right laugh. Jesus.

I tell him I like his shirt. He tells me his mum gave him the money to buy it and one exactly like it because she'd shrunk his others in the wash. I say, 'How chivalrous.' I mean, not only does he live with his mum and dad, that poor woman does his washing and then pays when something goes wrong. That's the thing with rich parents; it's all give, give, give . . .

The smoking rant was particularly fun – 'It gives you cancer, makes you stink and stains your teeth yellow.'

'DULL JUDGEMENTAL JOYLESS FUCKER' was Lady Jane's emphatic response when I filled her in on the goings-on. I'd say that just about covers it.

What a waste of time. I ended the evening appropriately by puking into a cardboard box.

Good times.

Friday, 15 January

It's customary for January to be a bit shit, but this year is taking the piss. I don't buy into New Year diet and exercise programmes, joining a gym and such, but I do indulge in a bit of optimistic thinking and the illusion of fresh starts. I've treated myself to a beautiful jade, croc-effect leather Smythson diary this year (a snip at £230!) and did get a kick out of writing on the first few unblemished days.

The Blank Page = new frontier. Today, though, it feels more like New Year, Same Shit. Then, to make it worse, the thing that *is* new about this year is Angel's leaving and that's not good new, it's scary new; sad new.

But let's stay positive, despite going out with dickwad last night. New Year is a time for dazzling new romantic adventures; fresh romantic hopes. Surely this year someone special will come along? I realise that this kind of thinking is verging on the superstitious, but it's also a numbers game. I mean, how many years can the bad luck go on?!

Angel and I are having a weekend in, just me and her, before her big adventure starts. Tonight – curry and *Cocktail*. Personally, I think this is an example of Tom Cruise's better work. I'm still waiting to have my own sex-in-a-Caribbean-fountain moment, but a girl can dream. She can also dream about having tits the size of Elisabeth Shue's – but you can't win 'em all.

Saturday, 16 January

A day of decadence with Don Draper. Day two of the weekend love-in and Angel and I are tucked under the duvet on the sofa bed in my lounge, gorging ourselves on cheese on toast and the first series of *Mad Men*. This is what heaven is like. Later we will go and eat delicious Chinese food at a place of Jay Rayner's recommendation and I will take a geeky thumbs-up photo of her outside McDonald's in Leicester Square drinking a giant fizzy pop to counteract the extreme spicy and salty effects of the Jay Rayner-recommended food.

I cherish the walk through China Town, under all the coloured lights strung between the restaurants, cutting down past the Prince

Charles cinema, where they do the Sing-a-Long-a-*Sound-of-Music*, into the madness that is Leicester Square. Keep going, past the National Portrait Gallery and St Martin-in-the-Fields church before catching your breath at the wonder that is Trafalgar Square.

Angel and I are link-armed, doing this walk we've done so many times together after drinks in Soho, catching the number 3 back home. We pause and look at the fountain, with the National Gallery all imposing behind us.

'It's Landan, innit?' I say to her in my best mock-cockney. A stupid in-joke.

She laughs. We keep going. I know she'll miss it. How could she not? It's London and it's beautiful on a night like this.

Tuesday, 19 January

Sing it from the rooftops, Music Man and I have *finally* set a date! The shock of getting that email today was up there with the time when a dead insect fell out of my pubic hair when I was in the shower after Benicassim festival.

So yeah, he got in touch and we set a date. A Sunday date. I'd given him the option of Sunday, Monday or Tuesday (then fretted over whether I'd given him too many options). He came back with: 'Sunday drinks could be good? But I can do any of those days.'

How refreshingly cooperative/keen.

So I said . . . 'Let's get slaughtered on Sunday then. Ha.' Slightly controversial, but funny, no?

'Ha. That sounds like an excellent plan. Sunday it is, then.'

RESULT.

Friday, 22 January

Tonight is Angel's leaving do in the Cave and I'm at home pissing about getting ready. Everyone else is already there, but I can't bring myself to leave. It feels so weird. I've put together a few mementos – photos and souvenirs from trips we've been on – for her to keep. 'The bears are not to blame' is a flyer from when we camped, freezing our arses off, in Yosemite National Park, when we did a road trip in

California. Grizzly bears are a big threat in those parts and we found the warning slogan funny. Then there's us in Ibiza, us at the Grand Canyon, us dressed as nuns wearing bright-red lipstick.

I can feel the onslaught of tears. This is not good for my flicky eyeliner.

I get a text. From her: 'Where are you Al? x.'

It's time to go. Wish me luck.

Sunday, 24 January

'Hot Hot Date' is an apt title for a date that has essentially been building up for six months. It's what I've been wanting for a long time. I'm genuinely interested in this guy. I'm excited, nervous and hopeful all at the same time. It's here!!!!

So how come I'm sat on my couch with Angel, chain smoking, wringing my hands together and plotting how bad it would be to try and rearrange it?! Why the fuck did I get so messed up when I've got a date, *the* date, to go on? Or, more to the point, why did I arrange a first date for the same weekend as I'm hosting the mother of all parties, Angel's leaving do? I mean, it began on Friday evening and the last person left at noon today, thinking he'd been in an airport lounge for the last eight-odd hours.

What I *should* be doing pre-date is bathing in ass's milk, buffing, scrubbing, ironing . . . I want to be employing loads of preening verbs. Instead, I'm emptying fag ends out of expensive scented candles.

This mild panic mixed with an overwhelming feeling of inertia continues until 2.15. Music Man and I have made a vague plan to meet, and allow me to quote myself, 'late-ish afternoon'. It's now early-ish afternoon and I haven't heard from him. I've certainly not been in touch with him, given that I'd not be safe operating machinery right now. *FUUUUCCKK!* What am I gonna do? Angel's no help, bless her, she just keeps asking me what I'm gonna do.

Would it be really bad to postpone? Now, this is such a turnaround for me. If I didn't feel so rough, it would almost be enjoyable. I'd normally be freaking out as to why I hadn't heard from him. It's all a bit last minute, isn't it? And it isn't even a battle of wills as to who texts first, because I don't have any will. None.

Then, bleep, a text: 'Are we still on for a few drinks later?'

Well, there we go. Like a big brave soldier I look at Angel and say, 'I'm gonna call him! We're going in!!' I know I'm not capable of texting back and forth the arrangements. I puff my chest a little at my sudden burst of bravery. I'm at the coalface, feeling like shit but calling anyway.

The call is a good move. I get to hear his voice, which is quietly husky (not too soft, you understand, and not squeaky like Fantasy Boy. Eew). I'm able to allude to the fact that it has been a big weekend and that I don't have the brainpower to come up with a venue. He suggests sustenance would be good (he's also been partying), so we settle on meeting at Liverpool Street and finding some food. On reflection, my pooh-poohing his original suggestion to meet in Stoke Newington as a 'ball ache' for me to get to wasn't my finest hour.

I shakily get ready – skinny jeans, chiffon blouse, fur coat (instant glamour hit). I know I'm not looking my best but look about a million times better than during the sofa strike. And I'm excited. Really excited.

Monday, 25 January

I see him before he sees me, loitering, smoking, at the Bishopsgate entrance to Liverpool Street station. I recognise him from his online profile pic. He's wearing skinny-ish black jeans, a tight-ish black leather jacket, pointy-ish brogues and a sexily dishevelled T-shirt to go with his shagged-out California rocker hair. He looks cute. And cool. Two out of two. I make my entrance.

'How are you?' he enquires, reaching out to do a two-kiss embrace.

'Bearing up,' I say sheepishly, reciprocating. I can feel the cold wind on my cheeks.

'That good?!' he inflects with a wry eye. I like.

We promenade to a pub of his suggestion, me trying not to think about two separate flirtations I've had with a couple of young barmen there. I clock one of them as soon as I walk in. Really hope he doesn't notice me. If he does, he takes my indifference as his cue to not notice. Good boy.

Music Man asks me what I'd like to drink. 'A pint of lager.' When in Rome (and hung-over).

'I don't drink pints,' he says almost apologetically, as if his manhood will be struck down right there on the ancient boozed-up tiles. Vodka and Coke it is.

He then worms his way into a really tight spot for us to sit rather than stand. A good move, and one I notice as a plus. He's not a pussy. Excellent.

I can't quite remember what we chatted about at this point, but it's pretty comfortable – a bit about my job, a bit about his Tokyo gig, a bit of laughing, a bit of exciting eye contact. Does he tell me about his family at this stage, or later? I can't remember. But that does come. He's got an interesting back story involving two very different continents, kidnap and unsavoury strip bars. I like hearing about it.

What'll we eat? We plump for Thai. I need something to remind my mouth that it's still alive. Angel has recommended a lovely little place in Spitalfields, which is all shiny these days. We comment on this whilst blatantly ignoring the smoking ban. Heck, it's cold enough to be outside. I love that he smokes. OK, maybe love is a strong word, but it just appeals to me more when somebody smokes. And it goes so well with his leather jacket. He's a musician, for God's sake. Give me a Keith over a Mick any day. Oh, I just remembered that we had quite a sweet encounter finding the place, him showing off an app on his iPhone, then using the map thingy to get us there. This prompts a funny men-and-directions chat and some close huddling over said apparatus. It's official, iPhone = romantic tool. Somebody phone that man in San Fran.

Dinner is cool. We share starters (cute). He decides my prawns are better than his crab, but then his sea bream main takes the prize. The wine is drunk without comment. I'm feeling A-OK. That'll be the booze.

What did we talk about? Er . . . that'll be the booze.

We split the bill. I think he would've paid, but I offer to go halfers. I think this is the ladylike thing to do.

I'm really trying to remember what we talked about, but I can't think on specifics. It was going really well, though. I remember that. So well that as we head outdoors, each crafting a roll-up, he grabs my hand and pulls me towards him and we have The Best Kiss.

Tuesday, 26 January

'Aghh!' I run from the carnage of tax receipts that is my living room, through my kitchen, into the communal hall and straight into Angel's flat.

'He just rang me, he just rang me!'

It's true. Music Man has just called me! After our thrilling first date, which I will continue shortly, we said we might meet up tonight, before he heads to Europe at the weekend to do some more dates.

'What did he say? What did he say?' Repetition is such a good enthusiasm tool. Angel, who is packing boxes and listening to the radio full blast, is excellent at enthusiasm.

'We had a lovely chat. He liked my picture message. He said I could go over to his if I wanted to, but we've agreed because we've both got to finish our tax returns to meet on Friday instead.'

I sent him a photo of my receipts and invoices, strewn all over my carpet. Rather boringly, we both had the annual tax return to do after our date. I like the fact he called me to have a little chat. So much more personal than texting.

Angel is reaching to turn the radio down. 'Did you say anything stupid?'

It's a reasonable question. I *always* say something stupid.

I'm pulling my best pensive face. 'Well, there might've been something.' He was telling me about a band he sometimes plays with, describing himself as their 'floating sixth member', to which I said, 'Floating sex member? Because that's what you are to me.'

Angel cracks up. 'That's fine. It's just funny!'

He did laugh and I guess it was funny, but come on! What on

earth was I thinking? *I* don't even know what I meant by it. Nerves and my sense of humour are not a good combo.

'I've got a good feeling about this, Al.' She comes over and gives me an excitable squeeze.

'I think I do too!'

There's something weird about the timing of this. Exciting new person arrives as adored best friend leaves. I mean, it's a rom-com, isn't it? Right, must put on a jaunty headscarf and finish doing those pesky receipts before retiring to a comfy armchair with a giant glass of wine.

The Kissing Date

The kiss. It was one of those great, natural kisses that happens because you're having such a good time. We exited the restaurant, caught each other's eye and he took my hand, pulled me towards him and bam! It was so good. Then we had post-snog fag. Also good, if both parties are smokers.

Kissing before the designated end-of-date time slot is THE BEST. It's the best sign, too. You simply can't wait. Love that. And from that point on it's like the floodgates are open and then kissing is just what you do. Order a drink, then a kiss, then a fag, then a kiss, then another drink, then a kiss . . . you get the picture?

So our date became a thrilling kissathon. We headed to another drinking establishment for a couple more drinks and Edith Piaf was playing on the stereo. It was perfect! But what next? We're in his neck of the woods – he asks me to go back to his. Earlier, when I was feeling like crap, I couldn't have imagined going back, plus there's the issue of the unkempt bikini line . . . what do I do?? He says to me, 'Come back, we can chill, we don't have to do anything.' I think that's sweet and also like something you might say as a teenager trying your luck. He then suggests we could hook up later in the week. Goodie, he's thinking second date.

Now, I hate that whole don't sleep with someone on the first date propaganda, but I had been thinking, I do really like this guy, I'm feeling post-party fragile as it is, how will it feel to wake up the next day with him? I think that's more the issue – the forced intimacy with someone you hardly know. It can be awkward. Heck, I could write a thesis on that particular subject.

Who am I kidding, though? This guy is hot, we're practically attached at the lips and I'm having too good a time to end it now . . . 'Taxi!'

We kiss all the way back to his – a really cool warehouse (where else do people live?) with a pool table in the main living space! Wow! It was a successful union. My best performance was the next morning, though, when I sat on his bed wearing just my fur coat and a roll-up dangling from my mouth before reclining, catlike, on the bed. 'You are so hot,' he lusted. I was half aware I was pulling a seductive Marianne Faithfull-type move, but it was still nice to get the recognition.

Anyway, the point is, the chemistry was all there. It wasn't awkward; he looked after me around his (shared) place. This is important, I think. Not to leave a girl hanging, skanking around an alien bathroom desperately trying to find something that resembles a towel, you know? Before we showered, together since you ask, he told me that he wasn't expecting me to be like I am (if that makes grammatical sense??). How do you answer that? 'What were you expecting?' I asked him, a bit worried.

'Well, for want of a better way of putting it, I thought you'd be posher. I'm glad you're not.' I think I know what he means. Brains, beauty and lack of up-own-arseness is a rare commodity. Ha.

Then later on, when we're skipping, literally skipping, down to the tube together, I say: 'You like me because I'm common.'

He says: 'I like you because you're like me.' Aw.

There were so many sweet things happened that morning after – like when the fur coat made another star appearance and we were cuddling in it at the bus stop. Like when we listened to music on his iPhone together – one headphone each – all cutesy. Like when he's asking me to teach him how to cook. Like when we were full-on snogging on the tube. I normally frown on such behaviour but, of course, when I'm doing it, it's fine. We also, over a lovely fried breakfast (my favourite meal of all), discuss past relationships, as in when we were last in one. This, I think, points to some level of future interest. Like me, his last significant one was about two years ago, to which I said, 'Oh, so you're not too fucked up then,' which he seemed to think was funny. Thank goodness.

Before going our separate ways – he's off to the Groucho to do what musicians do; I've got work to do, boring – we chat about when to meet again (tick!), then I dance off home feeling totally high and set to work answering the mounting number of texts from all my mates, demanding to know where the fuck I am. Res-ult.

Thursday, 28 January

'Wichita Lineman' by Glen Campbell came on the radio earlier today and really reminded me of the Big Ex, who left this very flat four years ago around this time. I think of him less now than I did, but it's sad-yet-illuminating songs like this that bring him back, or jolly, silly songs that I can remember him dancing around our living room to, like the *Minder* theme tune (random but true) and the utterly delectable 'Love Is in the Air', which I recently downloaded onto my iTunes. In fact, Angel, who's still packing next door, has fond memories of that song, too. She remembers dancing to it in circles with him in Old Street's 333 club (when 333 was good). They were happy days. They were.

Photographs are also 'good' memory joggers. I don't seek this shit out, you understand. That, in my wealth of experience of knowingly making myself miserable, isn't a healthy pursuit. But I came across pictures of the Big Ex and, worse, pictures of *me and the Big Ex* when I was ransacking a neglected cupboard to locate some invoices.

Anyway, I found these pictures and did have those thoughts of 'Ah, didn't we look happy in Sardinia/Egypt/Isle of Wight [where we are wearing matching cagoules]'. There was one picture, though, that really stood out. Me and him, link-armed, sitting on Mrs Jones's couch probably before we were due to go out in our blissful six-some (hey, I didn't just used to double date, I triple dated!). I'm smoking a spliff (at least that's what it looks like – I don't really do that now), he's looking at me in a really sweet way and I'm vaguely coquettish, resting my head on his shoulder. I know we were happy at this point – from the photo, but also the timeline.

So I'm looking at the picture, really looking, and thinking . . . I must dye my hair that colour again. It looks cool as fuck.

Closure?

Friday, 29 January
Angel left today. And Music Man cancelled our date.

February
Getting Comfort from Strangers

Tuesday, 2 February

Ronan Keating was right about life being a roller coaster. Geez. I've barely had a chance to come down from my date with Music Man before he's gone and texted me to say he can't get into anything right now.

Now, I'm the first to hit that excuse hard in the face with a heavy-bottomed pan, but in this case I'm inclined to believe him, be sympathetic(ish) and actually feel OK with it. I know, get me!

My initial thoughts wandered to the floating sex member comment, but as Lady Jane pointed out, if he can't handle that he's a pussy. I tend to agree and I know I can get way less appropriate than that.

We didn't meet up on Friday as suggested (by him) because he said he had to rehearse for his upcoming European dates. Fair enough, though his text to tell me this was unusually to-the-point, so a bit of doubt was starting to creep, smoke-like, under my door. I responded breezily to the news but thought, just 'cause you're being abrupt doesn't mean I have to be and I told him a bit about my week (I'd just had a teary goodbye with Angel) and asked after his. You know, being polite.

He responded well to that and sent a sweet text back commiserating with me over the loss of my friend before adding that his week had been, quote, 'weird' because, quote, 'a very close friend's mother is really ill'. Now, using my powers of intuition and imagination (in equal parts, I like to think), I decide that the very close friend must be an ex. Why else would you describe that experience as weird? Just saying.

Anyway, that was that. My suspicion and subsequent disappointment were aroused despite my dad urging me not to imagine every possible scenario before it happens. Whatevs, Pop. Then, yesterday, after thinking about it all weekend, I get the 'I had a really great time with you but . . .' text. Now, I know it's tiresome to get those texts, but I really did come away thinking that he was being straight with me rather than doing the 'It's not you it's me' bollocks. And I think it's ex-related – as in The Redhead From The Magazine. Whatever, he said he wasn't able to get involved and I tend to believe him.

I was super cool, sending him a great text back, saying all the right things – it's a shame but I understand, blah blah. I also told him I thought he was, quote, 'a really cool guy', to which he replied, 'And you're a cool and understanding girl.' Now, I don't know how this reads to anyone else, but I emerged feeling OK. I also said, quote, 'I'm sure there's a lot more drinking we can do in the future,' to which he said, 'By jove I think you're right.' Cute.

So that was that. I admit I did shed a tear or five in the immediate aftermath on the phone with Elfie. She conferred with her boyfriend (also a musician) and he was pretty convinced that the whole thing definitely had a whiff of ex about it.

I'm a bit gutted it's not gonna work out, for now anyway, but it really doesn't feel as bad when you feel like somebody's being straight with you. In a weird way, it's kind of restored my faith. And I feel cool for being cool. You know?

Wednesday, 3 February

I'm seeking comfort from strangers. A one-night stand could come under this category, but for now I mean something more innocent, and probably all the more perverse for it.

Last night, Rubles and I went to a screening of Jeff Bridges' wonderful *Crazy Heart*. It was a humdrum Tuesday. I'm still smarting a little from the textual dumping but also feeling periodically elated by my handling of it. You know, basking in the fantasy that he'll right about now be seriously doubting the dumping after my saint-like response.

I felt OK, but I also felt sad. But sad in a Hollywood way. Sad in a romantic, wistful way, where you still look pretty and you're playing the down-but-attractive role where people are watching you. Like you're starring in your own music video. Waiting for Rubles outside Twentieth Century Fox, smoking a perfectly rolled cigarette, with a light drizzle and noir-ish lighting, was the perfect *mise en scène*.

We go in, pick up the notes (bookish pursuits are always good during this phase) and take our seats. Some moron (OK, so I'm not fully in soft focus) noisily squats down next to us, declaring how the seats are just far enough back not to feel like it hurts your eyes, or something equally tedious.

Then – and you'd think I'd be more annoyed by *this* guy – an older, wild-haired gent appears. He bustles past the woman to my right, who's got the aisle seat, to plonk himself in the space between me and her. The screening room is not full by any means and he certainly doesn't need to be doing this manoeuvre, whilst crunchily trying to relieve himself of his trench (very 'old money businessman', rather than pervert). I'm watching him with amusement and giving him encouraging vibes. He acts, as he noisily keeps apologising – buffoon-like, Boris Johnson-like – as if he's bound to be getting on people's nerves. He probably is. People, i.e. journalists, are very easily annoyed at these things and he's the equivalent of a gang of hoodies at a multiplex.

I make it my life's work to smile, flirt almost, to make him feel comfortable and not like the rhinoceros he clearly is. He finally sits down and it's David Starkey, that mad-but-loveable historian off the telly. OK, it's not him, but he's a dead ringer. I think I'm in love.

We share the movie, sat next to each other: me in my supine, dreamy, reflective, music video state, him as, well, David Starkey with a constant itch. I have to say, I do kind of get off on those moments of bodily contact shared with strangers – the brush of the leg that you don't move away, a lingering hand exchange when you get your change. To place me somewhere on a continuum of such things, I'm not one of those people who carries hand sanitisers around with them, nor do I go cottaging (or the equivalent) on Hampstead Heath, but I do enjoy pleasures of the unknown's flesh from time to time. It's more my imagination that's the fun part – imagining we've shared some kind of moment. I like that.

Starkey and I have shared a few glances, a few brushes. I don't know, I think he feels my pain and I certainly feel his social awkwardness, so when our hands brush on the shared arm, we link our fingers together, like a couple would do. We don't acknowledge this with a sidelong glance, nor do we let go. We hold, for a good five minutes.

Probably not recommended behaviour in a dark place, but hey, you get your emotional highs where you can in this life.

Thursday, 4 February

My zen-like optimism from the other day about Music Man calling off our budding romance has given way to desperate disappointment and a nagging sense of inadequacy. I'm trying not to feel this way, but *I just can't help it*. I appreciate that excuse wouldn't wash with, say, serial killers.

I've discussed, I've analysed, I've re-discussed, I've re-analysed and, as a result, I've decided to impose a talking ban, on myself. I'm not phoning or talking to anyone for at least two days. It's for my own good. This was prompted after I re-told the story to Rubles's friend last night and got so annoyed with her response that I left the table abruptly to be on my own. It's not enough that I feel upset by the outcome with Music Man; I hate myself, too, for being so completely unable to 'just get over it'. I mean, we went on one date. *One* date. With an epic build-up, mind.

I've also got a pain in my neck. It's pretty bad. I wonder if it's related? Maybe it's my punishment. Punishment that sears down my spine and, when I'm really lucky, makes my left arm go dead. Is it a symptom of repetitive strain, or repetitive pain?

'Don't mope,' one well-wisher said.

'You can NEVER know what's going on in a guy's head – I mean, he could have decided he's gay,' another helpfully offered before concluding with 'JUST STOP THINKING ABOUT IT!' Ah, so *that's* what I've got to do! Silly me.

Do I sound bitter? Today I feel it. Well, I feel rejected, tired, rejected, stupid, rejected, confused, rejected, stupid. Stupid.

He, on the other hand, thinks I'm cool and understanding because I said all the right things – and meant them at the time, too. I'm all about being the best I can, reaching a rational conclusion, trying to understand, being cool (as all my friends constantly drum into me). That is until I unravel alone, like now, thinking, why am I such a fucking sap?

Self-intervention

This is the danger with trying too quickly to rationalise things that hurt you. It's actually bad to do that and something I do too readily. Gael Lindenfield, a therapist who wrote this brilliant book called *The Emotional Healing Strategy*, taught me this. When I came across her book, it really struck a chord with me. It's a five-step 'programme' that will, and I quote from the blurb, 'help you develop a toolkit for coping with any emotional challenge, great or small'. The idea is that you should give attention to the smaller knock-backs of life and – sorry for the therapy speak – devote time to heal from them in order to move forward. This is what I need to do now.

I met Gael about a year after I'd broken up with Cartoon Boy. The catalyst was when I met up with an old friend from home and he said to me, 'I've never seen you like this before – what are you so bothered about?' This isn't as heartless as it sounds. He just couldn't quite get his head around how vulnerable and insecure I was coming across. He thought I was cooler than that. So did I, mate! I'd become like a stuck record, so I decided to look into it.

The strategy is made up of five stages – exploration (I'm an A* student in this phase), expression (ditto – I tell EVERYONE), comfort, compensation and perspective. The idea is to work through each stage in order to heal the 'wound'. Until the conscious or unconscious healing of a wound is completed, she says, our physical and mental systems are running in a low-powered state. She likens it to a car that is in need of a service and not performing at its best. It applies to bigger hurts in life, like bereavement or childhood traumas, but also to lesser setbacks, like, erm, being dumped after one date. The point is that neglecting emotional hurts could cause problems later, which I'm realising is where I'm at right now. I'm jumping ahead to the perspective stage when I should actually be 'self-nurturing'. I'm pretty sure this all sounds pukesome, but I'm glad I've reminded myself of it – I need to stop myself spinning out sometimes. I'm going to devote the next few days to some hardcore comfort. Now, where's that curry menu?

Sunday, 7 February

I read a profile in today's *Sunday Times Magazine* on the poet laureate Carol Ann Duffy and, after a tough few days, feel the fug, along with the vow of silence, start to lift. She's brilliant. And inspiring. And this wasn't even her poetry, just what she said in an interview: 'My life is permanently erotic. Everything is, isn't it? Because everything has potential.'

LOVE that. And it's exactly the kind of pie-eyed romantic optimism I've been after.

She then touches on one of my favourite subjects: texting. In her most recent collection of poems, *Rapture*, Duffy traces the lifecycle of a relationship from its fiery beginnings to the fury of endless texting, likening her mobile to an injured bird in need of constant care and attention.

So true!

She's my new icon. For anyone feeling down in the dumps, it's worth taking heed of Duffy. Forgive my soppiness, but I think it's wonderful. Duffy believes every day is brimming with potential, and says, 'Don't you feel it? Every day I go downstairs and I open the curtains in my study, which leads on to a garden, and I go to the kitchen and let the dogs out and make a cup of tea. Every day feels like a gift.'

The interviewer says, 'Even when you're tired?'

And she says, 'Yes, because of that. Because of the harder times or the heartbreak or the tiredness.'

Of-this-world utopia – it doesn't get much better than that.

Tuesday, 9 February

In the manner of Gwyneth Paltrow in *Sliding Doors*, I'm getting me a new haircut today. That'll show him! Plus, Mr Scissors is always a welcome distraction in times of romantic carnage.

In another amazing twist of fate, and further proof that I am indeed On The Up, 'Pinkie', my German fashion friend, has invited me to go to Copenhagen Fashion Week as her guest. We fly this weekend! Woo fucking hoo!

The Getting-Over-It Index

1. Borderline pervy moment with a stranger? Oh yeah!
2. Self-indulgent alone time? Done!
3. New literature discovery? Tick!
4. New hair? Check!
5. European travel plans? Yas!

Friday, 12 February

Sex tourism is . . . a good thing, as far as I can tell. I've arrived in Copenhagen and the men here are FIT. I intend to get my map out and hunt them down later, like you might a gallery or place of worship.

Such is the quality of the men here, Pinkie, who's the pickiest woman I know, said the last time she actually did an about-turn in the street over a guy was right here in Copenhagen. 'And that was four years ago,' she added triumphantly. Theory proved, then. The men here are a cut above.

Now, my friends think I have a type. I don't necessarily agree because, as a rampant romantic, in theory, anyone has the power to provoke fire in my loins. In reality? It's more likely if they come slightly scruffy, long-haired, bearded, bespectacled and carrying a musical instrument.

Denmark has a ton of these, dare I say it, creative / thinker-looking types and they're a little more groomed than the equivalent in London, which is a definite plus. It's nice to make an effort, isn't it, Mum? In fact, I'd go as far as to say the Danish men (well, the cool ones, anyway) manage to look a bit fashiony without looking either gay or like total twats. Plus they're tall and nicely built. Yum.

Other kinds of tourism I like:

- Smoking tourism – Eastern Europe is brilliant, partly because you can smoke with the fervour of Don Draper.
- Meat tourism – Lady Jane's favourite kind.

Sunday, 14 February

On this very special day of love, kisses and hearts, let's be grateful if we have loved ones because that is truly a wonderful thing. But let's also be grateful if we don't have loved ones – that we are not suffering this day with some arsehole who can't handle his booze or has paranoid tendencies, self-esteem issues, a really bad temper or extremely shallow pockets. Or is that just me?

PS. I've been DYING to take the piss out of Magic FM's 'special' Valentine's screening of *Dirty Dancing* . . . 'Come along with your girlfriends in one big statement of single girly solidarity.' I think that's what they're getting at. I haven't taken the piss because it's for charity.

Fuck's sake.

Tuesday, 16 February

I failed in my mission to bag a Dane but did pick up a Swedish model at the airport. I kid you not.

So I spot this tall, blond, chiselled, pouting god in security, re-threading his belt. *I know* . . . He's unspeakably hot and, true to (my recent discoveries about) Scandinavian form, super stylish in his oversized military coat, grey hoodie, jeans, rocker-ish boots and a preppy tan satchel. I gather my belongings and myself where he's pitched up and I'm sure I pick up a vibe. It could, of course, just be my stranger sixth sense.

He disappears into the airport, leaving my tongue trailing behind him.

'He was hot,' I comment to Pinkie.

'Where's his mum?' she snaps, tiring, I think, of my constant Scandinavian sleazing.

We plunder the Kiehl's counter and pick up the obligatory airport Touche Eclat before sharing an apple juice (woo hoo!) using the dregs of our Danish money.

We sidle up to our gate and there he is! Excellent. I love a bit of airport interest. We get herded onto one of those buses via a revolving door – I know, unusual! 'Two at a time, two at a time!' the steward guy commands. Oh goody, I'm gonna do the door with the Swedish model! It's all lined up perfectly, two-by-two like Noah's Ark, when boom! I'm pipped to the post by a white-haired woman in a cheap parka. Shafted.

We get on the bus and he sits down towards the back. Fuck it, I'm sitting next to him. I brazen over and cosy up, offering my best nice-not-weird smile. He smiles back. There's that vibe again. Pinkie joins us, so we start chatting about whether she'd be jealous if her dog Pippa got a boyfriend. She reckons she wouldn't, but I reckon she would.

Anyway, all this dog-dating nonsense is eating into valuable chat-up time with 'Model Man'. What do I say? We're now climbing the stairs to the plane. He's right behind me and I'm super aware of his strapping presence. Is he lingering so that he's right behind me or is it just my rampant mind? Whatever, we're on the steps and I think it's now or never.

'Are you visiting London or going home?' I ask him. Not the most imaginative of lines but kind of apt given we're boarding a plane.

'I'm going for work, and to chill a bit too,' he says in a sexy Foreign Accent. 'What about you?'

I tell him we've been visiting for Fashion Week and ask him what work he's doing. 'I'm a model,' he says, somewhat sheepishly. Of course he is! What else could he be?! He's freakin' gorgeous.

'Cool,' I say, in the manner of Kevin the Teenager.

We're now on the plane. He takes his seat. I take mine. What next? What next? What's the next move? Model Man – how will you be mine?

We're about to ground at Gatwick and it's been an hour and a half since my and the fit Swede's titillating exchange. Pinkie and I have discussed the game plan and agreed that if I manage to speak to him again before dispersing through customs, I should give him my number and hope for the best. What's to lose, right? Apart from the usual dollop of dignity.

So that I'm nice and prepared, I write my name, the all-important digits and an 'x' in my notepad, tear it out and secure it in my back pocket with a little Asda slap. Now, I would try and tackle him while we're waiting to exit the plane – he's only two rows back – but I'm so painfully desperate for the loo, like abdominally challenged, that I can't concentrate on anything else. Moaning like a two year old, I rush through the maze of pathways (with really shit signage) and finally find the bog. Phew! Right, now I can concentrate. I speed onwards. Destination: carousel. Mission: talk to the Swedish model.

There he is, in all his Scandinavian gorgeousness, trying to spot his luggage. I loiter near to him and catch his eye, and he gives me the Best Smile Ever. This is my cue. He thinks he's missed his case and is frisking a live one that zips past. 'I think that one's mine,' he laughs, as it continues its lonely journey.

'Is *that one* yours?' I say, wittily pointing to a bright-pink monstrosity. He doesn't quite laugh, but he's definitely onside.

I ask him where he's heading. To a friend's in Baker Street. Very posh, I'm thinking. He asks if I live in London. We're getting warmer. I spot my case and grab it, noticing Pinkie all set to go with her luggage in hand. I can hear the *Countdown* theme going off in my head. Gulp. 'Er, do you fancy going out for a drink whilst you're in town,' I clumsily offer, not giving him time to answer before adding, 'Have you got a girlfriend?'

Now, I didn't mean to sound quite so aggressive – I meant it, believe it or not, as an acknowledgement that I was being a bit forward and should he indeed have a girlfriend this was his chance to bail. Anyway, whatevs, he said yes to the date!

'Shall I give you my number?' I suggest. My mind wanders to the note I prepared earlier in my back pocket. I realise, thankfully, that getting it out will make me look like a right twat and opt instead to fumble in my bag for my notebook, all spontaneous-like.

I hand over my love note (well, my number) and, elated, say my goodbyes. I don't want to linger like a weirdo.

'Have a safe journey home,' he says. What a lovely man.

Pinkie and I do the Nothing to Declare dash and I'm dying to explode with excitement. I don't. Restraint is the new black. We head to get the train and it starts to register what a crazy-ass stalker I've been to that poor foreign man. Geez, he'd have to be brave to follow this up, I'm thinking. Pinkie has to run to catch her train. I, it seems, have to spend a frustrating 15 minutes wrestling with the Fucking Ticket Machine.

Then a wonderful thing happens. Thanks to the Fucking Ticket Machine, I find myself face to face with Model Man again. 'I need to smoke,' he says to me. 'Wanna come?'

Er, does Liz McDonald like leopard print?

We're on the treadmill thingy trying to find a way out of the airport. Exit – super!

'Let's join our people,' I say wittily, before joining the other losers that are smoking in the rain. Model Man is telling me about his dancer friend currently enjoying the sun in Thailand with some Danish pop star I haven't heard of. 'We call him Kevin Federline,' he says. 'Ha ha ha.' Genius. Hooray, a sense of humour as well as unfeasibly good looks. I tell him about my visit to Copenhagen and he tells me he's partied out, what with being a genuine 'face' on the Danish fashion scene. He asks me where I go out in London – I offer up Shoreditch, Dalston, Soho and my very own South London mosh pit. After that it's all a bit of a blur. We finish up (our fags) and get back on the travelator to catch the train.

This is so exciting. Now we're sharing a train journey together! Very *Before Sunrise*. We climb aboard and grab a couple of seats. Cosy. Did I mention how HOT this guy is? He asks me about my work, I ask him about his. Did I mention – he's a model?! 'It's not hard and the money is good.' Fair enough. Sounds like a good philosophy.

He gets out a beautiful-looking arty fashion magazine he helps to produce and gets cross with the spelling mistakes (my kinda guy). He flicks through the pages slowly and it feels kind of seductive as he coaxes me through the pages, giving me ed's notes along the way.

'Let's speak in the week,' he says. 'We should definitely go out for drinks.' He suggests a Russian bar. Frankly, I'd go to an Irish bar with him he's that HOT. This is good, though. Now it's not just me accosting him – he's actually reciprocating. He gives me his email address and mobile number.

'What's that?' I point to an unintelligible symbol he's written down on my notebook.

'Er, it's a plus sign.' Oops. What a dick I am.

He then gives me a copy of his magazine. 'Are you sure?' I ask.

'Yes, have it.' I think that's very sweet and clutch the tome close to my heart as I exit the train a stop before him.

Did I imagine it, or when I'm starting to say my goodbyes did he lean in for a kiss?

Thursday, 18 February

Back on terra firma and everyone is loving the male model story. I even emailed Angel all the way in South America to boast. I always thought it crude to associate with people just because they're beautiful, but now I totally get it. It's like crack.

My mate has been in touch inviting me to her (very hip) magazine launch party at the Macbeth pub in Shoreditch. I spy an opportunity! I extend the invite to the Swedish model. I'll be at this party with some friends, why don't you come along? You know, cool as fuck.

What does he say? He only says yes!

Fuuuuuck. I'm dating a male model!

Friday, 19 February

We walk into the party like Reservoir Cats. There's me, Mrs Patz, Rubles, 'Minx' (Elvis's girlfriend, who I think I've got a crush on – she's naughty) and an old-and-rediscovered friend, 'Stella', who I've spent the day with at Portobello. We both bought wicked vintage shoes and I got a bad-ass biker jacket with tassels! I'm wearing the jacket and cowboy-ish shoes. I *think* it's cool, but I worry I'm working a head-to-toe look, i.e. Rock Chick, which is not so cool. Like I'm trying too hard to be Alison Mosshart from The Kills.

Anyway, it's too late now. He's there. Gulp. The girls have been primed on his gorgeousness – if you can't boast about pulling a model, then what the fuck? They form a line-up behind me and I introduce him to them one by one. When he's not looking, they all nod approvingly or contort their faces into 'he's well fit' expressions. Just the response I wanted.

He seems pretty excited to see me and he's very sweet, holding my hand. As there's smoking to be done, we disperse to the roof terrace, him with his friends, me with mine. Then it all gets a bit dull, as far as action goes. His mates are pretty desperate to leave to meet some other folks, so we have another little chat before he leaves. I don't quite know what I was expecting, this not being exactly a date, but after all the talk it's not exactly been fulfilling. He did say something about meeting up in the week. Alas, I'm heading northwards.

All is forgotten when we head to a pretty shit club to see a friend's band. Minx nearly gets us thrown out for smoking indoors, but it's fun having a dance and, dare I say it, getting home at a reasonable hour. I know, amazing. Then, in the taxi home, a text, from Model Man: 'Come to Dalston Superstore!'

'Too late, gorgeous, I'm a-going home . . .'

Saturday, 20 February

A night in with Rubles. My phone rings. It's the Swedish model! I'm shocked to hear from him after last night's anticlimax. He wants to know what I'm doing. I consider telling him I'm watching *Come Dine With Me* with Rubles, fridge fully stocked, then decide better of it. I do say I'm staying in, though. Even for one so fit I can't face another night out and another sort-of date with his mate in tow (I get the impression he would be).

Tuesday, 23 February

How many decisions are made simply with the preface 'Fuck it!'? I'd say quite a lot where I'm concerned. I've been working flat out since the weekend on a feature that culminated in me pulling an all-nighter last night in order to get it finished. The sleep deprivation and aforementioned fuck-it attitude led me to do the strangest thing.

The feature was a guide to cool websites and it was around 9.30 a.m. when it happened. I was wired. Delirious. Happy that I'd finished it. There was this particular website, about fanzines, which made me think to myself, you know who'll LOVE this? Cartoon Boy will love this. Cartoon Boy!

Christmas brought in a new phase to our relationship in that I still felt like shit when I saw him, but I acted in such a way that he no longer thinks I feel like shit and subsequently thinks that the fatwa has been lifted. We (sort of) moved on from the concluding email of our relationship, the one where I told him to leave me the fuck alone.

That's why it feels funny now, now that I've emailed him again, more than 18 months since *that* email. And so blithely, too.

> Hi,
> I'm writing a feature about websites and I saw this and thought you might like. If you don't know about it already. xx

What. The. Fuck. Am. I. Doing?

I know I'm guilty because I've told no one. No one. Which is unheard of. I tell everyone everything. I even told the booze shop guy I'd been dumped by Music Man, even though you can't technically be dumped after just one date. I just wanted to tell someone (else).

Lady Jane is going to kill me.

Wednesday, 24 February

The Swedish model has been in touch again. In all the stress of what's been the worst week of my professional career so far (don't ask), and the Cartoon Boy more-than-likely-to-be-disastrous connection, I've neglected the Swede.

'Hi, are you back in town?' goes the text, received while I'm sitting next to Lady Jane on her big orange couch in Manchester, scoffing Chinese takeaway.

I don't recognise the number, so ask who it is (cool, I know). He must have got a UK mobile.

I ping back: 'No, I'm not. I'll be back next week. How are you?'

'I'm good, thanks,' he replies. 'Text me when you get back. Big kiss.'

That works for me. He seems pretty besotted.

I reply with 'xx' and get into Lady Jane's bed, dreaming of models again. He will be mine. It's such a waste otherwise.

Friday, 26 February

I'm in trouble. My Cartoon Boy email fraternising has led to a kiss.

After that first email I sent him, when I was off my head on tiredness, he responded pretty much straight away with a typically upbeat, funny reply, prompting me to reply to him, prompting him to reply to me (you know the drill), ending with, and this is the significant part: 'When you've got your work done and had some sleep, get in contact??'

Shit. What does this mean?

Rather than picking up the phone and asking that question to everyone in my contacts book, I reply, *sans* harness, informing him of my imminent trip up north, and say: 'It would be nice to meet up, if you're around . . . ' Honestly, it's writing itself.

'Of course I'm around! Just let me know' is his reply.

Shit. What does this mean?

I leave it at that, thinking I'll probably get in touch with him a few days into my northern jaunt. I need time to think about how bad an idea it is, plus I'm going out with Roller Girl, so I'll think about him after that.

Good plan, except last night I walk into a God-awful bar in town and there he is, right in front of me, looking hot. We end up hanging out all night, with some other friends too, but he seems pretty keen to stick around.

Shit. What does this mean?

We go to a club. I know, ridiculous. It's Thursday night and the club is rubbish. I know this but go anyway. Roller Girl is getting entertainingly rowdy; we're having a laugh. I'm drunk enough to be chatting away to Cartoon Boy as if we never had a completely heartbreaking past. It must be the intoxicating mix of Red Stripe and bad R&B music.

A few hours into it, Roller Girl is swaying a bit too much, so we decide it's time to leave. I, thankfully, realise that this is the best plan of action, rather than stick around with my Nearly Love ex till the end of the night. Yes, cooler to leave. We say our drunken goodbyes to the rest of the crew and then it's time to say goodbye to Him.

I turn to face him. 'We're gonna go.'

He tells me, stuttering somewhat, to get in touch before I go back to London. Then we kiss on the lips for what in my inebriated state feels like around five seconds before I walk away.

Shit. What does this mean?

Sunday, 28 February

'Look at your hand.' I wake up to Roller Girl standing over me in her candy-striped pyjamas, smirking.

I squint to make sense of the black blob on my hand – the stamp from the club. It says 'Sex Wee'. Charming.

I decide to text Cartoon Boy. 'Have you got Sex Wee on your hand too?'

He replies: 'I just wiped it on my curtain.'

That's why I love him.

Spring, 2010

spring *(n)* the season in which vegetation begins to appear; the first season of the year

spring *(n)* the official mating season; a time for bold moves, experimentation and public displays of affection/embarrassment

Guest list:
1. Model Man
2. The Artist
3. Guitar Hero
4. Poet Pianist

March
Models and Artists

Monday, 1 March

After the Sex Wee exchange, I'm left wondering what my next move, if any, with Cartoon Boy should be. I'm staying at Mum's for a few days, so we're in the same place, geographically speaking anyway.

Lady Jane, who is now in on it, mock-scathed earlier over the phone: 'Don't worry, I'll be here to pick up the pieces again.' We both erupted with laughter at the barefaced cliché of her statement. She's right, though.

If I'm honest, I had started to feel twitchy as early as Saturday. Now that a few days have passed since our chance meeting and half-kiss, I'm starting to seriously doubt what I felt was pretty bloody significant at the time. Am I just imagining it? Or, more likely, is he doing his usual trick of seeming keen then backing off almost immediately?

Lady Jane, to her credit, because she's always hated Cartoon Boy, has patiently weighed up the 'evidence' and decided that I should probably explore it a little more while I'm up north. She justifies this later to Rockstar: 'What if he's the love of her life?'

She's referring, in part anyway, to the circumstances of their finally getting together second time around after a five-year hiatus.

'He's not the love of her life,' I can hear him shouting in the background. 'He's the dick of the decade.'

I plough on regardless and call him – yep, call not text – to see if he fancies an impromptu Saturday afternoon pint. Spontaneous is good, right? At least it would be, if he'd answered his bastard phone.

Luckily he calls back pretty much straight away – a good sign, right? I can taste my heart in my mouth and my stomach is dancing.

Alas he's not available – something about seeing a mate who's about to go to Afghanistan. What kind of excuse is that?! After a little chat – funny, as usual, because he is very funny – I tell him when I'm headed back to London and he suggests we could meet Tuesday evening. Before I have time to answer, he's already slightly backtracking (as I see it, anyway), saying I should text him first because I must have lots of people I need to catch up with.

Now, as is often the case with him, I get a funny feeling but can't be sure why. He's suggested Tuesday night, but then in the next breath is stalling. Is he backtracking or just being a bit wimpish, or, less likely, super polite? After all, I don't visit home that often and, yes, I do have a lot of people to see. It's not exactly what you'd call an excited response, though, is it?

I'm exhausted just recounting it. It's now Monday night and, after much thought, analysis and stress, I've decided to text him to follow up on our Tuesday half-plan. I fucking hate half-plans. They're the biggest pain in the ass and nearly always end in disappointment. Don't settle for a half-plan, I tell you!

I text: 'Hi, do you still fancy doing something tomorrow? I've got some time so could meet up for a pint or cup of tea . . . let me know x.'

That was at ten past seven – it's now midnight. In that time I've squeezed in two pints and scampi and chips at Wetherspoon's with my dad. He's been turned on to *the pub that doesn't play music* since he and my mum and both sets of aunties and uncles have been going to curry night on a Thursday. 'You can't go wrong' is what he says about the £4.99 curry-and-beer deal. Dad also likes this particular Wetherspoon's because of the building – a ridiculously beautiful nineteenth-century former chapel with stained-glass windows and a bar where the altar used to be. There's even remains of the organ pipes hanging reverently above the optics. My dad, the convert.

I check my mobile again: nada. Now, I know his phone could've died, he could be out or any other number of BS excuses we come up with in these situations, but I really feel, after all the crap I've put up with from this boy, the reason he's not got back to me is firmly from the 'because he's an arsehole' camp. Why do I not learn?

'Can you believe it?' Despite it being 12.30 a.m., I'm bending Lady Jane's ear for the fourth time today. 'I bet he'll be dreaming up some ridiculous excuse.'

I know this, because that's what he's done in the past. He'll stall and then come back with something outlandish. Lady Jane reckons he'll text back tomorrow at some point saying: 'Sorry for late reply, my phone died and now it turns out that I've got diabetes and I've just drunk a hot chocolate so I can't meet you.'

I can hear Rockstar shouting again, 'Dick of the decade.' Maybe that could be a song for his new album?

Tuesday, 2 March

True to form, Cartoon Boy has vanished. I don't even have a ridiculous excuse to marvel at, just my unanswered sent message preserved for ever in my memory because I can't stop looking at the fucking thing. I thought things, and him, seemed a bit different this time around. I let my guard down. Ultimately, it's not a bad thing; I probably needed another prod in the eye about it. My niece actually did poke me in the eye first thing this morning, so it seems an appropriate metaphor. That said, it's a bit too early to be getting philosophical, even for me.

In other, happier news, I have discovered not only is the Swedish model super fit he also has a GSOH. He asked me to text once I'm back in town, so I've decided to venture off-piste slightly and texted him ahead of being back in town with a view to making a date. You know, give the man what he wants.

So I said . . . 'You want to meet up either Weds or Thurs?' Nice and to the point.

And he said . . . 'Uh sure, I'm worst at planning, let's text each other tomorrow evening?'

So I said . . . 'Ha!!! Is it because you're foreign?' I mean, really. There's planning and planning, right?

And he said . . . 'Ha ha might be . . . we could also say Wednesday?', adding one of those smiley faces that seem to be all the rage.

So I said . . . 'We could . . . if both of us are still alive come Weds, let's try and hook up.'

And he said . . . 'Send me a text on Wednesday when u feel fresh and ready . . . Big kiss.'

Fresh and ready for what, eh? Am loving that text chat, though. He's so dreamy and I am officially back on the stallion again.

Texting. Part 7.

Why save text messages? The reasons for saving text messages from a love interest are, it seems, many and varied.

Asking around, Rubles says she keeps text messages if they're, quote, 'dirty'. What do men call it? The wank bank?

My cool-as-a-cucumber friend Stella reports that she saved one particularly choice message from her philandering ex to 'remind myself what a lunatic he is'. A sort of stun gun-style reality shot.

At the other end of the spectrum, a friend who recently had a break-up deleted all messages from her ex in an unbridled moment of defiance . . . only to break down in tears later feeling like she'd deleted him. Now, that's deep.

I said to her, and firmly believe, you should delete romantic text messages because post-break-up they're nothing but textual torture devices, the equivalent of scratching a scab over and over. The more you scratch, the worse the scar.

I should add, I'm the queen of scratching.

Thursday, 4 March

Dating a model is fraught. Last night we went out and he was literally fending them off – not women, men. And not gay men, straight men who just wanted to taunt him for his beauty. I couldn't believe it. We were in a little members' place on Greek Street in Soho where they play old-school rock 'n' roll music on a gramophone. It's like going back in time, like that TV show with Nicholas Lyndhurst, *Goodnight Sweetheart*.

We're smoking in the courtyard when these dickheads start having a go at him, calling him floppy head. Apparently he has floppy hair, which I guess he does. He does not, however, have shit hair, like them. Or shit clothes. Or shit faces. Or shit personalities. Or shit manners. Or shit for brains. They wouldn't let up. I ask them if they're comedians. One of them, the bulldog, asks me to go to the toilet with him. What the fuck? It's all aimed at making the model feel uncomfortable. I, of course, decline, prompting him to slur: 'Am I not good-looking enough for you?'

'No, and you're not funny enough either.'

Poor old Model Man says it happens quite a lot. And he's so sweet and nice, too. Men are bitches.

We finish our drinks a little flustered and that's when he asks me to go back to his, his being his photographer mate's studio in East London. Oh go on, then, you've twisted my arm.

It takes ages to find the bastard studio in the wilds of Hackney, but after various wrong turns and fending off at least three dodgy bastards we get there. Hooray! We're greeted by his mate, who I recognise from the magazine party. I'm trying to suss out where we'll be sleeping after, ooh, about 30 minutes chit-chatting in the mate's room. The suspense is killing me. Nice as the chat is, I'm kind of keen to get some alone time with the Swede.

'Where do you sleep, then?' I ask, casual as I can muster.

'Here,' he says, not batting a beautiful eyelash.

'Here?' I can't help but sound incredulous, looking around at the small room with one three-quarter-size bed and a whole lot of nothing.

'We can sleep here!' he says in his best can-do voice, holding aloft some Rizla-thin camping mats and pointing to the concrete floor next to his mate's bed.

Are you fucking kidding me? is what I'm thinking, heart sinking.

By now, I'm fast regretting my decision to schlep all that way to be basically transported back in time – this is real teenage stuff. Turns out, the photographer is actually a photographer's intern, which explains a lot.

I suck it up, though, and Model Man is sweet, trying to make it as comfy as is possible when faced with a flaccid mat on freezing stone. We listen to some tunes, look through a model's 'book' online who's got a one-word name. I try to keep any thoughts of *Zoolander* out of my head. Then we settle down to go to sleep. Oh goody. Not.

Model Man and I are snuggling, but it's hard to get comfy when your hip's sticking into concrete. I think all the alcohol I've consumed helps because I do doze off, but then I wake up absolutely fucking freezing. I'm basically in a concrete bunker with a flimsy blanket – not that surprising. I'm shivering uncontrollably. The model's asleep and, in spite of my predicament, I do manage to take a moment to admire his chiselled beauty. Then I stagger up, trying not to tread on him, in order to grab my fur coat. I've had a few sexy moments in a fur coat . . . alas this isn't one of them. I layer it over myself in the hope that I might start feeling my limbs again.

Model Man stirs and leaps into action. He's super apologetic before turning a heater on and wrapping his limbs around me protectively. That makes me happy. He's so long! I'm not sure whether it's romantic or if we're just surviving. I do feel him brush his hands over my bum, though, after a rigorous back rub. Whatever, the contact was nice and it's so not cool to start groping someone when his friend's literally a metre away. I should know, my mate once gave a guy a blowjob in our hotel room when I was in the bed next to them. I can still hear the slurps now. Ugh. That was Faliraki, though. What could I expect?

Morning came and I did manage to get *some* sleep. Model Man was very sleepy and kind, getting me coffee and giving me hugs. When the talk turned to hairstyles, though, I knew it was my cue to leave. *Zoolander* alert.

Now? To bed. In an actual bed. Heaven.

Friday, 5 March

I've woken up today with what Lady Jane calls 'floating anxiety' by virtue of the fact that it 'sticks to everything'. It's a feeling of unease, but you can't quite identify the what or the why. A bit like PMT. I was feeling it a bit yesterday, too, after the Model Man debacle. After my night on the concrete floor, I took myself off to bed for the afternoon, thinking I might wake up cured. Alas, no.

It's good to be aware of it when you're attaching a bit of crazy to everything. Put it down to temporary insanity. Always good for supportive but not softy advice, my ex Yorkshire makes a good point by email:

> What goes up must come down, and, conversely, therefore, what comes down must go up. Peaks and troughs, Ali-T. Avoid the plateau, you know . . .

That does give me some comfort – I'm a plateau objector! If I'm honest, I don't think the Cartoon Boy experience has really helped. That text I sent him is still out there, floating somewhere in the textsphere, unanswered; ignored. He really is something else. Actually, let me rephrase that, he's exactly the same – a cock, as I texted to Pfeiffer when she asked for an update earlier this week. I think I just underestimated the size of the cock, which is silly, because I've seen it plenty.

Saturday, 6 March

A new day! Specifically, Saturday. Even more specifically, Saturday morning. Is there anything more joyous? *Sound of the Sixties* is blaring from the radio, the bacon is doing its thing and Rubles has arrived from next door (her new home since Angel's departure), following its opium scent, like they do in cartoons.

'Oh, are you having bacon?' She's in a towelling dressing gown, peering over my shoulder as I shimmy and shake the pan. The Rolling Stones' 'Paint it Black' is on.

'Would you like some?' I put on my best talking-to-a-baby voice.

'Oh yes, please. Ta.' She loops her arms around me from behind, Patrick Swayze-style.

'You feeling a bit better today?'

I turn around to look at her. 'I am.'

There comes a time when you have to move on. I find it difficult identifying that time, but I think it is here. You have to take a hint –

mainly from yourself, because you're getting fuck all from them. I've been holding on to Cartoon Boy for way too long now. It's time to let him go, on this Saturday morning as I layer up bacon, cream cheese and cherry tomatoes on two lightly toasted bagels in the company of Rubles and the Rolling Stones.

To mark the occasion, as is only proper – with alcohol – I meet the gorgeous Elvis at the Cave for a few lunchtime vodka and pineapples (hey, I'm nothing if not exotic). You've got to turn to your friends during emotionally trying times and Elvis is certainly a tonic. Without doing anything, he makes me feel amazing. He makes me feel like *I'm* amazing. Then, to top it off, one of the old boys from the pub, the one with the handlebar moustache, bright-orange puffa jacket and tales of hanging with Dylan at Isle of Wight '68, gives me his late mother Florence's fur stole.

'It's a beauty for a beauty,' he says, looping the silky animal around my neck.

It's also *very this season*.

Time to move on.

Sunday, 7 March

The gung-ho way to tackle continued heartbreak is to go out on the tiles and not come back for at least 24 hours, with plenty of ridiculous stories to tell. The downside to this approach is that there's a really good chance you'll be sobbing into your Crunchy Nut Cornflakes come Monday morning. For now, though, Sunday afternoon, back home and chain drinking tea, I can't stop smiling. I mean, I went to a market, for fuck's sake. It was meant to be a *day* out. Me, Rubles and Minx met this artist guy and his mate in the pub and fell in love, in that way you do sometimes with people you meet and immediately bond with over ferocious piss-taking and shit-talking. We pub-crawled our way around East London, venues getting dodgier as the hours got earlier, until we finally gave up and collapsed, the three of us girls, into the artist's bed. He took the spare room like a true gent. We laughed ourselves to sleep and dreamed all the way home in a cab around noon today.

One of those great London nights filled with adventure and the thrill of the unknown around every corner.

Monday, 8 March

My email to 'the Artist' goes like this:

> How you doing? I'm feeling surprisingly chipper, I must say . . . just wanted to say, 'twas cool to meet you and hang out. Thanks again for letting us rowdy girls stay at yours. That was very kind, given that we literally just crashed out and were no fun at all.
>
> A x

The Artist is cute and curly and full of stories. It's only right that I follow up on our rendezvous. Do I fancy him? I'm not sure. But I'd definitely like to see him again, if only for more larks.

His response:

> Hey there, one of my new bezzies! I felt disgusting yesterday and today feel magic, what have you been doing since I last saw you?! x

Nice that. All in all, good work. I love it when a plan comes together.

Tuesday, 9 March

My hands are sweaty, my breath is short, I'm excited, I'm exhilarated – I'm in love!!! I just had THE BEST phone call of the last two months. Angel – my best friend, my long-lost friend – just called from South America. The landline rang out its shrill, unwanted call at around eight this evening. Rubles and I, almost two days into our slovenly movie and detective show marathon, heard its call for the umpteenth time. No one ever rings my landline. Correction – no one worth talking to ever rings my landline.

When the phone rang, we were watching the delightful film *Julie and Julia*, with our favourite actress Meryl Streep as the French cooking guru Julia Childs, but something told me I should answer. Why? I *never* answer the landline.

So I answered and there she was – my Angel. She's in the Bolivian jungle, which sounds a lot more interesting than where I'm at right now. I know, from her text messages and emails, that she's had the shits (her words), been attacked by mutant moths, showered below wasps' nests and had a near miss from being bitten by a crazy-ass dog, but here she is on the phone! You probably won't appreciate how amazing it is, but just hearing her voice is HEAVEN.

She's OK – going to Brazil now. Oh how I miss her, but she's there in the world and it's a wonderful thing.

Friendship.

Thursday, 11 March

'I'm harbouring Music Man desires' goes my first text of the day to Lady Jane.

It's true, I am. Why? *Why?* It's such an inconvenience. I think sometimes I look for things to make my brain hurt. Or else I'm farming for romance: raking and raking and raking to no avail.

'No no no no. You're bored, that's all. Do your work' is her *not-this-shit-again?* response.

'I was only thinking . . . ' I sulk back.

'He is ace and you will see him again. But if you text him before he texts you, it won't turn out right.'

'Why – what will happen?' I goad, hating the fact that she's right. 'Will my vagina implode?'

'Worse. A dick will sprout in the middle of your forehead.'

Gross.

Later I meet an old work colleague to go to YOYO, a club night at Notting Hill Arts Club run by Lily Allen's ex, the DJ Seb Chew. Everybody says it's cool, which I guess it is – kind of like being in an episode of *Skins*, as one of the parents. The music's good, though, and we do have a dance. We also get rather drunk, thanks to the 2-for-1 margaritas at the Mexican place we go to for dinner. I don't chat to any blokes (make that boys), mainly because it's so not my demographic. And this is not an age thing: I can handle a disco full of young indie kids or ravers, but not the baggy jeans and high tops crowd. We don't speak the same language.

Time to go home – well, back to my mate's place – and face the fact that it's 2 a.m., I'm full of tequila and, unfortunately for me, I've got a day in the fashion office tomorrow. Talk about bad timing. At least when you've got a full-time job you expect to go there every day. For me, it feels like some kind of practical joke, in a cab on the way to Shepherd's Bush, a million miles from home and only five hours before I have to get up.

Friday, 12 March

Wake up at my friend's house, in the spare room belonging to her boy roommate who's away. He works in media, or advertising, or maybe he's a web designer – he's one of those things because his room looks a bit like a concept store or urban museum, with graffiti art here and limited edition trainers there. I shouldn't complain, though, because as well being very keen on looking cool this guy is also a clean freak – the sheets were fresh; it's tidy.

Much better than the time I stayed over with Pfeiffer in Clapton at the house of the bloke she was seeing at the time. A sort of chancer/charmer/can't tell if he's for real type. He kindly offered to let me stay over because it was too late/far to go back to South London, which seemed like a good idea at the time. Clapton is never a good idea and I know this from experience, but still I went there and was given the skanky brown couch, a festered duvet and a doll's house pillow. The room was stuck in studentsville *circa* 1994, with *Pulp Fiction* posters on the wall and a load of mismatched furniture (not in a good way). I was woken from my four-hour horror sleep by the buzz of two Spanish girls fishing their clothes off the radiators, and every other surface that seemed to be covered in cheap laundry. Great. I had to go into the office the day after that, too, I seem to remember. I need to be careful; this is becoming a habit.

I make a quick exit from my friend's house without waking her –

she's a freelance stylist and isn't working that day, so there's no need to spread my misery her way. Plus, she's in her room with her boyfriend. I wouldn't mind a bit of that right now. Not with her boyfriend, of course, just someone resembling mine. I get to the office and find an email from her:

> How you feeling?
> My head's sore, I blame margarita madness! Xx

I bore her with the fact that I've agreed to go out again tonight to my mate's DJ gig at the Coronet in Elephant and Castle and that I'm not exactly feeling up for it. But then it will be nice to see them and an opportunity to meet new people and yada yada yada. Always thinking, *what if, what if*, that's my problem. It's The Fear Of Missing Out syndrome, coming soon to a self-help book near you.

'See how you feel later,' she advises back:

> Maybe just go for the dinner? Would be good to meet people,
> but unless you're actually up for it I always think you never
> come across well or have fun if you go because you think you
> should rather than because you actually want to. Xxx

When I'm hung-over, I always drag people into the minutiae of my social quandaries. It's a habit I need to shake, along with weeknight hedonism.

She's right, though. I'll decide later. I'm not keen on bailing – or bailers, for that matter – so I suspect I'll resist the couch and a takeaway curry in favour of hanging around backstage at a music venue, for a change. I might meet the man of my dreams (ahem). It's one of those terrible gremlins you have when you're single, that you should be making the most of such opportunities – that is social events with mates of mates – because it might be the start of your very own Pulp song. The one where you wake up in the morning with no way of knowing that . . . 'Something Changed'.

It's 5 p.m., just an hour to go, and I get a nice little pick-me-up in the form of an email from the Artist from last weekend. He tells me he's looked me up online (er, stalker alert!) and found some silly dating column I wrote a while ago.

'You'll have to hang out with me again, I might get a mention!'

Does everybody want to be famous, I wonder, before typing back, 'Do your worst!'

'Ooh exciting! When and where . . .' is his reply, by which time it's just about six and I've got the second round to contend with: I'm dripping wet from the swim, about to saddle up for the bike.

Saturday, 13 March

I made it out the other side last night at a totally respectable hour; there's no third-phase run to contend with, thankfully, so I'm enjoying a bit of at-home time. The yin and the yang:

Last night: shamelessly dancing on stage (yep). FUN.

Today: arranging my pens in the World's Greatest Daughter mug my mum bought me. FUN.

Last night: picking Elvis up off the stairs as he tripped from the backstage area before hurtling head first into an argument with a disgruntled drug dealer. NOT AS FUN.

Today: listening to an album dedicated to 'making science fun' by that professionally quirky '90s band They Might Be Giants. My favourite track? It's a toss-up between 'I Am a Paleontologist' and 'The Bloodmobile' – capillaries rock!! FUN.

Oh, goody. Rubles, who's marvelling over an advert for 'WaxiDoodles' (*hands-on, reusable model sticks that are great fun and mess-free!*) in *Guardian Weekend*, needs a pen for the crossword. I tell you, it's a rocking Saturday night here at Tudor Towers.

I brandish the World's Greatest Daughter mug in front of her, offering a choice of pens. 'What do you think of my new pen receptacle?'

She practically spurts with laughter. 'Where did you get that?!'

'Er, Mum.' Who else?

OK, we need to do something. Else.

Sunday, 14 March

Another glorious hangover-free day and another text from Model Man, en route to Paris: 'Gutted we didn't get chance to spend another night together.'

I do have to wonder, what is this guy on? Did he experience the same 'night together' as me?

Anyway, I appreciate his sentiment. He's hopped on the Eurostar to begin his Parisian stint – learning French and generally spreading a bit of his gorgeousness over that side of the Channel.

We didn't do a very good job of hooking up after the date where I nearly got into a fight. He got in touch twice on Friday night, trying to meet up with me, but I was far too busy walking like an Egyptian in Elephant and Castle to get my act together to arrange the meet. Shame that. But sometimes even a male model doesn't quite cut it.

Tuesday, 16 March

I've decided to give the Artist an opportunity to impress me with his company, so I ask him if he fancies being my plus-one for a gig tomorrow. Short notice, I know, but I don't really care that much, hence the spontaneous date suggestion. Alas, he's not free, something about a meeting, which makes him sound like a really go-getting artist. I thought they just stayed imprisoned in their studios all day, turning tea mugs a deep shade of brown. 'I can do Thursday, though,' he offers.

OK, I'll take that offer: 'What would you like to do?'

'Err, not sure, badmington?'

This would be funny if he could spell.

'Ha, I'm not sure I have the right wrist action. Am more of a tennis girl . . .'

'Right, then. What about Camden for a drink?'

That'll do, I suppose. He'll be in touch to arrange timings on Thursday. Is this a date? I'm not really sure. The beginnings are so ambiguous. At least if you get off with someone on the night you meet, you know where you stand.

Wednesday, 17 March

I had dinner tonight with Mrs Jones at Pizza East, the trendy East London eaterie from the owners of Shoreditch House – and we were struck by how fit the waiters are. I'm busy flirting with one of them – a green-eyed, asymmetric-haired blond god – asking him, suggestively, 'Yes, but is it good Chardonnay or bad Chardonnay?' and other similarly dickish questions.

After more mutual eyebrow-raising and pouting, he brings over said Chardonnay in a mini carafe and pours me a thimbleful in an even tinier glass. He then wafts away and glances back to give me his sex face (not really, but he's defo flirting).

I sip seductively on my wine only to discover . . . I'm drinking from the carafe.

Thursday, 18 March

It's the day of my date with the Artist and I'm surprised that I'm actually looking forward to it. You see, since we met on that Saturday at Broadway Market, and since we've exchanged a few emails and jokes, my mind's had time to create this person who I really, really want to go out with:

1. He's an artist; this is romantic.
2. He's a bit posh; this is foreign and therefore good.
3. Then there's the 'you never know' syndrome . . .

You never know what might happen, what magic might be in store, and if you don't try, you don't find out. I'm a trier. You know who else was a trier? Warren Beatty. I found this out when I interviewed Dustin Hoffman and he told me that was love god Beatty's whole shtick. Hoffman apparently asked him once, marvelling at the number of women he'd plundered, *Is there any woman you wouldn't go to bed with?* Beatty said, *No, because you never know*. Now, I'm not notching up Beatty's levels of notoriety, but I admire his chutzpah, and his optimism: the romance of possibility.

It's this cock-eyed relationship with romance that has left me, at six o'clock, really pissed off because the Artist has only gone and cancelled our date. In reality, I probably shouldn't be that bothered because I don't think I am that bothered about him. But, and it's a hefty but, I've spent the last two days on a crazy trip where Warren Beatty is my love guru and the Artist is, well, I don't know what he is, but in my fantasy he certainly doesn't blow me out by text with some story about artwork delivery. I am inconvenienced, to say the least, and now my brain has to rewire, which might take some time. Grrr.

Saturday, 20 March

It's Saturday night and I'm in alone. So is my dad. Mum's away for the weekend – with her fancy man. Not really, she's a Brownie leader and there's some do or other for the 100th-year anniversary.

I'm settling in with my new gas fire (that I finally got to freakin' work), a pizza, *Family Fortunes* (always good for a laugh) and a glass of vino.

I call Dad to see how he's coping without my mum and catch him midway through a cooking experiment. This is his culinary modus operandi.

'Listen to this,' he says excitedly.

I listen and hear precisely nothing.

'Did you hear?'

'No . . .'

'Oh, it's a gorgeous crispy sausage,' he carries on, sounding like a Yorkshire David Bellamy.

What a lunatic. And you know what he's having his gorgeous crispy sausage with? Chicken tikka masala – dug out and defrosted from the freezer.

'And I've got naan bread and a cold beer. What more could you want?'

True dat. I love my dad.

Monday, 22 March

I wake up in another foreign bed. And yet again it's at a female friend's residence rather than that of some hot new stud. This time, my location is Highgate, North London. I find it's good to keep 'em on their toes by switching up your geographical location at regular intervals. I'm hoping the map-hopping will yield new and interesting men.

Right now, though, the only thing I'm yielding is a hangover, along with my friend, the Elegant Ms S. We met some years ago in Italy on a press trip – bonded over cocktails in Fellini's garden, as we both like to tell everybody. She rocks that '50s bombshell look really well and has the platinum hair to go with it. She also has the biggest heart and most class of anyone I know.

'Tea?' She's half out of the bed, half into a robe.

'Yes, please,' I croak.

'Last night was fun.' Her manicured brow is arched. She's smirking.

Last night *was* fun. We went to a famous Camden juke-joint to see a gig. Ms S is friends with the guy who owns the pub – a charismatic local legend type. Ms S knows a lot of interesting people – mainly hell-raising music legends. One such person was 'Guitar Hero', so christened because apparently he is. He was solo acoustic last night, but, I'm told, plays with some pretty big names most of the time. Apart from me and Ms S, he was playing his set to a predominantly male audience of guitar freaks with nodding heads and adoring expressions.

'His groupies are middle-aged roadies,' sniggers Ms S, nodding to the assembled man-crowd. I mention this to him later when he joins our table and get the sense they aren't his ideal demographic.

I took a shine to Guitar Hero from the get-go. From the neck up, he's got the hair and face of Jim Morrison. The neck down is not as appealing, in that he doesn't have the Doors' front man's sexy hips and he's definitely 'showing' beneath his Americana checked shirt. He's also wearing bootcut jeans. Eesh.

I shoot him a few glances, flash a bit of shoulder; you know the drill. (Ms S did whisper in my ear that there wasn't exactly much in the way of competition. She had a point.) We had a lock-in and this is when Guitar Hero really started getting friendly. And when I say friendly, I mean pesty. It was unbelievable! And I thought musicians were meant to be cool.

Picture the scene: five of us sitting around a table – Ms S, the landlord, a dapper Irish gent, M, who's something of a local VIP, me and Guitar Hero. Now, I could handle a little light flirting, but Guitar Hero is insatiable – grabbing my hand to hold, linking my waist, stroking my hair. His demands for kisses come a little later. At first I'm completely put off and more than a little embarrassed. It's not cool to be copping off with the entertainment, is it? Maybe I'm not drunk enough.

The harassment continues for some time. Guitar Hero is now telling me I'm beautiful at five-minute intervals. It's all I can do not to burst out laughing. I know I'm looking at him like he's mad, between gesticulating to Ms S that I might've changed my mind about him. I successfully manage to keep him at arm's length, even turning down his delightful offer to nip off to the loos with him, but then he starts to grow on me.

How? I know. Unbelievable, isn't it? But I'm attracted to how he communicates with the others, more than me. M, who's a mature gent, is getting rowdy drunk, but Guitar Hero never once interrupts or contradicts or laughs. He has the utmost respect for this marvellous sartorialist, who's clearly well loved round these parts. I like that. He also obliges when he's asked to sing various songs on demand. A human jukebox – this is nice, too.

At 4 a.m. it's time to leave. Ms S lives nearby and I'm keen to check out her new flat. Guitar Hero is rampantly keen for me to check out *his* flat, despite the fact I've told him approximately a million times that it ain't gonna happen. He bundles into a cab with us, though, and we drop him en route. He's still trying his luck, bless him, but I manage to unlock myself from his lanky frame and propel him onto the road (there weren't any cars coming). He was so drunk I can't imagine he would've been much use anyway. We have a sloppy snog in the face of oncoming traffic, which is not as bad as it sounds.

Ms S and I get back to hers and set to work pillaging her fridge for morsels of cheese to decorate the baguette she's trying her damnedest to carve up (why do they go stale so quickly?). We get into bed and I notice I've missed a call from Guitar Hero. Sweet Jesus, he's keen! And there's a text: 'Please come out with me one day.'

Oh, I love it when they beg . . .

Wednesday, 24 March

Two things:

1. I should wear pencil skirts and heels more often. I look pretty damn hot. I had a date tonight. Which leads me to no. 2 . . .
2. What is it with people breaking dates? It's happened to me twice now in the past week and is getting on my freakin' nerves!

Guitar Hero got in touch and asked me out. You know, the guy who literally begged me to go out with him and the reason I'm shrink-wrapped into a pencil skirt right about now? He's only gone and cancelled due to being 'stuck in the studio'. Hannoying.

Lady Jane suggests I should date a man over 40 or a public schoolboy – someone 'trad', she says by text before adding, 'Breaking dates is a modern affliction.' By Jove, I think she's right. Still, annoying!

Luckily *The Simpsons* has pulled me out of my grump.

Is this not the best put-down ever? Old Woman to Grampa: 'You're more boring than my husband and he's dead.'

Thursday, 25 March

From one flake to another – I know, there's a definite pattern emerging: an email from the Artist comes through, apologising about the artwork delivery (at least he's sticking to his story) and what am I up to this weekend?

Can I be bothered with this, with two cancelled dates already leaving a black mark on my soul? With Mr Beatty's voice in my head and forgiveness in my heart, I suggest we meet up at Broadway on

Saturday. I had plans to go there anyway, so that's security of sorts. 'Yes, let's hang out on Saturday!' is his gushing reply. We'll see . . .

I then tend to the important business of settling a discussion Ms S has been having with her bloke mate about men and pyjamas, thus: *Do blokes get laid loads if they wear PJs? Or is it cos he isn't getting laid that he's wearing them?*

Random, yes, but certainly an engaging question. My response?

> Men in pyjamas are definitely not getting laid. Not by women, anyway. They're either into men or, I'd like to think of the retro silk pj types, opium. I'd indulge in the latter with them but nothing carnal. And as for those men that wear dog-eared dressing gowns – probably bought for them by their mums – NO WAY. It's the unsexiest thing ever. A definite deal-breaker.

Right, now that I've solved that particular mystery, I should probably do something useful.

Saturday, 27 March

Guess what? No word from the Artist. I mean, there's flaky and then there's all-out loserville. If he was a pupil in my class, I'd drag him to the front, tell him how he was wasting my time (and everybody else's), then beat him with a metre ruler. That said, I'm actually not bothered. Really.

Monday, 29 March

Had another shitty night's sleep last night, thanks to (I'm starting to think) working too much and not drinking enough. What's the point in not drinking, i.e. being virtuous, if you just lie awake (well, between getting up for mini-pees every five minutes) acting out various role plays in your head – namely how will I find the time to write up the interviews I've been transcribing all day and will that so-called Guitar Hero pull his plectrum out of his arse and actually keep our date this time?

After he blew me out last week, we rescheduled for tonight. Monday – the king of date days! I've pretty much been working the past few days so, yes, you could say I'm looking forward to tonight.

Guess what? He's blown me out again. How very dare he?

I texted him once I'd cleared my deadline around four-ish with: '????? What's occurring? Are we meeting later?'

You ready for this? He comes back with: 'Hi, I'm afraid I can't meet you tonight. I have a bit of a situation and now really isn't a good time. So sorry – I hate to mess you about x.'

Not as much as I hate receiving that sort of drivel into my lovely phone.

A situation? Perhaps the plectrum really did get stuck up his arse, or maybe his nose? That's feasible.

The text I wanted to send back? 'Yawn.' He's a legend in his own mind, this guy, if I can borrow Jay McInerney's words just for a second.

I don't reply. I blank him. What a tool. I suspect he has a girlfriend, hence why he's so droolly on a night out and not so much in the cold light of day, faced with an actual date.

I inform Ms S by email, flagging up the begging vs bailing issue (not to mention out-and-out rudeness), and she sends a rallying reply:

> Sod that, you really don't need it. Not one tiny little bit. Rude *and* keen equals wally. I think he is doing you a favour. You don't need it. It's not like you thought there was a deep connection, you were embarrassed by his embarrassing behaviour but nice enough to let it go. Did you reply or not bother? Please do NOT go there, there isn't enough intrigue to be going on with . . . xxx

She's right. I know this, but it still feels a bit shit to be blown out four times – that's *four* times – in half as many weeks. I reckon the odds on that would be so huge I'd be making six figures from the bookies if I'd put a bet on. I keep expecting Ashton Kutcher to jump out and tell me I've been 'Punk'd', but then I remember that I don't live in LA and I'm not a celebrity.

There's probably a lesson to be learned here that involves not dating musicians or artists and instead dating outside my comfort zone with, say, a banker or lawyer. That's advice I've read and been told on many an occasion. The rebel – or sadist – in me, though, just won't play along. It'd be like giving up. Also, there are wankers everywhere, no matter what they do.

Tuesday, 30 March

Because cockroaches never die, the Artist emails me today with a story involving a broken phone, something about feeling isolated without it and one tiny sorry. Not enough emphasis on the sorry, too much on the convoluted story, but he's an artist, what can I expect? He's complicated and terribly disorganised. He concerns himself with bigger things, right?

He's asking me out. Again. This time he's suggesting Kentish Town. I sense a North London bias developing, but I'm not free and also not mental enough to back a lame horse. Well, not for the third time anyway. After some email small talk about our respective Easter plans, he signs off, somewhat optimistically/deluded with: 'Let's keep in touch, hang out after Easter.'

Fuck's sake, I had a pen pal when I was 13 – I'm not looking for another one. She lived in Holland and there was more chance of seeing her. So long, sucker!

April
New Frontiers

Thursday, 1 April

After the cancelled dates car crash that was last month, I'm starting April with the philosophy, what would Debbie Harry do? In other words, I'm going to learn to give less of a fuck about the fuckwits.

As it's April Fool's Day, I've made up a fun-and-foolish game called 'Good Prop, Bad Prop' in honour of those two March fools. It's cathartic.

What are good props when it comes to men? Guitars are definitely bad props. Paint brushes, or some other tool of an artist's trade, are also bad props. Actually, that might mean banishing Mac computers or Adobe Illustrator too, which is perhaps a bit rash because then you wipe out all the graphic designers as well, who actually tend to be all right and not half as precious as 'artists'.

Anyway, you catch my drift . . .

Good prop: stethoscope? Now, this theory is yet to be tested, though I have been pursued by a doctor on one of those ghastly internet dating sites. An ugly doctor.

Good prop: camera? Now, this was Lady Jane's. When I was slagging off Guitar Hero to her earlier, she happily entered into my silly game. I know what she means, bookish guy with cool retro camera who likes taking cute pics on holiday . . . maybe . . . but photographers as a race? I'm not sure. I've had weirdos and also the best guy I ever went out with, so it's a tough one to call.

Bad prop: wedding ring.

Good prop: fish slice (or other more sexy-sounding kitchen utensil).

Bad prop: plectrum. Unless you seize it and use it to administer a short, sharp jab in the eye.

Capiche?

Friday, 2 April

Good Friday really is good! I'm in an inexplicably Good Mood on the train home and SO IS EVERYBODY ELSE. Posho grandpa opposite has just cracked open his second can of Stella, his wife – a spit for Jilly Cooper – is tucking into her gardening magazine with glee. Me and the really nice lady next to me have ordered tea and got cake for just an extra 25p! 25p! You can't go wrong, can you? That's what I said to Laura, who was manning the trolley, anyway. Then there's the tunes: 'Love Is in the Air' by that lovely hippy chap John Paul Young (what else did he do?) just came on my iPod playlist.

Love, of course, isn't in the air for me just now, it's kind of stuck somewhere hoping to escape, but there is definitely a lot of love on this train and you've gotta love that.

Saturday, 3 April

When I'm up north and socialising somewhere where they serve alcohol, I'm always struck by how much more forthcoming the men are, or maybe they're just shameless.

I'm home on family duty – three celebrations, to be specific: a birthday, Easter (a rebirth) and a pearl wedding do. After the birthday meal, we decamp en masse to the crazy alpine bar that is deep in the throng of one big fat Easter drinking session. The masses are marvelling over Nobby's (or some other ridiculous nickname) ability to drink eight pints of the 7.4 per cent cider.

I'm not sure what there is to boast about. Sure, he's drunk it, but as a result he's trying to get off with my 60-year-old auntie. Everyone is incredulous as he messily kisses her cheek and attempts to penetrate her ear with his tongue. She's a good sport about it, and she's a fine and glamorous lady, but still, it's socially awkward. He's now attempting to wrap his deadweight arms around her, prompting Rubles, the doting daughter, to intervene:

'Give up! You'll lead her astray . . .'

'I'd lead *him* astray,' goes my aunt.

Quality.

My favourite part of the evening is when one of the local boys I enjoy flirting with because he fancies himself as such a ladies' man gets up really close and whispers into my ear: 'You've really got the wow factor.'

Damn right.

Sunday, 4 April

Will I never learn? Shaving one's bikini line is *never* a good idea. NEVER. And, as I daub myself with Sudocrem, I'm reminded that, like going to the theatre, it's only ever painful.

Right, off to blow some eggs. Happy Easter.

Monday, 5 April

Because I haven't taken a guy home to meet my mum and dad for years, it's fun to imagine. Me and Dad have this thing where I propose a particular man (usually famous) who I would bring home, hypothetically speaking. Today the lucky man is Steve Coogan – a man I would love to pillage and drag home by his lovely long hair into my kitchen, laying him at my mum's feet, as she's no doubt scrubbing the lino. I think we'd all enjoy that. I interviewed Coogan once, some years ago, and asked him what he'd cook a lady for a dinner. He said he'd skip dinner and make her smoked salmon and scrambled eggs in the morning instead. Smoooooth. I like that.

So, me and Mum and Dad are sitting at the dining-room table eating leftover turkey and ham from Easter Sunday dinner, with chips made in the chip pan (theirs is one of the only homes I know that still has a chip pan). We're commenting on the number of condiments involved – salt, pepper, vinegar (for the chips), English mustard (for the ham), cranberry sauce (for the turkey), stuffing (ditto), apple sauce (ditto), ketchup (for the chips) and gravy (for everything).

I pipe up, once I've lathered my meal in all of the above, 'Me and

Steve Coogan would make a good couple, don't you think?'

Dad thinks about it for a bit, stabbing a chip and then beheading, chewing and swallowing it before saying, 'No, I think he'd be a bastard.'

'Really?' I was expecting various responses but not that one. 'Why?'

'I think he seems like he'd be a bit unsafe . . . in himself. He'd be too moody.'

I absolutely love that Dad is taking this seriously and giving me an answer based on whether this made-up Steve would be good enough for me. Aw.

But then because I can't resist shit-stirring a bit more, I say, 'Do you think he's a deviant?'

'No!' my dad says, like he's defending him. 'Perhaps *devious*.'

Interesting.

Interesting.

Steve Coogan, my dad and me are going to be just fine. I'm convinced of it.

Tuesday, 6 April

I take my eye off Pfeiffer for five minutes (OK, a week while she buggered off skiing) and this is what happens. Email, incoming:

> OK, so holiday goss.
>
> Met this loud Brummie, approaching 40, lots of tattoos, not much hair – amazing blue eyes and just so confident – nothing embarrassed him! So different from my usual type but also weirdly addictive. Met him on the second night and then he came and found me every other night after and I LOVED IT! Not sure why didn't go for all the hot young boarders but guess he was quite a hot old boarder – good clobber too!
>
> Can't remember what he said exactly much apart from he never thought I'd be interested in someone like him – also he would never live in the UK – France much better apparently – he would never work 9 to 5 – he also called me a hippy due to

some of my liberal views and the fact I chose to get the train there and back!

I think he is the resident drug dealer but he never mentioned this to me – he knew everyone, though – was everyone's mate and we didn't pay for a thing – suspicious!

He is supposed to be coming over in about a month (prob to pick up supplies!) so we will see what happens!

Email, outgoing:

I'm proud of you, Pfeiffer – you go on skiing holiday and manage to root out the criminal underbelly. Good work! Xx

Wednesday, 7 April

I'm lying on the bed in my old bedroom, wearing those fleecy boot slippers like grandmas wear with rubber soles. It feels like I shouldn't have them on my clean, cream duvet, but I haven't been outside so they're not dirty and I want to be horizontal right now. I like shutting myself off in my old teenage bedroom sometimes. It's a good place to brood: it's in the DNA.

I've got my lamp on – another shocking example of my attempts at interior decor back in '91. The base is made to look like an old Roman pillar or something. It doesn't, of course – mainly because it's turquoise and from BHS. I'm curled on my side, reading and facing the pitch-black window, which is open on the vent. I can smell the air and feel the fresh breeze on my face, entering my nostrils. The radiator's on too, so the hot and cold are competing for my attention. It's naughty, I know, to play the two off against each other, but I can't help it. I like them both for different reasons.

I remember my dad saying to me once how you get older but don't feel any different inside. Here I am, 32, on my teenage bed thinking, am I really that different? Looking at him then – I was probably about 14 and he was in his 40s – I couldn't get my head around it: *he's old, how can he feel the same?* Now I know exactly what he meant. As the months and years go by, especially since I've been single, it feels like nothing changes at all. The passing years blur into one. You've got all the trappings and social conventions of adulthood to deal with, but do you really feel any different? It brings to mind that bit in *Four Weddings and a Funeral* when Hugh Grant and Andie MacDowell are sitting in that café discussing how many people they've slept with – her numbers are creeping upwards and upwards, his are stagnant at eight – and he says: 'I don't know what the fuck I've been doing with my time.' That's how life feels sometimes.

Thursday, 8 April

I've been home for almost a week now and have managed to not run into Cartoon Boy and also not think about him quite as much. This is progress. The not bumping into him has definitely helped because that's when the trouble starts, though I'd also like to think I'm coming good on last month's resolution to move on.

On reflection, the big thing with Cartoon Boy is that he dumped me. That'd never happened to me before and, like a lot of new experiences – the first time you get punched in the face, for instance – you're not expecting it. I *really* liked him, too. And I think he did me, so it's hard to get your head around. And then you revisit and reignite hope, only to get let down again, and so on. It's a shitty cycle, which has to be broken.

You have to do something about it – force yourself. I think I've realised it can't all come down to the healing via the passage of time remedy. The reflective times are good, like yesterday when I was on my bed, as are times you spend with friends and family. There's so much comfort to be taken from those relationships. It sounds cheesy, but you have to remember that when you're feeling down in the dumps about a guy. You also have to remember to leave it the fuck alone.

'Shall we have a drink?' Dad's hovering at the bedroom door with an expectant look in his eye.

'Let's. It's five o'clock, why not?'

His whole face smiles, genuinely pleased I'm going to share in the teatime ritual. It's the small pleasures that matter, isn't it? Joining in, saying yes, being sociable. My friends joke that they find it hard to say no to me because I always look so disappointed when they do. I know where I get it from now – my dad. He's exactly the same. So be it, if we're going down, we're going down together!

Friday, 9 April

Me and Roller Girl are indulging our Vince Vaughn and Chinese takeaway fetishes round at her place, garnished with a shitload of San Miguels. Our love for Vince Vaughn began, probably like most people's, with *Swingers*. Perhaps not like most people, we watched *Swingers* for the first time in Paris when we were inter-railing students. We were so cool back then. Tonight he's reunited with his *Swingers* cohort Jon Favreau in *Couples Retreat*, so we're pretty psyched. We like them together in *Four Christmases*, too. It's our thing. The love is still there, but they'll never eclipse the greatness of *Swingers*, will they?

Anyway, it's a great night and I leave at a reasonable hour, feeling good to be getting in a taxi with my head held high. It doesn't always end this way when faced with an evening at Roller Girl's. There's that weird Twilight Zone thing where I don't emerge for days, if at all.

But just as I'm climbing into the cab, dead smug, it takes a turn for the weird.

I tell the driver where I'm going. He says, 'I know these roads,' which is about right for Yorkshire know-it-alls, though actually he was a Geordie, wearing a baseball cap. Gazza? There's no chat at first, which suits me just fine 'cause I can't be arsed really. Just wanna get home. Then he pipes up: 'Good day today, love?'

Fair enough, so I said, 'Yeah, fine thanks. You?' Not earth-shattering conversation on my part, but I didn't care to share my daytime's activities of doing a tiny bit of work (i.e. sending a few emails), eating pork pie, watching *Casablanca*, chatting to Lady Jane on phone, taking painkillers every three hours to deal with the mother of all period pains, blah blah . . . it's not that exciting, you know?

He said (thus demonstrating exactly why he asked me about my day in the first place): 'Well, I went to the doctor's today finally after about five weeks.'

Oh good Lord, where is this going? I have to say something, so I say: 'Five weeks. Blimey, is that how long you had to wait to get an appointment?' (A reasonable assumption from the way he phrased it.)

'No, I got my appointment yesterday, but I've had this chesty cough for about five weeks now, but that's what I'm like, just try to grin and bear it . . .'

Me: 'Yeah, er, did you get some antibiotics, then?' I am too polite for my own good. I'm asking for it, really.

'Yeah, really strong ones . . . I've got other underlying problems as well, you see.'

I'm thinking, no I don't see, I don't want to see, or even imagine ...

'Yeah, so I gave them a sample . . .'

WHAT?! Have I met my over-sharing match?

'I gave them a sample and they reckon these antibiotics should sort it all out, so we'll just have to wait and see.'

'Yes.' One word, that's all you're having. Weirdo.

Silence. I'm staring out of the window, literally waiting for him to get his knob out and show me his dose.

It's the kind of thing that would happen to me. Like the time I answered my front door to a guy selling karate lessons, door to door. What the fuck? He wanted to come into my living room and demonstrate some moves. True story.

Something bad will happen to me one of these days. It'll graduate from weird to sinister. I know it.

It's the last time I get in a cab not under the influence again.

Saturday, 10 April

The editor I write an online dating column for has asked me to try out some dating 'activities', by which I think she means organised 'fun' rather than heavy petting. When did dating become organised group-playing, like Brownies? Book club this, record swap that? Organised is bullshit. I mail Pfeiffer because it strikes me as something she'd be more into than me.

True to form, she's game to be my guinea pig in crimes against romance. 'Will have a think – I would def be up for trying stuff with you! There is this thing next Thurs – I can't make it as in Brum, but could be good for you?'

The 'thing' is – duh duh duh – speed-dating. And not just normal speed-dating, it's speed-dating at the Barbican – the trendy mixed-media arts centre. Does this make it OK? I'm not sure, but I've got an editor breathing down my neck so I might not have a choice.

In other Pfeiffer news, she bailed on a date she was supposed to go on last night: 'Felt bad but just wasn't feeling it and you can't force it. Went shopping after and then back to watch TV and eat spring rolls – much more satisfying!'

She told him she wasn't feeling it, too. That's one giant leap for Pfeiffer and a small step for womankind right there.

Tuesday, 13 April

My work life is strange sometimes. At the moment, I'm concurrently trying to track down stylish women who are over 60 to interview for a feature called Silver Stylistas; later this week I'm interviewing Ashley Banjo, that bloke who does street dance; and now I'm in the plush Soho Hotel waiting to have my bikini line zapped with the latest in laser technology. I never thought I'd take my knickers off for money, but here I am.

I do think the whole bikini line conspiracy is just that – a conspiracy. But then, at the same time, I still want to get rid of it. I would love to think that I could end it for ever at just the small price of a bit of pain and humiliation. It would be worth it. I've got three courses to do – like radiation or something – and then apparently the eyesore around my panty-line will be no more. We'll see. I'm not convinced. It's like waxing: when you first have it done, it looks like it will never grow back, but then, sure enough, after not much more than a week, those dark hairs rear their itchy little heads again and conspire to bring you out in a rash.

Wednesday, 14 April

I've been experimenting with a tinned food diet, or at least I'm sure that's what the guy at the local shop will be thinking based on my recent purchases. I've had a lot of writing to do, so no time really for proper food shopping or cooking. Today for lunch I bought a giant sausage roll and a tin of beans. Reminded me of lunches I'd have as a kid. Very comforting, I must say, but probably not high on a nutritionist's list of what's good for you. Then, tonight, I called in at the shop with a massive urge for tinned macaroni cheese. I mean, I love macaroni cheese, though I've never had it from a tin before. I'm intrigued. Intrigued and super aware that I probably shouldn't be making a meal out of it. But you know what? It's actually all right. Especially if you grate your own cheese on top and wash it down with a £9 bottle of Chardonnay, something I share with Lady Jane by text later on.

She comes back with: 'The one I'm drinking is fucking awful. Six quid from local offy. Feel like going down there and glassing him. Frankly, I've sucked cocks that have tasted more like Pinot Grigio.'

Thursday, 15 April

The time has come. I'm at the Barbican about to speed-date. Rubles is *my* date. I didn't have the balls to face it alone and I've only agreed to it because it's here, as a sort of live installation in the Ron Arad exhibition. For those of you not familiar with his work, Arad is the *enfant terrible* of the design world – messing about with chairs, bookcases and light fittings to create weird and wonderful items just perfect for a surrealist home. That's my take on it, anyway. I love that kind of thing and, I'm hoping, whoever turns up for this dating event will feel the same.

If I'm totally honest, I'm thinking the average punter at a dating event in a gallery will be cooler, more intelligent and cultured than your average speed-dater. Prejudiced, moi? Rubles told me about her only other experience of this brand of love-hunting at what sounded like a ghastly event at a bar in Leicester Square. Is it any surprise? Consider what happens on an average Saturday night in Leicester Square and then apply speed-dating. I shudder to think.

Because the advertisement for this event said 'subject to availability' we get there early. I really thought it would be popular – you know, amongst people who, like me, wouldn't normally be caught dead speed-dating. Sadly, as Rubles and I were tentatively signing up for the 'straight' round, it was apparent that boys were in short supply. Then came my moment of devastation – I spy a guy I've fancied for years. He's here to help organise the event, sadly not to take part. I skulk off to hide behind a curvaceous tipping chair. I'm showing my true colours now – not the brave dating experimenter but shamed loser caught in the act.

Because the event's a bit slow getting started, we head to the café for some food and Dutch courage. It is honestly not an exaggeration to say that I feel more nervous than I did before my driving test. All of them. Rubles persuades me not to bottle it and we go back up to the space, figuring it's better to hang out and be a part of things in the early stages, you know, rather than just burst straight in for the main event. Foreplay is everything.

Thankfully it's not as painfully quiet as it was when we first arrived. This probably has something to do with the drinks on offer: 'Love' cocktails comprising vodka and absinthe. A bourgeois love potion, if ever there was one. 'We'll have two!' The first round is about to get under way – we were chickens and signed up for the second. It's good to scope out the competition, I think.

The hosts are the Tenor Ladies – cross-dressing flamboyants who are the toast of the cabaret world. They keep things lively with some loud and lewd chatter – it's a good ice-breaker. There are 'stations' dotted about the space where the girls sit and wait for the boys to come and weave three minutes of magic (hopefully). It's kind of funny, because the daters, dotted between the sculptures and silver ping-pong table (another Arad creation), kind of become one with the exhibition. You can do quirky things, too, like send a text message to a suitor, which will be projected on the snazzy 'Lolita' LED chandelier. The event is named 'Speed-Dating with Lolita' after it.

After watching the first round and checking out some of the talent – I spotted two Little Boy Lost types that are right up my street – it's my turn to get involved. The Love potion has taken the edge off, so I'm (almost) raring to go. My spot, perched atop a sort of tower of foam building blocks, certainly makes for instant intimacy because you can't help but squish together.

Now, I don't mind the squishing, but I'm not sure my first date – a bumbling Louis Theroux type – feels the same. He's fighting a losing battle against the foam, which I find quite amusing. God knows how in three minutes we get onto the subject of adultery, but we do. I am pretty sure he's sufficiently scared. Next! There had to be an arrogant one. A Scottish guy who can't seem to make eye contact declares, and I quote: 'Yeah, there are a lot of fit girls wandering around the gallery, but none of them seem to be speed-dating.' Er, cheers. You idiot. Though I do have a nice encounter with a sultry Mediterranean guy fashioning a silk handkerchief in his breast pocket. He's intense in a good way and the three minutes race by as we discuss the exhibition and his love of Spanish cooking. 'Will I see you after?' he asks. I think you just might, love.

The other dates zoom by – no one in particular takes my fancy. One guy gets all psycho on me for asking what he does. I protest that I'm not interested in status, but he's having none of it. I guess I couldn't think of anything else to say and it just slipped out. That's a big problem with my dating technique, especially speeded up; things just slip out, like the adultery chat. Oops. The hapless boy I'd spied earlier in a blue blazer carrying a linen bag was sadly not in my round, but we manage to catch each other's eye and have a fun chat.

'I wish you'd been in my round,' he says, complimenting my Breton stripes. 'You look much more up my street.'

From what I can gather, he's a pianist, poet and sometime creator of music videos. Let's call him 'Poet Pianist'. He certainly seemed as baffled as me by speed-dating protocol, so we had that in common. I got his card, and Mediterranean boy's number as we shared a fag outside. Who said smoking isn't sexy?!

All in all, not bad considering I was a total speed-dating sceptic. I intend to get in touch with Pianist Poet, but I think I'll leave handkerchief boy for a bit. One at a time – I'm an old-fashioned girl at heart.

Friday, 16 April

'So am dying to know, did you meet anyone decent?! x.'

It's Pfeiffer, chomping at the bit at 9 a.m. Speed-dating does this to people. It makes them crazy. Anyone would think I'd done something important, like run a marathon or save a life or something.

I fill her in: 'Well, there were a couple who were OK – have two numbers, but not sure I'll defo follow them up. Really glad I did it. Was a big step for me! Xxxx.'

She's proud of me. I think I'm proud of me too, on the quiet. I often come back to the same point: you've got to put yourself out there, take a chance. Granted, you might square up to a surly Scottish psycho who wants to punch you, but equally you might meet a Spanish prince with a silk handkerchief and a gift for spices.

Sunday, 18 April

I thought I'd heard it all, but it seems a new hot topic in the world of dating relates to timings of dates. The Poet Pianist I met at the arty speed-dating thing has suggested we meet for a date at 10.36 a.m. on Tuesday. Now, I know he was being cute with the precise minutes, but 10.30 a.m. for a date? Really?

I responded immediately and truthfully with: 'Are you joking?'

He wasn't (well, apart from the 36 minutes bit, which he admitted to).

Now, to me this is a breakfast meeting, not a date. But then, is it a new dating trend I'm only just aware of?

Anyhoo, I declined. I had work to do and, er, sleep to sleep. Anything at that time sucks, unless you're already there. You get me?

Monday, 19 April

One of the things that can bite you in the ass from time to time when you're single is what your mates are up to in the name of being part of a couple. Pfeiffer's feeling the couples pinch when we chat over email, mid-morning:

Am OK but feeling a little weird – met up with Emma and Bex

on Sat afternoon – feel a bit like they are all moving on and I'm still stumbling out of bars drunk, looking for a decent guy! Also we are completing on the flat today so think that has made me feel a bit weird too.

The flat is one she bought with *her* Big Ex and is now selling because it didn't work out – never easy. I soothe back: 'I totally hear you. Just try not to abandon yourself to it. I feel that too sometimes, but it's just different timings, that's all.'

I want to add, don't forget so many couples are miserable and hate each other deep down, but I don't because that would be immature. But *it is* a conspiracy. It's like all the supposed 'sad' things about being single are what's advertised and the good things about couples. It's all, 'Oh look at her, she's drunk and falling out of a bar!' And 'Aw, they're getting married and she's pregnant.'

Fast-forward a couple of years and they might just as likely be getting divorced over a row about nappy bags. Or something. Sometimes I feel like there's this big relationship race that everyone's competing in – you start by meeting somebody, then the next lap you get married, the next lap you have a baby, and so on. It's noticeable if you're lagging behind, but that's bullshit. I think we all know it's bullshit, and we certainly know we wouldn't want to be in half the relationships we know; half the people in relationships probably don't want to be in them either, but they stick it out! Still, sometimes, if we're willing to admit it, we feel like we're lacking in some way.

So what's the answer? I don't know. I don't. I'm good at advising others like Pfeiffer but not always able to apply the wisdom to myself. I'm just trying to avoid the plateau and it's that which ironically keeps me on the straight and narrow.

Tuesday, 20 April

Well, tonight was a revelation! I had drinks and a burger earlier with my ex, Yorkshire, who's back from NYC, Elvis, Rubles and some other chums to celebrate the new pub Elvis and his brothers have taken on in Peckham. For some reason, Yorkshire and I were having a trip down memory lane – lots of conversations that started 'Remember when . . . ' The best/worst one had to be when Yorkshire addressed the whole table with: 'Remember when you gave me an envelope with a load of your pubes in it?'

WHAT??!! I honestly don't remember. But more to the point, WHAT??!!

Now, we're all laughing our heads off at this revelation but, really, I can't decide if it's cool in its all-out craziness or, well, gross.

Yorkshire said, 'That's what I loved about you. On the one hand, you were really studious, but then you'd do something mad like trim your pubes, fashion an envelope out of your notebook paper and hand it over with pride.'

I'm in awe of myself, I really am. I recount the story to Lady Jane on my way home. Needless to say, she loves it. We conclude that we were so much more emotionally brave back then (I would've been 19 at the time). Plus, pubes were so much more fashionable then. You'd have a job to harvest enough now to fill an envelope.

Wednesday, 21 April

That thing about men being like buses, I think it's true, but perhaps the tube is a more suitable analogy. The Artist, who dicked me about last month, is sniffing around again. He's like the Circle line – eventually he'll come back. Or herpes. He's like herpes! Anyway, because I'm a big softie I've entered into another email chat with him. It's amazing what a bit of flattery can do, isn't it? He reckons he tried to contact me on Saturday when he was at some book fair down on the South Bank. Is this guy pathologically useless? He's certainly phone illiterate. Long story short, he's gonna, quote, 'give me a bell' this Saturday, see what I'm up to. If that actually happens, I'll eat my phone.

Thursday, 22 April

The Poet Pianist and I have been texting again. A couple of things:
1. Beware use of sarcasm
This is not a new observation by any stretch but one worth

highlighting mainly because I worried about it for at least four hours after I'd sent the bleeding thing. We're trying to establish somewhere to meet and he said: 'Where are you in the Londres?'

Cute, and more sensitive to my location than most – it's usually a barked request to get your arse over to East London. I hit him back with: 'I'm south but do venture into town occasionally.'

Now, this was me being witty but, on reflection, could read like I'm borderline agoraphobic.

Then, the next day, he asks if I fancy tea that afternoon somewhere south. Now, I'm digging his willingness to come south (so to speak), liking for tea (he said he likes 'daytime tea-based fun') and spontaneity. It's the last point that raises my second point here:

2. Take care with spelling

Like an imbecile, when I turned him down because I wasn't actually in the city that day, I added a PS. 'Top marks for spontaeneity, though.' Spot the deliberate mistake.

Fuck's sake. Another spelling fuck-up.

I had this issue with Ant, the History Teacher: the complimentary/complementary debacle, but this one is a basic typo rather than usage issue.

'Do you think guys care about spelling mistakes in texts?' I ask Lady Jane later on the phone.

You see, I know that we've slagged off many a guy for it, even the dyslexic I dated. She decides that all things considered, i.e. how cool I supposedly am, he won't care and maybe even won't notice. We decide to leave as is, unlike with the complimentary/complementary mix-up, which I chose to rectify. Oh, it's like a scientific experiment!

It keeps playing on my mind, though, so to distract myself I email Lady Jane again about it. She suggests I resolve it by sending a text in the near future that incorporates tough-to-spell words, such as diarrhoea and chihuahua. Something along the lines of: 'Running slightly late, as on way back from Llanfairpwllgwyngyllgogerychwyrndrobwllllantysiliogogogoch after dropping off some diarrhoea medicine for my Welsh great-aunt's chihuahua.'

Alternatively, she said I could point out all spelling mistakes on the menu, if we were to go out for dinner. Even if we were in a 'foreign' restaurant.

Genius. Both great tips. But her infinitely more sensible conclusion was: 'If he is worth his salt, he will come to know your skills. Plus, he could have one bollock or something. Who made him Mr Perfect?' If we'd been in the same room at this point, we would've definitely high-fived.

Then, the funniest thing happened. He texted me again to try and arrange a meet-time. I didn't even notice, until he followed up his text with: 'For some reason, I put another m in tomorrow.'

So I said . . . 'Don't worry, I was pretty mortified at spelling spontaneity wrong earlier.'

We're meeting tomorrow afternoon. For tea. And a spelling test.

Friday, 23 April

Is the amount we prattle on about a guy proportionate to how much we like them?

No, didn't think so.

In fact, allow me to be so bold as to wager we prattle more when we like them less, if that makes sense. And you know for why? Boredom.

I'll often halt mid-sentence on the phone to Lady Jane when I catch myself boring on about a soon-to-be-insignificant.

'You know what? It doesn't matter. This is all crap,' I'll say. 'I'm just bored.'

Self-deprecating, yes, but also blatantly trying to find excitement when there probably isn't any. Like when the club's finished and you're desperately scratching around for an after party. Sometimes it's best just not to bother.

Some might call that attitude sad; I call it life. And a ridiculous, often misguided relationship with hope.

Right, off to go and meet that guy who I'm not that bothered about if only to have something to bore my mates with.

Saturday, 24 April

No call from the Artist again. Sweet Jesus!

Sunday, 25 April

Oh my gosh, I can't believe it . . .

. . . the day has nearly arrived, the one I've been waiting for. Angel is back! Well, she's back on Tuesday and I'm soo excited. She texted from the airport and we sent a few hilarious messages back and forth to the tune of 'Fuuuuucccckkk!'

It's gonna be big. I'm a bit nervous, if I'm honest. Will she have changed? Have I changed? (Well, that's a no straight off.) Will we have changed? Gasp.

Nah, it's gonna be AWESOME.

Places to Meet Men. Part 3.

The swimming pool. Now, bear with me on this one. I've only recently started going back to the pool (you know, since the asbestos scare) and it's for reasons of thighs and upper arms (oh and all-round good health) rather than to find romance, but I thought it an interesting discussion point, if nothing else.

So, I arrived hastily at the pool – hasty in that I still haven't purchased a new cozzie. The result of this haste? A saggy arse – the elastic's completely gone. Not a good look. Too late now – I just won't do any diving. It's lane swimming and pretty dead in all lanes, so I opt for the slow one – better to avoid the irate front crawlers that turn up in medium.

The talent, or lack thereof, becomes super-apparent as the slow lane fills with men with floats. Actually, make that balding men with floats, heaving their bulk through the imaginary waves.

One guy from the medium lane was checking me out, but he was wearing a swimming cap. I ask you, really? When has a swimming cap ever been attractive or, might I add, necessary for one who is clearly an amateur swimmer just trying to swim off his love handles?

In conclusion, the swimming pool is not a good place to meet men. Yet.

Monday, 26 April

Is dating the new networking? After my afternoon date with the Poet

Pianist on Friday, I'm starting to wonder if dating has become a super-strand of networking. Now, saying this off the bat is a bit harsh because I actually had a great time. The poet and I really got on, I really enjoyed his company – he's clever, funny, reflective (a bit too reflective, which I like) and sexy, in a quirky-crumpled-academic-studenty kinda way.

However, the fact that our 'date' ended with one of those two-cheek-kiss-things you do with foreigners, coupled with the text and email correspondence that has followed, makes me think networking. This *is* the guy who suggested a breakfast meeting, though, so I probably shouldn't be too surprised.

Now, when I called Lady Jane's Rockstar for some manvice, he reckoned no self-respecting guy would put in so much effort to network. That could be done over the phone, without the need to meet. He is, though – no offence – from a different generation.

The 'date' ended with the euro-kiss and a request from him for me to email him some of my work. Oh, sexy!!! To be fair, when we first met, at the art gallery, he had asked the very same question so was just following up. But it makes me wonder: is this gonna be some kind of arts-trading mission, or is it that he could only possibly be interested in me if my writing's any good?

I can't decide whether this is a legit request or not. Maybe it's just the over-achieving sister of Facebook stalking (I'm not a Facebooker, so that's not an option. Hmm)? Either way, I'm not convinced. I just thought of another, slightly less cynical possibility: he just wants to get to know me better.

I leave it and get very drunk with Rubles on Friday night to forget all. That works right through to Sunday, when – beep! – a text. From him. And it's very sweet – hoping I'm having a nice weekend, etc., etc., oh and he says my name twice at the beginning of the message. Cute! BUT he also gives me his email address so that I can, and I quote, send him 'my works of gold'. This is a metaphor. I am not a jeweller.

Tuesday, 27 April

Angel is now back in approximately five hours – that's back here at

Tudor Towers. All being well, of course. It reminds me how lucky I am to have the friends I've got. Like Mrs Patz, who I haven't seen in way too long. She's a thoughtful creature and texted me yesterday with 'One day to go. Woop woop!' because she knew Angel's return was imminent. I said I was feeling nervous and she said: 'Why nervous? It will be amazing. You two lovebirds will be romping in no time.'

It's nice that. And if this all sounds a bit too cutesy, I'll add: I've got a massive bruise on my arse today.

Wednesday, 28 April

When I finally switch my BlackBerry on at 2 p.m. today, feeling like a big pile of rotting compost, I'm greeted with this email from Lady Jane, reminding me how old we're getting:

> Yoyoyo!
> BIG WELCOME BACK LOVE to Angel! Hope you're having
> mega fun times. I'm off out to my SECOND 40th birthday party
> in two weeks. I remember when my dad was 40 . . .
>
> xx

It's true, isn't it?

It's so good to have Angel back, though, even if she's only in London until next week. Until then, she's mine!!

Friday, 30 April

Tonight we're going Out Out.

May
Employing the
Etch A Sketch Approach

Monday, 3 May

4 a.m. and rising. Me, Angel and G are in a cab on our way back from the opening party at Elvis's new pub in Peckham. We're done. Officially done. We've been partying since Friday, with the odd disco nap in between, but pretty much going full throttle. We screech to a halt in the petrol station foyer just near my place. Angel is ravenous for snacks. G and I wait in the car, in our dreamlike state, basically just giggling. Angel reappears from the shop clutching pasties and crisps and walks towards us, grinning, before going straight past our car and into the back of another one that's pitched up by the pump. She climbs into the back, oblivious, before jumping straight back out as this massive, mean-looking bloke – a spit for Marsellus Wallace – climbs out of the front and asks her what the fuck she's doing. I've never seen her move so quick. She dives towards our cab, jumps in and we laugh for at least two hours once we're safely locked and bolted back in the house. Funniest thing. Ever.

York Notes on the past few days

1. Photo booth messing about at Rough Trade record store.
2. Pizza and rosé at Pizza East.
3. Beers in the Griffin, Leonard Street.
3a. Beers at the Strong Room, Shoreditch, for old times' sake.

4. Karaoke at the Birdcage on Columbia Road – a place that's famous for topless ladies, alcoholics and clubbers. Mrs Patz belts out 'Kids in America' by Kim Wilde and everybody loves it.
5. Party back at Mrs Patz's in Hackney – muffled memories, people in every room, sick in the bathroom.
6. Saturday? Saturday? Saturday?
6a. 'I'm not having a shit time, but I'm not having a good time.'
7. Barbecue at J's house on Sunday. People smoking weed. Making phone calls ready for the night. A new mad friend with blonde hair and liquorice papers pushing for the phone calls to be made.
8. Taxi to Peckham.
9. Smoking outside.
10. Dancing inside.
11. A gold-curtained stage reminiscent of *Phoenix Nights*.
12. Soul and disco. Because we do believe in miracles, and Everyday People.
13. Laughing.
14. More dancing.
15. Taxi.
16. More laughing.
17. Sleep.
18. Finally.

Tuesday, 4 May

Pfeiffer has been seeing a bloke who works on *Newsround*, which I know shouldn't be funny but it is. I keep imagining her striding out with John Craven, who used to present the show when I tolerated it in order to watch *Neighbours*. 'All going well so far, but famous last words!' shrills her email today. We're arranging to meet up on Saturday with him and his cricket chums – 'Not sure if your type but one I've met is quite fit!' Bring it on. What I don't know about cricket isn't worth knowing.

Wednesday, 5 May

It's been almost two weeks since my 'date' with the Poet Pianist. Since then we've exchanged a few emails about our respective work (yawn) and then this comes through:

> Dr Taylor,
> How's it all going?
> I hope this finds you well and brilliant and fab.
> A close friend of mine who works for the BBC has started this interesting project and he's looking for some help with press.

Then it goes blah blah blah until:

> Anyhoo, have a look when you have a mo and let me know what you reckon.
> Let's have tea/a drink soon.
> xxxx

Jesus. I think I might've been right about the networking thing. To be a bit fair to him, the subject line of the email was 'A cheeky question'. I forward it to Lady Jane for her thoughts, which come back thus:

> Hmm yes, poss slightly odd that this is his first comm with you in a few days . . . BUT it could be an excuse to get in touch too . . . I do like the way he calls you Dr Taylor and he uses lots of kisses.
> I say, ignore it for now! Reply in few days, as if you're really busy. After all, it is primarily a work-related thing. Then say sorry but you've been busy, it does look interesting, you will mention it to peeps. But you're not his personal media pimp. And if he isn't even going to suggest a date, then he can stand in line with your other professional commitments.

She's right, you know.

PS. What's with the tea thing? What kind of self-respecting man asks a girl to go for tea? Unless he's gay or we're meeting the grandparents. Hmm.

Thursday, 6 May

I've decided to take an Etch A Sketch approach to my love life – I'm cleaning the slate.

I think it's true that most women have some guy lingering that they've dabbled with, or considered dabbling with, but aren't quite sure what the status is now. Well, that's true for me with a few. Like Poet Pianist, who, after some deliberation, I've decided is just a rampant networker and, mutual work-wanking aside, there's not much giving, so I'm letting him go.

Then there's the Artist, who might as well be an illusion artist, the number of times he's presented himself and then promptly disappeared.

So it's a swift and satisfying sideways wipe for them – new picture coming up.

Saturday, 8 May

Anyone for cricket? Well, I was all ready, until Pfeiffer decided to be too hung-over to go. I'd put on my best Aran jumper too. Not really, but I had greased up my bat. Not really. So here I am in Crouch End, having – wait for it – tea and cake. What's with all the tea at the moment?! Arrive home by 8 p.m. Not the night I had planned, but hey, shit happens.

Tuesday, 11 May

I keep having dreams about Alexa Chung and Alex Turner – you know, the fashion–music superpower? Now, this isn't all *that* weird, in that I do from time to time check in on their relationship status online. You know, because Alex Turner should rightly be mine. I love him. I do. It's that gift of language + northern guile + long rock hair.

But let's not forget Alexa – there's a crush of sorts here, too. Because of my work I'm (sort of) forced to keep up to date with Ms Chung's latest fashion forays (espadrilles are on my recent radar).

I've actually interviewed her in person before, which makes it even weirder that in my dreams I'm blatantly, unashamedly, trying to get off with her boyfriend.

It's not sisterly at all. If I had to commit either way, I'd say I'm more Alexa fan than foe – but Alex, he wants it. He really does.

Best celebrity couples, past and present, in no particular order:

1. Jay-Z and Beyoncé
2. Kate Moss and Johnny Depp
3. Kate Moss and Pete Doherty
4. Marilyn Monroe and Arthur Miller
5. Elizabeth Taylor and Richard Burton
6. Mick Jagger and Marianne Faithfull
7. Brooke Shields and Andre Agassi
8. Humphrey Bogart and Lauren Bacall
9. Charles and Camilla
10. Niles and Daphne Crane

Wednesday, 12 May

I'm in the fashion office and catching up with Mrs Patz, who has had two dates this past week – good going in these times of recession. It's doubly good going because Mrs Patz never goes on dates. Never ever. Never ever ever.

I should add that she's not been the least bit excited about either of them. Does anybody look forward to dates any more, I wonder? It's more a case of feeling relief when they're over and you can just puke up and go to sleep. Or is that just me? A lot of my dates seem to end with me slumped over the toilet. It's the stress.

Anyway, this guy, let's call him 'Dry Boy', whom she met in a Hackney Road skuzzer joint, called Mrs Patz to make arrangements on Monday night while she was shooting the shit in my kitchen. She came back from the phone call red-faced, head shaking.

'So?' I say, proper excited.

'I don't think I can go out with him now. Not after what he just said.'

'Why? What did he say?'

'I don't know if I can tell you, it's so embarrassing.'

As you can imagine, my mind is racing at this point. What could he have said? Is he into something weird? Has he told her he loves her already?

'I told him I was at my sister's for a barbecue on Saturday but that it rained . . . '

She inhales on her fag. I'm expectant and a little confused. Can't quite see where this is gonna go.

'And he said, "I love the rain. I love how it smells."'

That's it? Bit try-hard, yes, but surely that's not a deal-breaker? At which point she's making puking noises before finishing up with: 'I'd be less offended if he slapped me around the face with his knob.'

Wow.

Thursday, 13 May

We have a new fashion season and a spot of better weather, which generally means that guys are attempting to display their style prowess a bit more. This is enjoyable, particularly when one is bored and crossing London on the shit-tram that is London's Overground.

In the last few days, the biggest trend I've noticed is for jeans or chino-ish trousers rolled up and paired with some kind of brogue or, for the more dandy, deck shoe. Think Dickie in *The Talented Mr Ripley*. I like this look, in a patronising 'Aw, they're really trying' kinda way.

Now, this is not a trend so much as a warning: there are increased numbers of tanned sporty types, erm, sporting wraparound shades. Think Shane Warne. Twats, the lot of them. Never trust a man in wraparounds.

Finally, special mention has to go to the Steve Jones-a-like, wearing the Aran cricket jumper. It was like my mum's old knitting patterns had come alive in front of my very eyes.

The mating season has officially begun. I can smell it.

Friday, 14 May

It's always good to wake up on a Friday morning to find your front room fogged with smoke and stinking of an all-nighter. It's even better when you've not been part of it and you're up to go to work feeling relatively spritely. Elvis and Rubles, on the other hand — they're not going anywhere any time soon and nor should they. My little cousin the Nurse is visiting from home with her mate Red and we probably showed them too much of a good time last night at a gig in Camden, hence this particular car crash. The youngsters took themselves off to bed, though, unlike these two reprobates.

'Do you think you'll make it to *Dirty Dancing* this afternoon?' is my fog-coated question to Rubles on my way out the door.

'What do *you* think?'

I think not. I've managed to swerve the West End show too, because I'm working. Can't say I'm gutted. Loved the film — what girl doesn't? — but the musical is a step too far.

'See you later?' We're having dinner in town. Allegedly.

Rubles grunts and gets on with her discussion with Elvis about the Catholic Church.

Sunday, 16 May

The Nurse and I have somehow managed to get involved in a gambling ring in a (very) local pub I never frequent. The Nurse is a sports fanatic, which is why we're sitting on threadbare banquettes, lone girls amongst a smattering of around 15 lonely boozing men and betting on the cricket. It's the 20:20 tournament and the Nurse couldn't bear to miss it. I'm here, just to make it even more confusing for the pub's regulars, with my MacBook, because I'm also on a deadline for tomorrow. A strange afternoon, indeed. Red and Rubles are back home dying from Saturday night. The Nurse and I are facing our hangovers and doing it anyway. We're going to round off the weekend's proceedings with a delicious curry — a day-after tonic — before those two clear off back up north in the morning.

All in all, a satisfactory weekend with just the right mixture of fun and weird.

OMG I can't believe I missed out the best bit of the weekend! We saw Niles from *Frasier* having a drink outside a pub near Leicester

Square on Friday. My hero! He's doing a play in the West End. I love it in *Frasier* when Daphne says to him: 'I'm feeling a little like the good china . . . '

Then Niles gazes at her longingly and says, 'Somebody should be eating off you every day.'

Tuesday, 18 May

As much as I meant what I said about the Etch A Sketch approach to my love life, it seems that some men just won't disappear and I'm not sure I want them to. American Boy is one such specimen. He's been enquiring after my well-being again. It's like we're war sweethearts, abetted by email.

It's got me thinking about the coming and going of men – the men merry-go-round, if you will. How they drift in and drift out of your life sometimes, or come along and then leave (or you leave . . .). Sometimes you think, 'I'll never hear from him again,' then boom!, he's back – whether you want him to be is another matter.

I take comfort from this in those 'fuck, where is he?' moments I have from time to time. Because that's what it is – a sometimes thrilling, often unreliable, but continually moving carousel. Movement is good, so you may as well be merry.

Deep, I know.

Wednesday, 19 May

Remember that rubbish TV drama that was on years ago about a NY–LON relationship? You know, New York and London, like, combined? Clever shit. Well, I emailed American Boy back and, probably because I'm a bit bored and should be working on something else, I'm having my own NY–LON fantasy. I have been known to share with most of my girls, and I quote, 'I could see myself with an American.' And what's even more hilarious than that is they all agree! Women are so supportive, however cock-eyed the theory.

You see, this guy really is great. He's hot (I know, I keep going on about that), smart and also a bit serious. I like that. I'm sick of guys who just piss about all the time because they're basically so deeply insecure they pretend they don't care about anything. He's bothered about stuff, you know? It's not all One Big Joke.

On a much more superficial level, there's so much fun to be had with phrases that get lost in translation. Woo hoo! It's not exactly hot sex, but it's something. Like when I used the word 'cheeky' and he said, 'I don't speak the Queen's. What does that mean?' He's funny, too. Try translating what cheeky means, though. Not easy, even for a wordsmith such as myself. The best bit? He might be coming to Europe later this summer. I do hope so.

Friday, 21 May

The men merry-go-round I was on about the other day? Well, it's gone berserk. Actually, perhaps the ghost train is a more appropriate, still fairground-related comparison. I bumped into two exes this week and it was at once unsettling and joyful. The first one was a very early boyfriend from sixth-form college, let's call him 'Rugby Boy'. I know, I know! Me and a rugby boy: unthinkable! Hey, I was into sports once and the rugby lads in my northern town were like the T-Birds, you know: 'ard.

So, Rugby Boy bounded over to me when I was in Brixton en route home yesterday and shouted my name in my face, as if he was reminding me what it is.

'Yes,' I affirmed. I didn't keep him hanging long because I did recognise him – our paths have crossed a couple of times over the years. My first line wasn't my best, though: 'Oh, aren't you big?' I said, giving his bicep a playful squeeze like Babs Windsor in the Carry On films.

'What, you mean fat?' was his immediate response.

Oh God. 'No, I mean packed.' What? I don't even know why I said that, but he did look like he'd been on the protein shakes. I then dig myself into a deeper hole by explaining that he looks a lot different from the rakish 17 year old with long hair that smelled of apple shampoo and had a lovely slim neck that tasted of Fahrenheit (whenever I catch a whiff of that scent, I'm still reminded of him).

So, I'm spewing all this forth and realising, slowly, as he gazes fondly into my eyes, that it seems like some kind of nostalgic come-on. It's certainly pushed his buttons a bit because he wants to take me out. I said yes, but only if he uses the apple shampoo first.

I bumped into the other sort-of ex earlier today while walking to the shop and chatting on the phone, as is often the case, to Lady Jane about her Fucking House Renovations. I see this guy coming towards me and think, oh he's quite cute, before thinking, oh fuck, it's him.

He flashes me the most sheepish look, like EVER, and I say, 'Oh, hello.' Imagine the most disappointed tone of voice you've ever heard, add an air of disgust and a negligible percentage of Kenneth Williams and you've got it. He pauses, presumably thinking we might chat. Not today, darling. I keep walking, my sunglasses acting as a sort of cool-as-fuck armour. At this point I'm talking absolute gibberish to Lady Jane, who's baffled, to say the least.

'You'll never guess who I've just seen?'

When has that game ever worked, by the way? After running through a ludicrous list of people who would never be wandering around my neck of the woods, I put her out of her misery.

'Oh, him,' she says, as if she's just chewed a paracetamol.

Now, this guy, let's call him 'Mr Sleaze', was, as my mum would say, a bit of a one. He worked in one of the local pubs and charmed me over my scampi (*you had me at tartar sauce . . .*). He asked me out and we had one of those great dates where you snog like mad. He was fit, young and enthusiastic – like a puppy. I accept! We went back to mine and he became a man. Ha.

But then, a few days later, when I was back in the pub with some mates, all hell broke loose. Turns out, Mr Sleaze has got a girlfriend as well as a jilted (bulldog-faced) lover who also works in the pub. She's learned of our tryst (probably because she's been following him, because she's CRAZY) and she's practically trying to bite me, from behind the bar. It's brutal, like *EastEnders* or *Neighbours From Hell*.

But then the funniest thing happened. I get a text off him – the longest, most ridiculous, grovelling, comedic text I've ever received.

You know when Russell Brand does that silly Victoriana chat – all highfalutin'? It was like that. He told me he thought I was titillating! Ha, never a truer word spoken. Then he came round to mine, to further grovel, apologise and basically inform me that he really loves his girlfriend, he didn't want to lead me on, he thinks I'm great, he couldn't resist, but he loves his girlfriend, yada, yada, yada. Did I mention, he loves his girlfriend?

After one date I find this overblown speech a bit unnecessary, not to mention disingenuous. Why the big I-love-my-girlfriend bit? Personally, I'm looking more for the Sorry-I-nearly-got-you-maimed-in-the-pub grovel. Now, don't judge me on this, but I have to test his resolve, so I'm lounging on my sofa, bra-less (I do that sometimes), and he's still dribbling on about his girlfriend, so I say, 'You still want to shag me, though, don't you?'

You know, to make a point.

Saturday, 22 May

My cousin's had a new baby, so I'm on the train on my way up home and doing a bit of BlackBerry admin to pass the time. Another email comes through from the Poet Pianist with a link to some coverage his mate got in the *New York Times* in case it's 'of interest'. You know what I'm interested in, love? I'm interested in how much your mate is paying you to be his personal PR.

Annoyed.

Sunday, 23 May

I'm out at the local pub, 'wetting the baby's head' with my cousin's baby's dad, the Nurse and her mate Red. We're shooting the breeze over a few shandies and Red keeps sniffing her fingers (between trying to soothe her burned shoulders crispened by the Caribbean Breeze tan accelerator oil she'd been slicking on all day).

'What you doing?' says the Nurse.

'My fingers smell of garlic. Or gas,' Red replies before taking another sniff.

Nice. We're all laughing.

'It's better than last week,' she carries on. 'When they smelled of arse.'

Priceless.

Monday, 24 May

I've been struck down with a mouth infection, the pain from which extends to my neck and shoulders. Is that even normal? I've been to the dentist, been speared with two jaw-disabling injections and been prescribed really strong antibiotics. Needless to say, I'm feeling a wee bit sorry for myself. I'm also slightly concerned that I won't be well enough to go on my solo trip away to the seaside this weekend. I'm planning a three-day writing-and-reflection jaunt and am actually looking forward to some time alone. It's all been a bit hectic with visitors, silly boys and working full time in the fashion office (well, for two weeks I was). I'm staying in a gorgeous B&B in Hastings on the East Sussex coast, as I inform Yorkshire via email.

Always looking out for my welfare, he comes back with:

> Do NOT drink on those painkillers. Dental ones are lethal. OK
> . . . not literally lethal, but you will be sick on 'em if you drink.
> And no fags. Not good for mouth infections, as I told Jay who,
> on his eternal quest to find out for himself, found out.
>
> Hastings sounds all romantic, nostalgic, historic, etc., but in
> all actuality it's got one of the highest numbers of asylum
> seekers in the country and, therefore, probably one of the
> highest locals vs comer-inners levels of conflict since . . . er . . .
> 1066. You'd be wise to stop in.

Talk about killing the romance.

Tuesday, 25 May

Roller Girl came round to my mum's to see me this evening and was telling me what happened to her on Saturday night. When she told me, I couldn't help but crack up because it's so ridiculous and also so typical of her, as an accident-prone lush. What did she do? Hit herself in the face with her own fridge door when she was foraging for her next hit of vodka and tonic. She actually burst her lip. Her husband was worried it'd look like he was knocking her about. I literally doubled up with laughter at this story because it's her to a tee. Hapless. Ridiculous. Like the time she went to casualty in a bathrobe with no knickers on.

I think there was something in the air this weekend, though, because there were other good performances from my friends.

Lady Jane: Went to a wedding with Rockstar and took air guitar to new limits – the two of them got into such a drunken frenzy dancing to 'Living on a Prayer' that they actually poured beer over their heads in order to fashion the bottles as guitars. 'We were in soft rock bliss,' she said to me yesterday when we were catching up in a Manchester beer garden. Rockstar is now in a mild state of paranoia that said footage might make it onto YouTube.

Another friend, who shall remain anonymous, emailed to say: 'You'll like this. Tim and I did the dirty deed in the toilet on the Virgin train.' Nice!

I totally pat her on the back for that one, but personally I reckon I'd be more up for sneaking a fag in one of those grim toilets. Anyway, fun times, girls. Good work.

Wednesday, 26 May

Do you ever wonder if you'll ever have sex again?

Friday, 28 May
What happened in Hastings

So here I am in my Hastings garret, trying to write but apparently not able to stop myself from posing for self-administered photos on my BlackBerry to send to friends no doubt busying themselves with actually having a life this filthy-wet bank holiday weekend.

I've made a conscious decision to come away alone to write and yet here I am texting, emailing, BlackBerry messaging and photographing like some kind of lunatic. It's funny, though, going solo. It takes a while to acclimatise – a bit like being single after being in a couple, I suppose. Going away on your own is The Next Big Step, after the hellish Going To A Wedding On Your Own, etc., etc. Those things don't really bother me any more, but taking a one-woman trip? This is, well, a whole new trip.

I arrived to a glorious reception from the landlady – she lavished me with a cream tea containing meringues. Meringues! It wasn't even 12.30 – a promisingly decadent start. After settling into my 'turret' room (if that's not a garret, I don't know what is), I decided to brave the wild streets of Hastings. I email Yorkshire to let him know and he whizzes back, 'Out to bag a Kosovan?' Funny, if a tad racist.

As it turns out, I have a rather brilliant afternoon that takes in some of my favourite things:

1. Fish and chips – consumed in gale-force conditions, but I'm going on that beach if it kills me – you know the drill.

2. Weird pubs – treated myself to a Coke, as still on the strong drugs, at a character-filled local pub in the old town. Think Captain Birdseye and Sam Elliott, Patrick Swayze's cowboy boot-wearing mentor from the movie *Road House*, and you'll have some grasp of the clientele. I also did some actual writing on a picnic table outside and observed said locals smoking weed. Left proud that I managed to not get involved.

3. Crazy golf – OK, I didn't play, but I did observe some rowdy pensioners having a go and vowed to be like them when I grow up.

4. Shopping – now, I don't need any encouragement to spend money but being on your own means you literally haemorrhage it, on the basis that you 'deserve a treat'. Man, if I had saved a pound for the number of times I've justified purchases for that reason, I wouldn't still be deferring my student loans. The shopping was surprisingly good. Cute antique-y places selling awesome kaftans and oriental plates, and an excellent 'dress exchange' shop where I bought three new items. The best, though, was my foray into the Only Health Shop In The Village, where I parted with the best part of £40 on organic skin cream and facial wash. The woman working there had barely thrust a tester in my hand before I was gamely buying up the entire range. To be fair, I've decided natural skincare really is the way forward, so it was only a matter of time.

5. Cinema – now, this is an activity that's perfect to do alone and if you want to know why, well, you're stupid. I watched *Sex and the City 2*. I had to see it. I won't bore you with my review but, needless to say, I felt very let down. Still sat all the way through it, though. It's like you really care about what happens to these women – even if they do look weird as fuck traipsing through the desert in comedy heels.

So, I totally managed to be on my own in Hastings. I didn't come a cropper with any local ne'er-do-wells, though I couldn't help but smile to myself when I was climbing back up the hill to my weekend residence and passed two sportswear-clad yoofs who had a proposition for me. Did I want any speed? *What a kind offer, young sir, but no thanks, not today*.

Back to the more glamorous end of the spectrum – and I do like to flirt with both sides. In that dress exchange, I bought what can only be described as a 'fabulous' knee-length cardi-coat trimmed in antique lace. It's gorgeous – in an old Hollywood kind of way. I put it on over my jeans and T-shirt when I left the SATC crime scene and stood out like Grace Jones at Morrison's deli counter, where I'd gone to get my supper to eat back at the B&B. I know, the glamour. But then when I got back to my room I flounced about in it and really had one of those moments where you feel like a better person because of something you've bought. It really is super.

Saturday, 29 May

I just spoke to Angel on the phone – oh, how I miss her! Not because I've been away, oh, all of a day, but because she is now away, permanently. She has officially relocated to Manchester and was moving into her new city centre pad yesterday, the very same day I was schlepping off to the seaside.

Because she's as much of a goon as me, she sent me a photo of her new front door; her stood next to it with characteristic enormo-grin. I texted back 'Nice door!' but couldn't ignore the pain pang in the pit of my stomach. As you know, she lived next door to me in London for many years and now she's gone. When some time last year she told me of her plans to move, I think my heart broke a bit and I don't think that will alter.

But that's change for you. It happens. All the time. Whether you like it or not. I think that's what makes being single a little more challenging too, sometimes, because often the mates you used to see all the time, your sparring partners, bugger off to 'settle down' and could potentially leave you feeling a little bit left behind. I urge anyone who feels this to reject it immediately. It's not about being left behind, it's just about change. And timing. I need to not see my life as having something missing. Would I really want somebody else's life? No, I don't think I would.

Being away this weekend just brings it home to me more. It's actually lovely to chat to Angel about her move and my weekend away. When I told her about the motley group of guys from the pub, she saw it how I saw it. So, in some ways, it's still the same: the same, but different.

There are times like that, and I said this to Angel and Lady Jane, when you wish someone was with you to share the fun. I know if one of my best girl-mates was here with me, we'd have been getting up to all sorts of ridiculous high-jinks, and I do hanker after that. Importantly, I long for their company more than I do that of a man. Don't get me wrong, I have a glorious double bed just ripe for some hot sex and, given the right guy, I'm sure I'd be having a swell time in and out of the room. BUT for me, a lot of my memories of being away with a boy are actually pretty awful. If we're honest, I reckon most people have more memories of scorching arguments than hot sex. Not that most people would admit it.

I actually came away to Hastings many years ago with the Big Ex. I struggle to remember the details because it was a long time ago. I think we thought it was a bit rough and we certainly didn't stay in a chic B&B like I'm in for Hastings Mark II. As a couple, we did go away a lot and at first, in the early years, we had a great time, with the hot sex and everything. But for too long into the dark years I had some of my most miserable times away with him: screaming and crying in the pouring rain in Paris; screaming and crying in the blistering sun in Barcelona; screaming and crying on a windswept beach in Kefalonia (*Captain Corelli's Mandolin* fantasy crushed).

You've got to think, where's the fun in that?

I surf through the not-so-nice centre of Hastings to find a picnic bench in front of the sea to sip my double macchiato (I know, get me). It's funny what you notice and overhear when you're on your own. Nobody notices you, or at least I don't think they do, but they become your ensemble cast in the movie where you're the lead. Given that I'm in a gritty British seaside town, the director is probably Mike Leigh or Ken Loach.

It's also fun to observe people. I couldn't help but snigger when I walked past a woman talking loudly on her phone about her rampant bladder infection and the fact she 'felt like shit'. I hear you, love, but you did just put me off my coffee, given that I was drinking out of a receptacle resembling a sample cup.

Hastings is ripe with life, which is just the way I like it – a little bit rough around the edges. There's the disproportionate number of really overweight people whizzing around on mobility scooters ('Therein lies crushing irony,' quips Yorkshire, remotely from NYC). And the women guarding two trolleys filled to the brim with Iceland carrier bags having a massive row. And the skater kids. I LOVE the skater kids. And the cool-looking young couples obviously visiting from London.

My favourite, though, has to be the wiry-and-wily-as-fuck-looking guy with a vagabond tan, wild hair, bandanna and metaller T-shirt, pulling along a flag-adorned cart behind him containing a cute little lad dressed as a pirate. Thinking about it, the guy totally had a whiff of the Jack Sparrow about him. As a kid, you wouldn't have a clue of the prejudice sent this guy's way, i.e. your dad's way, for being a crusty, or a druggie, or a drop-out, or a gypsy, or whatever, you'd just be thinking, this is brilliant – I'm a pirate! And I don't have to walk.

I hit the beach again and switch on my iPod to tune those people out and my thoughts in.

Seaside playlist

1. 'Cornerstone', Arctic Monkeys – still LOVE this for reasons mentioned before.
2. 'Down in Albion', Babyshambles – a rousing ode to Britain and all its quirks never goes amiss at Brit-by-sea.
3. 'All or Nothing', Small Faces – because for me, it does tend to be all or nothing. Yeah, yeah.
4. 'Never Went to Church', The Streets – this is a beautiful song that Mike Skinner wrote about his dad dying. It makes me super-grateful that I've still got my dad, and reminds me what's important. It also reminds me of Angel. We both love The Streets and have seen them several times. I listened to this particular song on the train travelling back home with her and her boy two days before she left London. She looked across at me and I was all glassy-eyed – over the song, but also the fact that she was about to leave and change everything. She shipped to the seat beside me and gave me a sideways squeeze. She's good like that.

Sitting now, looking out to sea and listening to it again (hey, I'm a sucker for revisiting pain), I have to text her: 'Reminds me of you.' I'm not half soppy sometimes.

The music, the sun, the view, the fact that I'm alone is having a stirring effect. Being able to be on your own removes the need to be with someone else, thereby removing any hint of desperation or inadequacy you might sometimes feel (not a good look). There's a difference between need and want, you see. I want – *oh I want* – but I don't need. Not when it comes to men, anyway. Sitting on this picnic bench, contemplating and dreaming, I feel like this imprints a bit deeper. And I'm proud of myself for it.

I'm also officially off the antibiotics, so I'm off to have me a whole pint of lager.

Sunday, 30 May

I'm flush with wine and watching, on ITV2 (that bastion of brilliant cinema), *The Holiday*. The unashamed – some may say shit – rom-com starring Jude Law, Kate Winslet, Jack Black and Cameron Diaz (notice how I list the Brits first?). Anyway, *The Holiday*. This is (whisper it) actually the third time I've seen it. I know it's cheesy as fuck, but I just love it. I do. And I'm thrilled that Lady Jane feels the same way. It's her first time and she texted me to say as much after I suggest she watch it to shake off her fug.

It's a bit sad, but we're texting our comments as we watch, her in Manchester, me in my seaside B&B. It's romantic. You see, though it's schmaltzy, the characters pull off the fact that they seem to fall for each other. They do. Also, Jude is FIT.

After he's slept with Cameron Diaz for the first time, they're both doing the do-we-don't-we-want-anything-more dance, you know, because she's got to go back to LA and he's saddled with two kids that she doesn't know about yet. But then he says it, the killer line. He says: 'You're lovely.'

That just works.

Monday, 31 May

It's been a weekend full of solo fun and enlightenment. I'm about to check out of my garret and leave Hastings. I text Lady Jane about the unsightly bite I've discovered on my forehead. I knew something was nibbling at me!

'How is that fair?' I wail electronically.

She pings back, quick as you like: 'There'll be people leaving Hastings this weekend with a lot worse than a bite. Think yourself lucky.'

September 2010
Paris

I turn up at the Paris apartment and feel . . . almost sick with nerves. It dawns on me that I've, somewhat recklessly, arranged to let a virtual stranger, albeit a handsome stranger, stay for four days in my borrowed Montmartre loft, albeit a sweet loft.

How the fuck will this work?

I walk in and he's still HOT, if a little tired (hey, give the guy a break, he's been flying all night). He's wearing a grey button-down and that unbelievably sexy fringe of his. I feel mixed emotions – I've nursed a rather silly crush on this guy for a couple of years but what will he actually be like? And what will he think of me?

How the fuck will this work?

Let me fill you in.

Back in July, I get a call from American Boy, my long-distance fantasy lover from New York City. A beautiful, beautiful man.

'What you doing in September?' he asks in his sexy, Julian Casablancas drone. 'I'm finally coming to the UK.'

My reply? 'Seeing you, hopefully.' Cool. Even if I do say so myself.

I then add that I'll be in Paris at the beginning of the month, swanking it up in a Montmartre loft. After some swilling around of dates, we decide to hang in Paris for a few days before the London leg.

Being the romantic that I am, I couldn't have written it better myself: meet a hot guy in New York more than two years ago and indulge in hedonistic heavy petting; become sustainable virtual pen pals interspersed with daydreams of giving it all up to move to Brooklyn; then meet up 27 tantalising months later in The Most Romantic City In The World to rekindle the flame and, hopefully, shag in a toilet somewhere again. It's a beautiful thing, it really is. You know what else is beautiful? What happened when I called Eurostar to push back my return journey.

As it stood, I was due to leave on the day he was due to be touching down. Nightmare! I wanted to delay my return journey by a few days – four, to be exact – but had a feeling this would mean buying a whole new ticket since mine was one of those cheapo non-refundables.

As suspected, when I got the Eurostar woman on the phone to check she confirmed my ticket was indeed non-refundable/non-exchangeable. Shizer!

'Can I ask why you want to extend your stay?' she asked.

Well, you did ask . . . I proceeded to tell her the story – the fantastic, romantic story – and you know what? She only bloomin' changed my ticket! I could've kissed her. The start of My Very Own Romantic Happy Ending.

Back in the room. American Boy is still lounging nonchalantly on the couch. I'm still doing a good impression of an absolute moron.

I blabber away for the first ten minutes, saying God knows what and thrusting beer into his hand before blabbering some more. American Boy is very sparing with words. I can say this now after our crash-course relationship. It's very becoming. He counterbalances my alarm clock shrill with his sexy snooze vibes. I won't say I feel comfortable, but I feel *more* comfortable.

He takes a shower (I know!) and then we head out. Me and the sexy American. It's like I have to keep reminding myself what I'm doing, voiceover style. We walk up the steep and winding hill to Sacré-Cœur, passing the carousel featured in *Amélie*, and squeeze our way through the assembled crowds of tourists, buskers and beggars.

It's a freakishly bright day. We're both wearing sunglasses to shade ourselves from the rays and palpable frisson. We reach the final stage: the white steps of the temple, where people are sitting eating sandwiches and taking pictures of the amazing view. We're shoulder to shoulder, taking it all in. This is nuts, I'm thinking. I'm stood, Paris all around and below me, with American Boy.